LOVE AND INDEPENDENCE

The Struggle to Attain Two Ideals

Love and Independence

The Struggle to Attain Two Ideals

Paul D. Spörer

Anza Communications
Post Office Box 453
Highland Mills, New York 10930

Copyright © 2000 by Paul D. Sporer
All rights reserved.
No part of this book may be reproduced, stored in a retrieval system, or transmitted by any means, electronic, mechanical, photocopying, recording, or otherwise, without written permission from the author.

ISBN # 1-58721-338-9

1stBooks - rev. 05/16/00

About the Book

This is a landmark work which specifically addresses the core problems facing the contemporary family. The book, entitled **'Love and Independence'**, investigates an area of critical significance, namely the relations between men and women. This work's conclusion is that the current destructive conflict between men and women is caused mainly by an inability to find compromise between personal concepts of 'love' and 'independence'.

The findings of several hundred studies and analyses of international data are used to illuminate the ongoing effort to find reconciliation between the desire for companionship and the desire for autonomy. The author hopes he can stimulate the readers's perceptions and provide thought-provoking information gathered from his extensive research. Whether you are looking to expand your knowledge, or to find the answers to particular questions, the material that you read must be accurate, complete, and timely. You will find the observations and commentary in each chapter to be unique and enjoyable to read.

A critical work on family life must grapple with the universal dilemma of meeting the demands of full partnership in a loving and affectionate relationship, and at the same time remaining free to think and act as one pleases about career, entertainment, friends, housing, food, clothing, and so on. Many works trivialise this dilemma, often attributing the cause of marital conflict to mere 'miscommunication', with the solutions being equally as facile. As relations with people become more distant and unstable, marriage appears to be the only relationship where the ideal of love can be satisfied, and society has offered a life path of succession of accomplishment in order to fulfill this ideal. Yet there is no guarantee of reaching these goals in life, and natural aptitude, not choice, often affects career and social pathways.

The many failures resulting from cheating and selfishness have led people to believe affection in no longer needed, and that autonomy and materialism are the only concerns one should have in life. Paradoxically, the stresses of modern life push people to begin having dependence on one another from an early age, even though their immaturity precludes lasting friendship. It is a lack of understanding the underlying factors that coalesce to form personal concepts of 'love' or 'independence' that cause an inability to find compromise. Hence, the ongoing conflict between men and women.

Every person needs advice that they can depend on. Please take this opportunity to avail yourself of information which will give you the power to make your own decisions that will change your life.

*To Cassandra,
beloved wife and true friend*

Contents

CHAPTER 1

INTRODUCTION 1

CHAPTER 2

SACRIFICE, COMMITMENT AND REALISM 25
Outgoingness and Courtship 25
How to Best Build a Family? 42
Tradition's Compromise: Marry for Money, Work for Love 60

CHAPTER 3

EMANCIPATED CHILDREN 101
Now a New Pattern: Good Fortune Gives Way to Skill 101
The First Step: Leaving Home 140
Alone but Not Alone 155
The Perception of Privacy 166
Household Size and Lessons Learned 186
Substitutes 200
The Weight of Many Influences 217

CHAPTER 4

A SEARCH FOR SIMPLICITY 227
Don't Waste Time: Think Alike 227
Education, the Great Equaliser 237
Is Marriage Just Another Friendship? 253
Social Disruption, Family Order 271

CHAPTER 5

IN THE AFTERMATH OF PRAGMATISM 295
A Balancing Act 295
No Way to Win at Love 298
Apathetic Dependence 311

CHAPTER 6

CONCLUSIONS 329

APPENDIX A
STATISTICAL ANALYSES AND REPORTS, INTRODUCTION 357

APPENDIX B
VARIABLES USED IN STATISTICAL ANALYSES 375

REFERENCES 383

NOTES 403

TABLES

Table 1. Factors involved in deepening a friendship: Entrustment and concentration of attention 27

Table 2. Probability of living with an unrelated individual and age of marriage, by income and sex. 150

Table 3. Propensity to marry as a function of residence status at age 21 159

Table 4. Effect of mortality on marriage age and propensity to never marry. 209

Table 5. Comparison of ranges of opinions on married life. 242

Preface

Terminology concerning married life would appear to be straightforward, as the expressions used are so common. However, a lack of precision is evident. People make what sense they can of them, and often there might be disagreement about an issue simply because the parties involved have not settled on basic nomenclature.

In our discussions, various terms pertaining to marriage age are used frequently, and it would probably help the reader if example expressions were interpreted into a precise meaning:

Expression	Meaning
'She married early'	Marriage under age 21.
'She married late'	Marriage over age 30.
'She did not marry late'	Marriage under age 30.
'She did not marry early'	Marriage over age 21.
'She married at around the average age'	Marriage between the ages of 21 and 30.
'She did not marry at all'	Never marrying during one's life, or marriage over age 45.
'She married'	Marriage at some point in life, whether early, average or late.

The following abbreviations are used in this book:

SA: US Bureau of the Census, 1989, *Statistical Abstract of the United States*, 1989, (109th edition) Washington, DC. (For this source, references to a table will be as follows: SA:105, wherein the reference is to table 105.)

HS: U.S. Bureau of the Census, 1975, *Historical Statistics of the United States, Colonial Times to 1970, Bicentennial Edition, Parts 1 and 2*, Washington, DC. (For the above source, references are made to a table and column number, such as HS:B25 refers to table B, column 25.)

Proverbs and aphorisms of different cultures appear in this book passim. They are taken primarily from:

Mieder, W., 1986, *The Prentice Hall Encyclopaedia of World Proverbs*, Prentice- Hall, Englewood Cliffs, New Jersey.

'European data', wherever it is referred to in this work, refers to a database of information compiled by the author and taken from various sources and analysed using various statistical tools. Note that the catholicity of the word 'European' is challenged by our primary focus on Western Europe, but its implied broadness might still be preserved through the inclusion in our purview of the numerous descendant cultures living in North America and Oceania. Specifically, the countries in this database are: United Kingdom, Ireland, Norway, Sweden, Norway, Denmark, Finland, France, West Germany, Austria, Netherlands, Belgium, Spain, Portugal, Italy, United States, Canada, and Australia. Not all these countries are used in every analysis, as data are not available in all categories in every nation. The names of variables and sources of data are listed in Appendix B.

Chapter 1
Introduction

Independence, freedom, liberty — these are, when given fullest expression, proud, bold, resonant, defiant concepts. They represent an almost ineffable feeling; being without restraint indeed strikes a unique impression on the mind. Like a free-fall, liberty is an intoxicating rush that goes to one's head. Doing exactly what one wants and not having to obey rules about what to think, what to do, what to say, where to go, what to wear — these are the things that humans innately seek. Being released from a dreary obligation creates an extraordinary moment, most potent while still in the full memory of what has transpired. Whether it is leaving an unpleasant home life to live on one's own or becoming one's own boss or going on an extended holiday, the casting off of shackles can be exhilarating. The mind reels at the tremendous possibilities that independence finally bestows, and one is only limited by one's imagination, hopefully not grown dull by years of complacent servitude.

Is this concept of freedom without peer? Many would say that the only thing that equals it, indeed, competes with it, is being in love.

Love — a word that can conjure up great emotion, but one that quite frankly wavers when confronted with 'emancipation' and 'free choice'. Love invariably involves being dependent on someone, and someone being dependent on you, and that is its main problem. However, no matter how much one has basked in the glory of cutting bindings from oneself, the shadow of emotional desire, of affection, can never be left behind. Western cultures have repeatedly made it clear that we cannot experience total fulfilment in life unless there is also love. In a modern world that promotes and rewards autonomy, freedom can come cheaply, yet love then comes at a premium, because the bold concept of independence comes at the risk of injury to the most crucial dynamic in a relationship, the spirit of cooperation. Today, we seem to have crossed the line, where there is a cost not only to individual well-being but to social stability as well. To counteract the tidal forces of instability brought on by independent minds each pulling their own way, companionship is more necessary than ever. The solidity of two in deep affectionate embrace can overcome all waves of change. But love cannot flourish where people press for self-determination; it is hard to strike a balance since, compared to love, the costs of independence are relatively inexpensive and the returns are immediate.

Are love and independence therefore implacable foes?

From the dream-like world of childhood, autonomy rises up as one of our great primary visions. Love is usually taken for granted, unless it is withheld by guardians, relatives and others in one's social circle. It occurs naturally as simple a concept as independence, but always strongly prone to subjective emotional forces. Quite in contrast, independence revolves around material questions and factors, which appear in various guises at different psychological phases. The desire for freedom grows out of the failure to satisfy basic personal needs. We would not need to discuss the concept of independence if we could always find easy success in our endeavours. Thus, when we say one has obtained 'freedom' from something, that something must have made significant impositions on one's time, resources, intellect and emotions. The sequence of liberation is often the same: The first freedom is from the household of origin, the second from school and teachers, the third is from an occupation, the fourth is from community and institutions. Thus, autonomy is a relative concept, entangled in context, dependent on other questions that are pertinent, such as happiness, security, friendship, mature love, self-respect, equality, comfort and accomplishment. Love on the other hand stands alone, being dependent simply on the interaction between only two people.

It does not take long before the maturing individual discovers that life always demands a combination of freedom and service. It is not so much striking a balance between the two, but using each wisely. All people want the freedom to choose their destiny, but this does not entail having a destiny that is free. A person might choose to work in service to someone, with hardly any free time of his own. The choice to work there was entirely his, but after this free exercise of choice, the rest of life is largely given over to the decisions of his superior. This individual is indeed free if by this he is able to avoid worry, self-doubt and conceit. He might be able to achieve all the respect and appreciation he wants in this lifestyle in spite of the criticisms and ridicule of others about his 'despised' state. Hence, one can be truly free and still sacrifice for another, if that is his choice. The *context* of the situation must therefore always be borne in mind.

There is no guarantee that the individual will develop the concept of 'freedom' or 'love' as an integrated whole. Precepts about these issues might be based on a few aspects, not one's whole existence. A key question is: How much freedom can an individual give up and still be 'free'? People often focus quite understandably on the end result; autonomy however, is *not* the end result in life, but only a means to achieve something that is. Thus, when asked directly, 'What is the most important goal in life?', the consensus is overwhelming: *happiness*. We cannot easily separate happiness, family, love and freedom as they are all are interrelated concepts. Clearly, each component has its own rewards, but freedom and family can also be methods to fulfill the other two. In a general survey that asked people to rank a large number of life goals, family came first, then freedom. In another survey, young people put happiness before freedom or love.[1] Thus, if we are properly to examine the issue of independence, we must accept the fact that most people see it as being of secondary importance. Love might or might not be of greater importance than freedom as a means of securing happiness. People interestingly choose to focus their attention on results, such as contentment, over methods, such as equality, democracy, and marriage.

Let us now follow the sequence of events which leads to love in relation to the need for independence. The desire for affection usually arises from realisation of the coldness and sterility of autonomy. Love develops as needs become complex, as the individual becomes vulnerable and understands he cannot go it alone. One has no problem accepting the advantages of affection, but one must initially determine the costs linked to independence. Ideally, there would be little or no cost, but this is highly unusual. More likely, love takes a significant portion of one's freedom. However, we should also see that a loss of freedom due to other reasons can be compensated for by love. People sometimes do so successfully, but as love is the superior dynamic, it does not work the other way around, that is, freedom cannot make up for a deficiency of affection. People living in countries disrupted by totalitarian systems and war experience less freedom, and so desire companionship as compensation. Perhaps this is the reason why people in some parts of the world are more strongly in favour of marriage than in other parts.[2]

More than just temporary affection is needed, however, for the individual to feel fulfilled. The affection must last a lifetime, and indeed, from the individual's perspective, it must be *eternal*. There is no doubt that as all things pass in this world, and in order for love to be transcendent it must be different in some substantive way from all other artefacts of existence. This means that love between two people must never end, even though we all know that this possibility always remains. In other words, a husband and wife must have *absolute* faith that their love for one another will never end, no matter what circumstances appertain. If there is even the slightest doubt that the consideration will end, then it is *not* true love. Such statements appear are harsh, but we have no control over the rules of this reality, we can only report on them.

The basis of love is the desire for good friendship. Friendships are formed naturally and easily, often without much thought behind the process. Note the causality: There must be a friendship before there can be love, but love does not necessarily arise from a friendship. The relationship which is uppermost in the minds of everyone is the unique *bond*, a genuinely mature relationship that can only exist between a man and a woman. True love, which is to say lasting love, can mutually occur between any two people, but it is most keenly felt and most extensive when it is between a man and woman, because each possesses what the other desires in order to be complete and perfect. We should not underestimate the power of this relationship. Despite of the rush of mundane business, in the midst of all the commotion and clatter of worldly matters, the allure of the opposite sex never seems to falter. Hence, no matter where a man or woman finds himself or herself, even in isolation, even where the sexes are in a great imbalance and a mate can hardly be found, the conception faithfully, perhaps irrationally, lives on. With growing maturity, one realises the uniqueness of a male-female friendship, and one understands that it can transcend all common or conventional facets of life. Work, school, the neighbourhood, relatives, obligations to company, family, state, and church, can all be places where this relationship begins, but ultimately the relationship always grows bigger than the place where it began. Nothing can ultimately keep it from growing and nothing can ever ruin it. The only end to the true love between a man and woman must come from the inside, not the outside. And, of course, if a supposedly true love relationship ends, then it was not true love to begin with. The test of a relationship is its ability to be resistant to threats and stresses; it must be profound and long-lasting.

Friendships are founded on mutual respect, without which there is no trust and thus no exchange of knowledge, resources and validation. *Respect* is ultimately built on the belief that the individual is in control of his or her life. This will lead to one being impressed by the cool, rational, and thoughtful manner of the other person. Further, one can learn from the other how to be in control because respect and admiration breed a desire to imitate the best characteristics of the other. Respect is a highly significant fundamental concept where the binding effects act in a recursive fashion. Thus, if a wife says 'my husband does not listen to me', we can gather a great deal from this deceptively simple statement. We know that she and he are both not in control; she is not, because no respect of her if forthcoming from the husband, and he is not, because she has clearly not learned from her husband how to be in control.

Conscious control over various areas is essential, and such control is manifested in one's traits. What traits are sought in the opposite sex? Clearly, there are many personal characteristics that are derived from one's background and personality. There are literally hundreds of such details relating to emotions, intellect, physique, career, education and habits that can be subsumed into categories. We can fortunately say, however, that aspects exist that are universally attractive and that are objectively superior to other attributes. These traits are called *virtues*, and the esteem that one bestows on a virtuous person of the opposite sex, one could bestow on anyone, male or female, whether they come from one's own family or community, or whether they come from anywhere else in the world. The virtues are described using many different terms, often depending on whether the discourse is considered religious or secular. They can, however, be distilled to seven essential concepts, which we enumerate:

- Purity; clarity of mind and cleanliness of body, a desire not to have one's intellect dulled by chemicals, social striving or material desires, or to have one's physical strength impaired by overindulgence in food, drink or nocuous substances
- Objectivity, honesty; a search for all the relevant facts in a situation
- Perfectability; a need to eliminate all ignorance, all ugliness in character, and all wastefulness; a search for understanding and practising correctness in all situations; a desire for self-improvement
- Caution, reservation, scepticism; a desire to carefully study and test all things, especially before a large investment of resources is made, in order to prevent neglect, exploitation or destruction
- Devotion; the desire and discipline to hold on to what is good and shunning what is bad, and to be prepared to make sacrifices to accomplish this
- Empathy; an automatic or reflexive mental action whereby the individual puts himself in the place of others who might be affected by his actions.

- Integrity: the ability to look at oneself as a complete individual, a stable integrated persona; the desire to maximise one's reputation and the desire to see all the other virtues be maximised and exist simultaneously

Whatever way you care to describe virtue — trust, dedication, cooperation, generosity, loyalty, truthfulness, purity of motive, confidence — all are approaches and attitudes that will yield the *best* results, no matter what the situation. These virtues are self-evident. Can anyone say that they find devotion or sincerity a negative trait, or selfishness or dishonesty a virtue? Can anyone say that, even provisionally, one esteems liars, sycophants, cheats, layabouts or traitors? There might be people who cast some small regard upon those who do not conform to conventions, but this confraternity of iconoclasts is but weakly allied. The closest ties always rest upon the continual witnessing of highly regarded attributes.

Why are virtues so important in a relationship? The virtues reveal above all a love of oneself, because they are all designed to allow the individual to make intelligent, constructive decisions that will bring far more rewards than losses. Those who poison their minds and bodies, those who become involved in deceit, those who care only about short-term expediency, those who rush into making decisions in order to please or impress their friends, those who are not interested in the truth but only status, power, or sensuality, they without exception make key mistakes that bring misery. How can one expect to have someone love them when they do not even love themselves? How can someone who acts self- destructively, that is, someone who treats himself with malevolence, be expected to treat someone else with kindness? How can someone who does not care to seek the best in himself and in his own life be expected to elicit what is best in someone else? When people possess the virtues, then and only then, can genuine love occur.

These fundamental good attitudes provide the engine for developing and grounding other ideas, such as attitudes towards the group dynamics, economy, education, social customs, and politics. Simply put, economic and social exigencies often clash with emotional and intellectual needs, and how a person resolves these conflicts in favour of a positive result for himself and others is a measure of his character. Surety of similarity in views between two people of good moral character, although desirable, is not guaranteed, however. In the area of politics, for example, a person among whose virtues is honesty might think that conservative politics can have a major impact on moral values, whereas another person of equal probity might think it might have little. The fact that there is a divergence of opinion does not negate the fact that both people are upright, and thus potentially true friends; because of their virtue, each gives his viewpoint sincerely, without concealed motive. Virtue acts as a mechanical system, a dynamism that produces other attitudes, an impetus for seeking rectitude in all areas of life. The fact that all such people of virtue do not agree might be due to differences in education, intelligence, perspective, or most likely, specificity. It is a misunderstanding that with gainful discourse can be remedied. Thus, amongst people who possess virtue, and thus command respect, we can say that the major *fundamental* factors of belief will always be analogous, the *derived* factors might or might not be so. Further, high virtue does not necessarily mean possessing the same set of viewpoints, but it does mean possessing the same set of behaviours.

It is essential that we now stress the fact that, although allure for the *whole* person is what makes for true love, it is the attraction for only *part* of a person that is far more common. Why should this be? Simply because one is more likely to favour one member of a set than most members of a set, other things being equal. Whereas many traits are ignored or even treated with suspicion, only a set of a few traits is what most people feel attracted towards, and therefore, only a few traits constitute the a person's image in the mind of the average person. Consequently, attraction between the sexes is more likely to be a fascination with a part of an individual's set of behaviours and attitudes rather than the whole person, resulting in an inability to make sacrifices because respect has not been established.[3] Those who do understand true love do not require any lessons, for the details come easily. But few are so endowed, and everyone could stand to benefit from learning about the pitfalls of the superficial infatuation. No matter how much the reader might think himself rooted in love, attractions to an incomplete set of *traits* are still problematic. Indeed, this dynamic is no respecter of class or status, so anyone can easily confuse this type of attraction with an attraction for the whole individual.

In order to maintain a focus on the whole person, one should strive to accurately perceive all attributes, place them into larger categories so as to make identification that much easier, and then to ascertain how each sex interprets these attributes. Attributes or traits are simple observations about another person, such as 'generally placid except at work', 'very sensitive about appearance, but otherwise takes criticism well', 'thrifty in all areas', 'easily swayed by friends' requests', 'likes to read complex novels', 'very good musician but does not have discipline to develop talent'. From these observations we gain an understanding of the forces inside a person, and these forces we relate to our own drives, desires, goals, hopes and views. All traits can be classified as facilitating, non-facilitating, promoting, or not promoting a constructive relationship between a man and woman. Yet, because many desire maximum independence, those traits that interfere with independence, even if they facilitate companionship, will be ignored or made negative. It is absolutely essential to understand how the desire for independence and the desire for love interact. Independence creates restrictions on the way in which another person is viewed. The more keenly one desires independence, the more likely it is that one will view a possible love interest only as a subset of attributes. Because of this strategy, maximum freedom can occur, and there is the potential for establishing a basic relationship with the intended person. However, *as true love can come only from full respect, and as respect can come only from an evaluation of all traits, this simplified view of another person will definitely not lead to lasting, deep affection*. A full assessment of all factors must be made if one is to be happy in matrimony and it is the aim of this book to bring to the reader's attention life situations where such improper valuation of traits can arise. We fall in love with someone because we find their attributes worthy of respect, but the recognition of these attributes is affected by our desire for individuality and autonomy; thus, it is critical that we make certain our evaluation of another is not affected by our particular material and emotional requirements.

If an attribute is studied at all, it must have some attractive qualities. The attraction to this attribute might be the result of it being congruent with one's own qualities or being non-congruent. Due to the diversity of traits among people, even in the most homogenous culture, there is a low probability of making a perfect or near-perfect match. Therefore, if attraction between human males and females is nearly universal, then this attraction must be the result of a *combination* of similarity and diversity. Attraction in the human realm is unique, however. We can easily observe nature: Animals will invariably attempt to mate with those opposite-sex animals of like physical characteristics, keeping sexual activity within the same species or breed. No prompting other than from physiology is required for an animal to select another of its breed and to mate, which is based upon matching through the senses various external traits to it's own. However, animals, unlike humans, have no comprehension of 'self' and so the matching that occurs is purely mechanical. One could extrapolate this to the area of human nature, deducing that as humans have similar fundamental physiological attributes to animals (mammals) that they also have an innate proclivity to mate with their own species, and possibly their own 'breed' or race. In regards to this, we can cite a certain natural human narcissism portrayed in the arts, made obvious in the tendency for artists to render subjects in paintings with physical characteristics similar to that of the artist himself.[4] However, fulfilment in human relations must integrate dissimilarity, an issue that is difficult to discuss rationally because disagreement in opinions and behaviour is far more likely to cause conflict than agreement. It is this diversity, however, that puzzles and aggravates, because all too often it is that which first attracts, and then is abandoned as the couple seek similarity, either real or imagined. In essence, similarity draws a man and woman together, but it is a constructive *diversity* between them that pulls them in beyond the 'outer perimeter' and keeps them together. Similarity is easy to live with, but differences can be difficult to tolerate and negotiate, yet one is eager to find the essential differences that compensate for failures and that make similitude secondary.

This book seeks to present all the pertinent aspects of the problems mentioned here: The conflict between virtue and self-centeredness; the mistake of being attracted to only a few traits and not to the whole person; and most importantly, the struggle to reconcile the desire for independence and the need for support. Although there is no shortage of books on the subject of marriage and relationships, they have for the most part failed to inform people about the real problems that exist. Ideas on independence and marriage are spread through society informally and through the mass media, so it is not as if there is no attention paid to the various factors governing the relationships between men and women. Indeed, academic works deliberate a wide variety of attributes. However, no one mentions *independence* as a major source of this conflict, nor does anyone mention the often-seen corollaries of selfishness, mendacity and greed. Instead, essayists attempt to act as clearinghouses of demands, providing information about what the various groups in society are seeking to establish, without passing judgement on these demands. Men attempt to learn about women, women about men, young about old, old about young, shy about extroverted, extroverted about shy, and so on. This is not surprising in our age when most people for the first 20 years or so of life seek to find out what 'I' really means. Eventually, they will have to learn about others for their own advantage. Only when both authors and readers focus on a subset of personality traits do we get such a situation. Humanity will however always find ways and means to discuss all-important issues of love, but most works presently deal with making clear and, to a certain extent, validating the self-orientated attitudes of most people. Ultimately, seekers of truth need to be their *own* guides, to tell if any significant adjustment in life is necessary; if it is possible; how long this adjustment will take; what underlying principles are involved so the individual can develop his own techniques of dealing with problems. One would think this varied approach to be common in a society that places so much value, ironically enough, on independence of thought. Yet, people depend on others for critical answers because they have become so 'self-governing' that they now are without moral foundation, and therefore, without knowledge of the social rules necessary for attaining happiness.

Independence as a concept is simply taken for granted in most discourse, and so none of these works get at the heart of the problem, which contains *material life issues that conflict with the ideal of love*. If the ideal were settled, then behaviour would follow. But the ideal of the happy fulfilled relationship is under revision, and in this form it engages in a contest with other ideals. Further, the material issues of life have always provided both a support of love as well as its hindrance. Understanding these fundamentals, these hard realities of life, and how they relate to the relationship between men and women will pave the way for true love, that is, if the individual is ready for the sacrifices that are necessary.

In spite of the many difficulties in matching attributes and ideals, the elusive dream, to love and be loved, is not impossible to secure, however. There *must* be ways to make the dream come alive, as many quite obviously do, even in our fractious age. What secret methods are used to achieve the ideas begun by those fleeting glances, idle daydreams, and hopeful imaginings? What does one do when the remarkably clear vision of the future fades? In order to find out, we must show some courage and don the outfit of the explorer, for there are evidently no easily perceptible answers. The danger is that as explorers the temptation is to stray, to fall into the false belief that one can become independent of love. If there were easy answers, there is little doubt that the actual relationship between man and woman would routinely match the vision. Instead, the vision is so often violated that special citations and awards should be handed out to the few who reach the ideal. We must venture throughout all the areas that men and women find themselves, all the areas that affect their friendship. The aim is to find these concealed properties, to ascertain what founds and rules the relationship between the sexes. Just as men and women currently have no limitations placed on them as to what they are, where they go, what they buy, what they wear, and what influences them, so an enquiry cannot have limits. It is necessary for the explorer to take a comprehensive look at every important facet of a love relationship.

The matters that enter into properly founded relationships can challenge individual lives, but should not and cannot shake the relationship. This can be stated simply and directly; no great tome needs to be written. But so as to alert the wary as the potential obstacles that might befall them, it is necessary to discuss each area of possible conflict so that these can be defused quickly and with definitude. Relationships have to be examined, including material, emotional, intellectual, and personality concerns. It cannot be overstressed that *true love is ineluctably a function only of virtuous behaviour*. For those who still do not understand the necessity of virtue, this book shows the dangers of relying solely on personality and material factors. For those who do understand and practise virtue (to the few left!), this book means to reinforce your wise decision, and to preempt the problems that will arise in those areas that are still weak.

Thus, the focus of our discussions on relationships, even when not explicitly stated, is always to give the reader the means to achieve true, non-sexual intimacy and affection, which is indeed the greatest achievement of mankind. 'Pure love' is undefiled dearness or being cherished with an emotion unadulterated by social obligation; material and pragmatic factors, such as status, are never more important than the love itself. Such love is beyond mere attraction, and moves into the deepest realm of human existence. It is our goal to see that men and woman can attain this through their own efforts, whilst still operating within the boundaries of propriety and decency, *and* still in keeping with their own needs.

Whilst pondering all of the ways in which the individual can be swayed, it should always be kept in mind that human beings exercise free will in regard to their decisions, this being as true in the history of our Western civilisation as it is today. People can however give up their own minds and bodies in return for what they consider to be spiritual satisfaction. Free will is tied to autonomy; when one has no binding ties, one is then theoretically free to make choices amongst viable alternatives. Certain factors, often economic, interfere with choice and also might interfere with living a virtuous life. Compromises might have to be made to moral principles in order to support the vitality of the industrial apparatus.

It is fair to point out that we will use terms relating to marriage and married life as indicative of the close relationship between men and women, even though such a relationship can take place under any social circumstance or arrangement. Western society, or the English language at any rate, does not have any other convenient expression for 'a close bond between a man and woman', beyond that of calling the persons involved a 'husband', 'wife', or 'married person'. Thus, when we say the tendency to 'marry' this in reality means the tendency to become emotionally and intellectually devoted to another, whether formally married, only cohabitating or some other arrangement. The concepts of 'devotion' or 'companionship' in no way imply that sexual contact is required, although that might voluntarily become a corollary.

The issues that are addressed in this work can be summarised as follows. It is self-evident that love and independence are two universal forces, which although always in competition are not mutually incompatible. The key to accomplishing a balance of the two areas lies in discerning the nature of each. For love to exist there must be respect, and respect grows out of witnessing virtuous behaviour, such as honesty, integrity and purity. On the other hand, for personal independence to be maximised, the individual must properly manage financial, educational and other external factors, in addition to reifying advanced concepts such as social reciprocity, self-examination, perfectability, and empathy. Affection, a major component of love, begins with friendship, and two factors in reference to the independence of the other person are involved in the decision to deepen it to romance: level of commitment and probability of loss. Thus, marriage entails a rational search process which requires objectivity and, more importantly, flexible and innovative use of resources. Yet, substantial pressures from the outside to marry, especially to stabilise autonomous individuals, make the 'ideal' marriage seem less a question of choice and more of destiny or luck.

External material changes have traditionally exerted a moderate effect on marriage patterns, through an interrelationship of occupation, income, savings, lack of available partners, and mortality. Society has offered a succession of life path accomplishments in order to fulfill the love ideal and the materialistic apotheosis. There is, however, no guarantee of expected success in this path, and natural aptitude, not choice, often affects career and social pathways. The first major announcement of a person's independence is leaving the home of origin to begin a new living situation, an event which is influenced by social pressure to contribute to the economy, but also more importantly by the personal dynamic of dissatisfaction with home life. Thus, one's experiences at home, good or bad, will considerably impact one's attitudes to married life and society in general. Poor upbringing, poor social skills, or witnessing bad parental marriages often increase the desire for a companionate relationship, as a means of providing the love one never received at home.

Since marriage decisions are often affected by experiences unrelated to a future spouse, and the dynamic of achieving wholeness through joining similarity and complementarity is often ignored, various neglected psychological and personality issues must be investigated in order to understand the actual processes involved and to estimate the damage that is being done. Two critical personality issues, personal sacrifice and the willingness to change, have been abandoned due to mass migration and the demands of the modern economy. These alterations in society succeed in creating an emphasis on beliefs which assure larger group solidarity and not marital harmony, the basis of which is virtuous action. Further, they bolster concepts of autonomy, which in the modern context produces exploitation of the kindness of others and a derogation of constructive inter-dependence. Because of these negative actions, it is now believed that, although friendships of all kinds are important, marriage is the only relationship where the ideal of love can be satisfied because relations with people have become more unstable and distant. Unfortunately, the selfishness which operates so freely in this world cannot be contained to life outside the home, and thus callous self-interest weakens and degrades the husband-wife relationship. Although both sexes have undergone significant changes in personal ideals, it is specifically the feminine that has experienced a major transformation, from reflecting idealism to embodying pragmatism.

In life there will always be something of a contest between love and independence which can and should be worked out into balance by compromise, hence the subtitle of this book. By independence, we mean the *constant* desire to change one's life circumstances in the pursuit to have the things and surround oneself with the people that one desires. By dependence, we mean the emotional, intellectual and material support that others can give a person, including advice, validation of ideas, direction, inspiration, and financial support. These two forces always act against the background of the ideal of love, which is that most profound desire to have an intimate, fulfilling, pure and undefiled relationship with someone of the opposite sex. Throughout time, independence, dependence and love have co-existed, and this will continue to be true as long as human beings exist. In the past, people struggled to attain an independent livelihood, to find a position of respectability in society. They also needed support from others, and they needed to have a close, reliable relationship with another that would be clearly different from all other friendships. In our day, the theme of independence has become a preoccupation, which in turn has made it difficult to be loved because there is a lack of elemental respect. People have made themselves 'unlovable' because of the deceit, frivolity, aloofness, self-centeredness and promiscuity that society expects of the fully 'autonomous' person. This has made it impossible to achieve true love, and instead they use dependence as a substitute. Instead of a couple's activities being carried out on the basis of cooperation and convergence of interests, they are carried out on the principle of a cold *quid pro quo*, where the two take turns satisfying each other's selfish needs.

The detailed strategy to the problems discussed herein must be worked out by the individual reader. I attempt to set the *context* wherein resolution of challenges to one's concepts of affection and autonomy can fruitfully occur but only the reader is responsible for correct application of conclusions reached in this book. Thus, I alert the reader to the hazards that are on this part of the journey of life, the long road that leads to a compromise between independence and love. This road, however, unlike many others, can be travelled quite within the capacity of the average individual, and it is not particularly arduous; there are traps of course along the route, although not that many in number. The turns and twists are easily comprehensible because they are so basic to individual life: Material aspects, education, family of childhood, love, affection, freedom. Sovereignty over one's affairs is possible not because one merely knows about these issues, but because one authoritatively controls the ramifications of these issues by accepting the universally known ideas of virtue. Thinking about social influences is highly important, and we should not take anything for granted. The wonderful thing about the sociological study is that everyone can bring something of his or her own to it. Indeed, one of the best ways to determine whether a theory is correct is simply to see if it can be applied to one's own life. This is what sets the social sciences apart from all other disciplines, which demand laboratory or controlled scientific examination for verification.

Unless one understands all the basic factors involved in the relationship between men and women in reference to one's own personal needs, one will undoubtedly risk great failure. But if one understands as much, and it is not a sophisticated task, one stands an excellent chance of protecting oneself from emotional and material injury, if not finally achieving one's ideal of love. In the last chapter of this book, we will put together the information that we have compiled and attempt to sort out the cross-influences to reach a larger, more comprehensive understanding, set in the framework of personal development and cognisance. We should always bear in mind in our investigations that although love never requires justification, attempts to reach it without addressing the need for independence leave one's character and life all too often emblazoned with failure and sorrow.

For this cause shall a man leave his father and mother, and be joined unto his wife, and they shall be one flesh.
~EPHESIANS 5:31 (KJV)

*Up there on the mountain,
there is a tall house,*

*And every morning...,
three fair maidens come out*

*The first one is my sister,...,
the second is my friend...*

*The third has no name,...,
she must become mine...*
~DORT OBEN AUF DEM BERGE
(song, early 1500s),
Ludwig Senfl[5]

Chapter 2
Sacrifice, Commitment and Realism

Outgoingness and Courtship

We first lay out several principles that we shall be addressing throughout this book. Before we understand anything else, we should know that humans crave affection in whatever form it comes, or from whatever source. Children, insecure and defenseless, will seek the affection of parents and relatives, hoping to receive the security they desire. If the attention is adequate and instrumental, then these children will be less likely to seek acceptance outside the home. As they grow older, they gradually become more interested in gaining independence, but if home life is attractive, there is little reason why they should seek out friends from the social environment unless they come up to the standard to which they are accustomed. The background to all this, however, must contain the freedom to choose and explore relationships between children, parents, relatives and friends. Freedom in home life becomes a critical component in the development of healthy concepts of love and affection.

The general parameters of relationships are established early in life and are in many ways based on experiences in the household. However, many of the requirements that the individual desires in a relationship are not affected by home life but are highly personal in nature. Males and females often come together because they find that the similitude in thoughts and feelings cross-validate individual ideas. The ideas of one person are echoed by the other; the seemingly impermeable wall that prevents understanding can be demolished by the knowledge of the other; observations can be taken and completed and given insight by the other. The gregarious liaison between a man and woman can thus be extremely consequential. As Lucretius observed: *Consuetudo concinnat amorem*, that is, habit causes love. One is intuitively drawn into deepening the relationship for these reasons, magnifying and expanding the positive experiences one has had. At some point there must be a resolution to the question: Are we to go forward into intimacy, or are we to remain merely friends? If substantial resources are expended on behalf of the other person, usually the inclination is to go forward and open oneself up emotionally, materially, intellectually and physically. Thus, all intimate relationships, including marriage arranged freely, must begin with *friendship*.

Logic would seem to indicate that love falls on a continuum of relationship closeness. Before we can convince ourselves that love is truly a part of the relationship, a considerable investment of resources must be made, although according to La Bruyère we would be wasting our time: 'Love begins with love; friendship, however warm, cannot change to love, however mild'. This overly- idealistic attitude towards love posits that compatibility is *instantly* recognisable, so one knows immediately if a relationship is bound for love or for mere friendship. But to believe this would indeed be folly, for as we have said, it is absolutely essential that we found our affections on the basis of evaluating all of a person's traits, and it is impossible to know these traits before numerous meetings and discussions have taken place. No one, unless he is a suspect in a criminal case, is compelled to reveal details of his life, thus such revelations must come under the aegis of friendship. Thus, since friendship is not compulsory, whilst the evaluation process is going on, there are two basic questions that must be answered in order to determine whether our investment is prudent, and whether the friendship bond will be deepened into love: The degree of commitment one can expect from the other person in pursuing and maintaining the relationship, and the risk of losing that person's friendship to another. These questions, of commitment and stability, are made reasonable because they stem from a fundamental knowledge of human nature, and relationships cannot go further without them being resolved. It is rather self-evident that they form the overarching themes for every companionate relationship and are present whether acknowledged or not. Within a dyad (two-person relationship), there are four possible issues:

Table 1

Factors involved in deepening a friendship: Entrustment and concentration of attention		
	Degree of commitment of the other person to this relationship	Probability of the other person forming another relationship
Man	A	B
Woman	C	D

Each cell contains an intensity of response, such as 'high' or 'low'. The cells contain the following definitions:

A. Man's expectation of a woman's commitment
B. Man's expectation of a woman going to another man
C. Woman's expectation of a man's commitment
D. Woman's expectation of a man going to another woman

The best relationship would be one where both the man and the woman feel that the other is highly committed to the relationship and is at low risk of becoming involved with someone else. The worst relationship would be one where both the man and woman feel that the other is poorly committed to the relationship and is at high risk to become involved with someone else.

Commitment, or more accurately entrustment, is a pledge to take a certain course of action in the future, with implied penalties if one does not. Male-female relationships demand a larger set of promises than other relationships; they must abide by certain rules concerning the amount of time, support, praise, consideration, advice and money one person gives to another. Further, the loss of someone involves a complete or nearly complete abandonment. There might be some future contact, but intimacy is limited and information and opinions are restricted.

The two factors of commitment and risk of loss are largely independent. Let us examine a few unexpected combinations. One could be poorly committed to a relationship, yet not be very prone to start a committed (exclusive) relationship with another person (low commitment, low risk of loss). This scenario is more likely to occur when independence is an important goal in life. When independence is high then there is a tug of war between two factors: The individual and another individual, or the individual and a situation, such as a career. For example, if a woman is caught between two men, A <- F -> B, and she wishes to obtain satisfaction from A, but also likes to do the same with B, then there can be little or no commitment to either lest they bog her down. It should be understood, however, that she might not wish to leave either man, thus her chance of ending a relationship is low, although her level of commitment is also low. Also, one could be highly committed to someone and still be attracted to another person (high commitment, high risk of loss), a situation which occurs when there is a sense of duty but inadequate knowledge about and valuation of the first relationship. Thus, self-centeredness is the source of the problem in the first situation, and ignorance is the source of the problem in the second.

Once a friendship is established, and the individual feels that there is a future for the couple, the themes of entrustment and fidelity become even more significant as the level of investment increases. The level of continued entrustment is often predicated on how easily an individual can find another person that will be at least an equal substitute. Based on utilitarian concepts, if the male presence is low, and female presence high, then it is easy for any particular man to find another woman, thus making his commitment to his current female partner fairly low. When companionship is valued highly and people become 'cost-conscious', each individual assigns a certain approximate probability to finding another friend of the opposite sex if the present one is lost. If there is, for example, a 20% chance of losing a man due to a small surplus of females, and taking a man's commitment into account, then a woman for example with a very high educational attainment will have reason to worry, for she knows the difficulty that awaits in finding another man with similar educational status if this current relationship misfires. She could well rush to engage in physical intimacy in order to deepen the bond and increase his commitment (a situation which creates a form of pseudo-marriage). On the other hand, a woman of average education, such as a high-school graduate, might not turn to such a manipulative enterprise in order to 'capture' a man, because if her boyfriend leaves her, the loss would not be excessive. The cost of finding another man of *average* education (as opposed to high education) is low, as there are greater numbers of such men compared to the numbers of men of *low* or *high* educational attainment.

Thus, there are two types of cross-sex relationship: Friend and lover. The greatly divergent responsibilities of each leaves a clear social dichotomy that only the most foolhardy would dare to ignore. Although it is common for single men and women to go out frequently on dates, any longer term dating relationship necessitates reflections on marriage. There must be a change from one of friendship to one of love relationship. Unfortunately, in an independence driven society, 'deepening' a relationship, usually results in a deplorable and offensive vacillation and wavering in attitudes and behaviour. Thus, any deeper relationship must proceed with the perhaps unsaid understanding that both partners are readying for life-long entrustment.

The form of the relationship requires resolution to enquiries, but not necessarily commitment. Courting is a series of informal meetings between members of the opposite sex, that fundamentally are a loosening, if not a rejection, of the individual's independence, and are usually as a prelude to more intimate relations and marriage. The goal of courtship is to provide a period where the couple get to know one another, their backgrounds, their likes and dislikes, their attitudes, their hopes and fears. If the couple feel that they are then able to live with each other, and if they feel that they cannot live without each other (a somewhat romantic notion), and if the fundamental pragmatic factors are in place (namely the availability of housing, job, minimal income for food and clothing, furniture), then they would consent to marry.

The context and timing in which such meetings occur are socially and culturally determined. There is great variation of form, ranging from meetings planned and supervised closely by parents to fully independent decision-making by young people. In times past, men and women met in informal situations at people's homes, at gatherings, and in church. There were no clubs, bars, dating services or other means, and connections were usually arranged by family members. Such contact through personal networks meant that the door of one's home could admit many potential partners and suitors in safety and discretion. In European cultures, the tradition has been one that stressed close supervision, but it has never included or tolerated actual decision-making by parents as a general rule, except in certain unusual circumstances. Unless a society was on the verge of penury or relatively great fortunes were involved, people saw fit to allow their children to marry whom they wished, although voicing an opinion was not uncommon.

Dating forms only one aspect of courtship. Courtship can be seen as a process encompassing a number of factors: Understanding each other, increasing desire for each other's company, establishing the rules of the relationship and preparing the way for marriage and lifetime companionship. Mental adjustments must always precede material changes, and so time must be given for rearrangement of internal and external resources and dynamics. Independence is an asset in this case as it allows an individual the time to complete the phases of courting and to walk away from the relationship if serious problems come to be revealed. This process can be broken down into the following phases Exploration, Assessment, Building, Execution:

A. EXPLORATION. To *find* another person that meets the minimum criteria of goodness for a mate.

The individual searches for a person that will meet his standards, which might include level of extroversion, ambition, career plans, material philosophy, views on children, home life, social life, politics, morals and ethics. He can use a variety of resources, such as friends' recommendations, personal statements, or biographies. Although it can last several years, this phase is probably the most important since a high achievement here will mean much lower level of effort in later phases. There is no a priori time limit, apart from the one culture imposes, because there is no control over the variety of people one is likely to encounter. Much is based on probability, although one can increase the odds of finding individuals who meet the requirements by engaging third parties in the search. Care must be taken to verify all pertinent characteristics; untruthfulness and inaccuracy, things one must always guard against, can be very common in self- descriptions.

B. ASSESSMENT. To *discover* what the individual will find necessary to adjust in order to have a successful marriage.

Needless to say, no one will ever perfectly fit one's criteria. No matter how well one explores, one will always have to make certain sacrifices to accommodate the essential hopes of the other person. Thus, the individual must now understand what he will have to do to please the other person. This could mean changes in school plans, career goals, leisure time, time spent socialising; it might mean delaying certain activities he now takes for granted. If he is able to accept these changes then he can move on to the next phase, if not then the courtship should be ended.

This phase can last a few months. Since the particulars of his potential mate have been verified in the previous phase, the individual, who presumably knows himself better than he knows anyone else, can fairly quickly resolve what changes must be made and whether he can or cannot tolerate them.

C. BUILDING. To *prepare* to implement the changes in lifestyle and personality.

The individual must now make allowances in his behaviour and possibly find alternatives to his original life goals. If his future wife insists on getting a better education, for example, he will have to look for a school and the funding. If she wishes for him to stop spending so much time with his friends, he will have to ease himself out of these relationships without giving offense. He will have to prepare himself psychologically for a new life. The temporal extent of this phase is the most unpredictable. Depending on what changes were agreed upon, it might last from a few weeks to many years. In previous generations, couples would remain engaged for years until they felt that they had obtained a requisite amount of education, secured good employment and had saved enough money to buy or rent a residence that was to their liking.

D. EXECUTION. To *implement* the changes in lifestyle that a person has agreed to do.

If both people have made earnest attempts at change, if they have fully cooperated, there is an excellent chance that the marriage will be successful, more successful, in fact, than either could have imagined. This phase should clearly begin before marriage, although realistically it will probably be several years before all the changes have finally been made. It is not uncommon that in the first three to five years of marriage husband and wife tend to maintain a significant variability in traits, after which they tend to converge more.[6] *A* succeeds in pleasing *B*, which works for awhile but then *A* finds it difficult so reverts back to old ways or turns to another equally unacceptable manner of behaviour. *A* tries again but this time with a different approach, which might then succeed in the longer term.

Thus, we go from a cursory examination of another person to a friendship, on to deeper friendship and then finally to marriage. At all phases there must be the consideration of how likely it is that this friend will leave for another, and how seriously this person takes the nature of the relationship. Further, the pace of the phases is predicated to a certain extent on one or the other finding alternative partners; this probability might actually increase with growing friendship, as one can look for someone new as weaknesses are revealed in a friend. There are few modern cultures that have been examined in detail about their courtship practises, and surveys of previous cultures themselves often mention the fact that whatever practise is described might be highly local. Further, these surveys view the courtship situation from the outside, focussing on material considerations, not emotional or psychological changes. A community in Andalusia[7] is probably representative of a modern culture grounded in traditional mores mirroring a pre-modern rural society, especially one which tolerated marriage later in life. People in this region tend to have conservative social values, separate roles according to sex, but young people still easily fraternise with one another, limiting this social intercourse after courtship begins. They show great care in choosing a mate, going through a lengthy courtship process that might easily last five to seven years. There are three phases: The secret phase, lasting six months to a year, where a man and woman meet informally, usually without the knowledge or approval of parents (corresponding to phase A above); the romantic phase, lasting one to two years, where the formal courtship begins (as a lead-in to marriage) and the couple intensify their relationship, become comfortable with each other's personalities and temperaments, and where the families get to know one another (B and C above); the contribution phase, lasting one to four years, where arrangements are made procuring the a house, bed, other furniture, and so on (D above). During this last phase, the economic status of each family is quietly assessed, and the families come to some kind of an agreement as to what each will contribute, with an emphasis on complete fairness. The woman and her family are often expected to contribute furnishings and the man and his family are expected to contribute the house itself. Preparation usually begins even before the couple begin their courtship, but intensifies once the couple decide to eventually marry.[8]

The social focus is on phases C and D, and courtship is an informal, but by no means casual, contract, where each party is expected to provide certain minimum contributions as set by culture and other contributions as promised. It is apparent that people are not especially fearful of losing a potential mate to someone else, nor do people seem to lack commitment. Starting the marriage out well materially is uppermost in everyone's mind, and indeed, the problems of adjustment that occur in the first years of marriage can be magnified if the couple struggles to find acceptable living quarters, buy furniture and other items, or to live up to a desired standard. In this particular culture, inheritance is a troubling issue, the root of many family problems, with siblings quarrelling over shares. Community members are careful to be quiet about their household affairs as envy is rampant; even the realisation of small differences between households can precipitate acrimonious relations.

These observations might very well be true in many other regions, but to a certain extent reflect the temperament, and thus the innate character, of the people. Hence, it would at least appear that an *exogenous* variable or variables have a major influence on the courtship process, that it is the economy and culture that 'call the shots' when it comes to the courtship process. People must abide by the demands of material necessity as to how long it will take to reach the personal ideal. The better the economy, the shorter the courtship period, other things being the same. Psychological factors are often not specifically addressed, with the old assumption being made that the couple will 'grow' in love.

Naturally, the psychological needs of the individual are paramount, but many other factors could produce the desire to marry than simply to maintain a deep friendship with the opposite sex. We can see, however, that the specific primary needs for companionship can be buried under other considerations, which can ultimately wreak havoc with those primary needs. Consequently, from this point on in our discussions, we shall examine many of the significant factors that are external to the specific decision to maintain this close friendship, those mentioned above and others. It should be understood that the basic psychological principles of evaluating entrustment and fidelity, as discussed above, are always active.

To first understand the processes of courtship, the main regulators of the phenomenon must be sought. We can observe that courtship *length* is a common factor in many aspects of this process, including level of emotional intimacy, finances, family relations, and organisation of life plans. Economic, cultural or personal factors are mainly responsible for the length of courtship, and the rules of courtship can be both causes and effects. When the process is longer, greater attention can be given to developing understanding of the other's personality and needs, greater closeness can be achieved, and greater augmentation of material resources is possible. If a particular social situation requires waiting a long period, then the sexes must be rather aloof; if they were not, early infatuation and love interest could spark early marriage (if premarital sex is strongly condemned). However, where the ideal material life can be reached quickly (standards are low, and/or the economy is doing extremely well), then such a sex division is not necessary. In this culture it would appear that rigid general separation of the sexes (though not necessarily precluding ordinary friendship) is necessary if people are to be able to court for many years. However, this same separation encourages and facilitates independence, since one is presumably freed from early marriage. From a circle of female friends, a man chooses one that he wishes to be his wife. He and she both work and save to put together a home that is consistent with their ideals of comfort and aesthetics; when they accumulate all that is required, they then marry and move into their new residence.

A plausible sequence seems to obtain: Standard of living forces young people to wait for quite a while before marrying, but the culture forces men and women to remain apart, somewhat fairly distant from one another. The sequence might be as follows:

Economic situation -> create new social rules -> extend courtship -> restrict cross-sex relations -> delay marriage

In the Western world, although the economy has some role to play in how people socialise (there is a non-significant positive correlation of +.5117 between number of close friends and GNP per capita), the argument that economics is an extremely significant or crucial factor regulating contact between the sexes is evidently false. What could then influence the size and depth of friendship interaction? It is quite possible that the parameters of one's friendship circle are almost entirely determined by personal choice. The length of courtship in turn is thought to be influenced by the degree to which the sexes fraternise. However, if the intention is to delay marriage by restricting access between the sexes, then it does not work. Possibly Andalusians are by nature more restrained, thus holding back on forming intimate relations. They might also be culturally more predisposed to take care in going through the phases of courtship, without undue pressure. This would explain the long courtship. We could assume, therefore, that the fewer friends one has, the later one's marriage. However, we learn that among the larger Western nations, having relatively *few* male and female friends is associated with a *lower*, not greater, likelihood of later marriage.[9] In other words, people who have few friends do not put off marriage, and people who have many friends delay marriage. Further, the strength of this relationship makes us think that this is indeed a major *determining* factor in late marriage. The stronger the correlation with a measured external variable, the likelier it is that a population or some segment of it is strongly affected by one variable and that one alone. Other internal influences, not easily measured, might very well be responsible for this association. This is not to say that there is not some other segment of the population that will indeed marry earlier (there is no clear correlation for marrying at ages below 30), but there is at least one segment that will see friendship as a substitute for marriage. *Temperament might determine the strength of desire for opposite-sex friendship, which in turn affects marriage age.*

If we accept the notion that the act of choosing one's friends is one of the freest things one can do, not affected by economic considerations, living conditions, and so on, then the possibility arises that friend choice is genetically (temperamentally) influenced. In addition, if a strong correlation between friendship choice and late marriage exists, other factors are of little or no influence; with no other factors that would work to possibly affect the choice of friends (and so indirectly marriage age) the idea that it is the product of some individual innate dynamic is strengthened. Thus, it is probable that an 'aloofness' in relations between the sexes, and indeed the courtship process as a whole, might be the product of innate ethnic genetic trait, and it is the individual's personality then that 'calls the shots'. The rules of courtship are both a cause and effect in many matters in a young person's life, but in light of these observations about personality, it would now appear that they are more an effect than a cause.

Even if there are rigid rules of manners and etiquette that draw boundaries on physical intimacy, this does not mean that men and women cannot have close emotional relationships which adequately fulfill their innate desires so that marriage is made unnecessary. Friendship is thus not only used as a way to bring about courtship and attract a potential mate, but it can also act as a substitute for marriage itself. During courtship, however, the couple might isolate themselves from their friends, focussing their attention on one another.

The true sequence of events might be as follows:

Temperament -> restrict circle of friends -> lengthen courtship or delay marriage

If cross-sex relations are limited in scope by personal disposition and/or social rules, and courtship is the only legitimate context in which a close friendship can take place between young men and women, then courtship would likely be extended and the saving aspect is simply the best use of this time, but not an end in itself. In addition, restraints placed on trysts between long-affianced couples might be a prudent measure to reduce the temptation to engage in sex now rather than wait for marriage. Thus, separation might be more necessary between engaged people than between opposite-sex friends.

One major aspect of personality is level of extroversion. Those who are introverted will presumably have fewer opposite sex friends and not marry early. An introverted individual will prefer the company of people he knows; since other persons of the same sex will be more likely to share his beliefs and attitudes, he will more likely fraternise with them than with the opposite sex. The introvert has fewer friends than the extrovert, which leads him to seek marriage, but his *personality* prevents facilitation of this. When he finally does find an opposite-sex close friend, he is more likely to formalise the relationship by initiating courtship, and this often leads to marriage, since he would not wish to lose this close friend. We would then think that having a greater number of opposite-sex friends would *increase* the likelihood of early marriage, with an extrovert having more potential partners to choose from than an introvert. Based on the above analysis, this would be logical, but further analysis reveals that this does seem to be the case. Extroversion is strongly related to having a larger number of close friends and is only modestly associated with early marriage.[10] As mentioned above, the individual can focus on the ability of friendship to act as a substitute for marriage. Extroverts tend to have more friends than introverts, but extroversion does *not* lead to earlier marriage, instead leading to later marriage.

The personality trait of extroversion deals with freedom of personal relations and the width of a friendship circle. The extrovert might call upon a number of opposite sex friends for advice, comfort, and so on, not necessarily imposing himself on any one friend that much. An introvert might obtain all of his friendship from one other person; such a relationship would entail a formalisation because of the sacrifice involved. When the level of closeness and sacrifice demanded by another person crosses a threshold, the relationship then moves from friendship to romantic love interest, and to maintain it courtship must begin. However, courtship and marriage narrow the friendship circle, regardless of whether one or both people are introverted.[11] Thus, the size of the friendship circle affects marriage, but marriage also affects the size of the friendship circle. We can now see a close connection between companionate relations and social environment.

The extrovert's tendency to speak openly and freely widens the circle of friends, making reliance on any one friend unnecessary. The same tendency, however, allows the extrovert to become very close with a one or two people in this circle, especially with the opposite sex, necessitating a reduction in the size of his circle. Naturally, the extrovert could find immense satisfaction in just one very close friendship, but he also prefers having many other friendships, admittedly shallow but nevertheless rewarding. The natural outgoingness of the extrovert makes him varied friendships, but his eye will fall on one girlfriend who recommends he forsake the others so he can spend more time with her. He experiences a widening of the circle, then a narrowing of it, and then possibly again another widening as the close friendship ends. We can formulate a general principle which describes the inherently mutually exclusive nature of the phenomenon we have been exploring. Succinctly put, *it is in the extrovert's nature to desire and have many friends, but it is this wide circle and ingratiating nature that quickly allow him to gain the confidence of a single companion, who then demands more exclusive use of this time. After awhile, the temptation is then to go back to the larger circle of friends.* If excessive independence is linked to excessive extroversion, as it often is in modern society, then this principle describes, in rough outline, the current struggle in relationships, the harmful tension between the outside world and the couple. Three factors—extroversion, size of friendship circle, and marriage—are critical in defining personal autonomy, as these cover personality, social and pragmatic variables. We shall examine the concept of autonomy from this perspective in further detail later on.

HOW TO BEST BUILD A FAMILY?

An individual's level of entrustment and assiduousness are discovered through the process of courtship, which is taken at a pace decided largely by the individual himself, in accordance with his level of extroversion. Thus, *the role of materialism appears to be secondary to that of emotions and personality.* Attention should therefore be paid to the mental factors, as enumerated in the four phases above, that figure into adjustment during courtship as much as the economic factors. The process will not function correctly unless and until both people substantially cooperate with each other, and as with anything else there can be no great return where there has not been significant investment. Of course, one can always be lucky and find a mate that has total compatibility. But in most cases there must be give and take, without which each person will increasingly irritate and disappoint the other, leading to disagreements and animosity. Further, this procedure will often not work, when one or both have a psychological disorder. Particularly troublesome are various personality disorders which make people unstable, impulsive, defiant, weak or indecisive. Whereas many might emphasise the joys of married life, it is the role of scholars, researchers and writers to emphasise the costs as well as benefits.

How easily the individual gets along with other people, and the depth and number of friendships he has, are indicative of the dexterity with which he forms relationships. The proficiency of relationship management is an important consideration determining the extent to which one methodically follows a long-term plan. If relationships are formed only with difficulty, then people will be loathe to expend large resources on analysis, as the results will often signal rejection of one person, and the search starts for yet another. It is easier, if not wiser, to eschew any complicated search process and take whatever seems good. Realistically, though, how easily men and women make meaningful social contact with others similar to themselves is a critical factor, albeit indirect, in the long-term stability of relationships.

We have seen how phases C and D are prone to personal adjustment, and we might very well expect that the first two phases of courtship are similarly characteristic. Indeed, the methods used to find a spouse can be as varied as the human imagination can allow. As a way of overcoming the problems presented by shyness and poor access to the opposite sex, and as a kind of strange antipode to the rational search process, many cultures might emphasise certain alternatives to extended courtship, such as metaphysical procedures that 'reveal' the inevitable truth about potential matrimonial candidates, and thus obviate the problems of choice. Indeed, because of the high ideals many have about love, any error in judgement, no matter how seemingly trivial, might be fatal. As Proust said, 'It is a mistake to speak of a bad choice in love, since, as soon as a choice exists, it can only be bad'. A woman might resort to magic in order to uncover the name of the man fated to be her lover, or to reveal to the unwitting male the 'truth' about their inevitable future together. Thus, the belief that choice of marriage partner is *destiny* and not really in the hands of mere mortals. Psychics, numerology, astrology and other parapsychological fields have commonly been used for many generations as both the means to secure a mate and as a means to sustain true love. People, particularly women, living in rustic cultures have been using such methods for many generations. We find that where this indirect approach to finding true love flourishes, men are more likely to obtain a mate through aggressive tactics.[12] However, knowing that force is typically used between people who know each other,[13] we can say that restrictive rules of courtship might not be at fault for this retreat into the mystical. Force of one kind or another is often used by impatient and socially unskilled individuals to get what they want when negotiations turn out to be fruitless. It does not appear, however, that the faults and limitations in the courtship process that cause isolation produce aggression, since negotiations are not likely to have occurred to begin with. Aggressive tactics are more likely to be used when satisfactory contact is present between the sexes but obtaining commitment becomes difficult because of the new demands of modernisation. Lacking physical prowess, women in primitive societies manipulate preternatural and 'unseen forces' as a way of controlling men, a mysticism which men evidently accept, but which they counter with physical domination over women in everyday life. A vicious cycle arises in which men fear the 'occult power' women have over them, which in turn spurs more aggression, which in turn makes women even more likely to rely on potions, spells, and so on. No doubt the infatuation that sometimes seizes men when meeting a woman appears 'irrational' and so contributes to the feeling that mysterious forces are at work.

Notwithstanding the inherent romantic qualities of such 'moonstruck' relationships, it is, of course, much more instructive to see how a rational plan operates, especially one that artfully combines psychological factors with pragmatic ones. W. A. Mozart, the great composer, lodged for some period of time with a family whose household situation deteriorated after the father died. With the approval of the mother, he struck up a friendship with one of the Weber daughters. Mozart came to know the manners and personalities of the people involved: The oldest sister was insincere and something of a flirt, the youngest sister was rather dim, but the middle one, Constance, was competent enough to run the whole household, yet received no recognition or reward. He believed here to be a virtuous woman, with common sense, facility with domestic crafts, and above all sincerity and honesty. Much of her maturity and proficiency he attributed to her having to compensate for the indolence of the others.[14] Like many others of his time, Mozart believed that difficult challenges, and with it hard work, build character. Constance's honesty appears to be more of a natural disposition, which led her to achieve other skills out of necessity. A proposal of marriage was made by Mozart not only for his own sake, but in order to 'save her' from two bickering sisters and a widowed cantankerous mother. For a young girl, losing a father, and living with a mother and two other siblings without much financial support, would surely have created a certain loneliness. No doubt it was tempting for her to make a close friendship with a respectable, artistically talented boarder.

Thus, Mozart developed his friendship with Constance within the domestic situation, as was very common at that time. His career took him to many cities, which allowed him the opportunity to meet eligible women and converse with them at length, but without any obligation on his part, although in some cases his convivial nature led some women to think he was serious in marrying them. He made a point of looking for virtuous women, those who met his very traditional, Roman Catholic standards. This virtuous woman would find her reward in a devoted husband and father trying his best to balance his ambitious career and his domestic life. Upon his marriage he did not appear to make any real changes to his life; he fell into married life easily. Mozart evidently did not plan on changing that much for his future wife, except perhaps travelling less. We do not know if Constance insisted on any other significant changes in his behaviour, but there is little doubt that the similar backgrounds of Amadeus and Constance helped reduce the number of extraordinary demands in their married life. How would things have turned out had they been of very different classes, or one highly educated and the other not, or one English-speaking the other German-speaking? We surmise that it would have been much more difficult, as Mozart himself was highly critical of places and people, showing great discrimination and a distinct preference for things that he understood.

In any relationship, the key to long-term success is to first objectively determine if there is enough compatibility between the partners, and if there is enough flexibility on both sides. The loss of independence must be made up by at least an easy flow of social relations within married life; in essence, the freedom one gives up must be at least compensated for by equal cooperation from a spouse. In a study of how pressures and strains in courtship affects life after marriage, ORBUCH ET AL (1993) use satisfaction in the third year of married life as a guide to whether a match was successful. It was found that if men *initiate* courtship and/or propose marriage, there is a *higher* chance the relationship will succeed than if the woman initiates and/or proposes. It would appear that men are more objective in mate selection than women. Women operate under more unrealistic assumptions and evidently force a match, whereas men might be somewhat more cognisant of the probability of a good marital relationship. It might also be true that women show more flexibility in accommodating themselves to a husband's personality. Mate selection is always a *two*-way process; a man might be well-satisfied with a woman's looks, background, education and temperament, but the woman might not be satisfied with the attributes in his life and she might indeed choose someone else. If men are the ones who are expected by society to make the choice, then women might be less likely to reject their offers of marriage. The natural pliancy in women functions to reduce stress in the marriage by making allowances for their husband's behaviour, increasing the chance of fulfilment. Although women might willingly make these allowances, over the course of the marriage daily experience clashes with personal belief so much that wives eventually feel that they have lost their identity, an event which in turn contributes to disruption later in conjugal life. Men must be initially more content with the choice of a spouse since they are less willing to undergo a metamorphosis as a concomitant to marriage. Whether it is the man or the woman making the choice, if it is not a wise one, conflict will ensue. As the Dutch have said, perhaps more in regards to men, forced love does not endure.

However, these two factors, objectivity and flexibility, are not equally strong. The best satisfaction comes when a third party initiates or proposes and this would indicate that it is not flexibility that is most important, but *objectivity*. A third party can often be more objective in analysing compatibility and they would have an opinion closer to the truth than either man or woman, ceteris paribus. These third parties might be relatives, friends or acquaintances. The use of matchmakers in the past made sense, and so leaving such matters to 'destiny' was not the conventional method of handling such a complex situation. Since matching two people with similar characteristics is difficult, having an extended social network is definitely a major advantage. In any social setting of young people, most people will have only 1 to 3 close friends, whereas a few, perhaps about 25%, have four or more friends.[15] If *A* is able to associate with *B* who has a considerably large network of friends then *B* would have a much better chance of finding a suitable partner for *A* than *A* would on his own.

Thus, the search for a marriage partner is a much more efficient enterprise when the aid of others is enlisted. These potential matchmakers could be constantly scrutinising eligible people for signs of compatibility. If *B* is particularly gregarious, he could even enlist his own friends in the search, widening the network even more. Furthermore, compared to dating services, these friends of *A* know more about his personality and temperament than any simple form or survey could discern. People have a tendency to exaggerate or lie on such forms in order to make themselves more attractive. Friends, especially ones of long-standing, know the individual as they are without the pretensions and so are more accurate in making matches.

In this regard, the protocols of modern society have made it anything but easy to follow a logical procedure. It is interesting that of all the myriad institutions modern society has established, not one has been created for the development of friendships, especially for marriage. Instead people resort to haphazard methods, such as more or less randomly asking for a date anyone that fits in with their minimal standard of attractiveness; the office, a store, a theatre, a bar, or the street have all become places for 'romance'.[16] There is no clear boundary or time when or where it is appropriate and when it is not to ask for dates. Far from bringing men and women together, this inevitably creates hostility between them, and since women, as the ones being sought out, cannot find a place where they can be left in peace from male advances, sometimes quite aggressive, must erect a tough exterior as a defence. In the past, friendships were made often through more congenial methods, such as one friend referring to another friend, who in turn could refer him to another, etc. Such connections could be used whenever one liked, and relations between men and women could be more polite and less intrusive. As an adjunct to conventional means of finding dates, single people are eager to make whatever environment they are in more 'social' by making friends with everyone there. Widening the circle of friends obviously increases the probability that a suitable mate will be found, but drains away precious time that could profitably have been spent with the few close friends actually met through private personal connections. The deficiencies of modern social life sap energy, and fear and insecurities displace the capacity for finding meaningful relationships.

Various adjustments to personality have been made in order to increase opportunities for finding a mate. Frequent social introductions continue to be important. As a way of smoothing the awkwardness between men and women, sex role behaviour has come to incorporate the traits of both sexes. In addition, improving social skills and lessening the importance of negative evaluations by peers, and reducing the emphasis on physical attractiveness would increase the level of interaction by dropping barriers.[17] In recent times, in order to increase the chance of a good match, women have become not at all shy about asking men out for dates. Intrusiveness, it seems, now can work both ways. In spite of the increased social contact engendered by abandoning etiquette and more casual conversational forms, create greater emotional and intellectual isolation of individuals, which actually all contribute to difficulty in forming relationships.

How individuals assess others and build a marriage strategy is a private process, more attributable to temperament than economics. This procedure is used to determine another person's level of commitment and their interest in other members of the opposite sex. By eradicating ignorance, one can determine whether one is committed to a relationship, and a thorough examination of another person's life is therefore prudent. However, the extent to which a person takes the time to learn is dependent on patterns of energy expenditure, which can flow within, such as in the case of mental reflection, or outwardly, as in the case of socialising. Courtship requires a certain environment wherein growth can occur, where the couple seek new and significant ways to interact. In this way men and women learn more about one another, building up the esteem that should be the bedrock of any companionate relationship. It should be apparent that although having a knowledge of form is always very profitable, honesty, integrity, devotion, caution, and perfectionism, are all essential for good relationships of whatever type; no amount of strictness in protocol and formality in courtship can ever make up for a deficit of virtue. Thus, the standards that people use are important, as are the standards that go into planning for engagement, wedding and the first year of married life.

Since assessment is so personal, preferences must be deliberated upon continually throughout the period from early puberty until the building phase of courtship. Upon entry to middle adulthood, a greater awareness of one's own and other people's preferences gains momentum in the life of the individual. Ideas about what matters and does not matter in life become more fully elucidated, reducing time and resources wasted pursing unfruitful attachments. This not only helps in the courtship process, but establishes the operational machinery of marriage. Yet, especially for women, increasing age also brings pressures external to the relationship to unify, to entrust. The careful evaluation of traits brought by maturity might be rudely interrupted by larger social requirements. Whereas the former might increase the number of months of courtship, the latter might well do the opposite, making it less likely that the individual will marry a well-suited person. Losing one's best opportunity for marriage due to indolence or fear is a thought troubling enough to cloud the most sensible person's reason. The dilemma of the period of life between gaining full adult rights and losing choice, between continuing independence and sacrificing for love, was articulated simply by William Congreve this way: 'Say what you will, 'tis better to be left than never to have been loved'. One could state more prosaically: 'I should not let this one go, because there might never be another chance'. The pragmatist, however, who disdains romantic notions might look at the situation somewhat differently: It is better to have married at least once, then to have never married at all.

It should be obvious that a wide variety of considerations, both personal and social, must be taken into consideration before men or women accept the responsibility of marriage. We have already considered the fact that there should be emotional closeness, and a willingness to satisfy urges of procreation if they exist. Other practical and financial matters must be considered, where the couple will live, what occupations they will have. The concern here is with the larger issue of how to plan for marriage, who should be doing it and when should one begin.

Many people believe that marriage has only the illusion of free choice, and in reality is actually a 'Hobson's choice', where the attributes of lifestyle, such as number of children, housing, and work habits, have already been socially determined. The only way to avoid the pitfalls one sees in married life is to simply refrain from it all together by remaining single. Thus, according to this view, the *substance* of the marriage is for most not a matter of debate, but only the *timing* of its inception. However, as we shall see, nothing could be further from the truth. In any society, the individual has always been given choices that he might work out within the context of marriage. Certainly there are social expectations about what constitutes a 'normal' marriage, but not being 'normal' is not necessarily equivalent to being deviant or anti-social.

This idea of a Hobson's choice in marriage arises when external circumstances push an individual into marrying when they are not yet emotionally or financially capable. Pressures from parents, relatives, friends, media or clergy might act to encourage individuals to overlook serious flaws in their partner, or to adapt their beliefs about the realities of married life. Needless to say, rushing judgements about marriage could only cause disruption, disappointment and heartache.

Why would there be a push to marry? We should understand that marriage is a *social* union that makes certain fundamental and unavoidable demands on people. Marriage can be used instrumentally as a way of achieving a certain envisioned lifestyle. Many women desire a stable emotional relationship with a man, and although they prize the spontaneity and allowances of unmarried romance, they might consider marriage a reasonable solution for the problems caused by a vacillating and uncooperative boyfriend; persistent persuasion is used, along the lines that one or both sets of parents and friends feel that the couple 'look really good' together, and that it is time to wed. Stability in a relationship can be attained by commitment, as devotion to another's priorities will sometimes mean relinquishing one's own. Many women rush men into marriage because they feel the responsibilities of running a household will make their inconsiderate boyfriend more mature. If the completely ad hoc relationship becomes burdensome because of the thoughtless and aloof antics of men, women will put their faith in another, more socially controlled, type of relationship. By marrying and surrendering some of their personal freedom, men, it is thought, will take on a new view of the world, settle down and deal with dissension fairly, openly and confidently.

Women attempt to use traditional concepts to make a man substantively conform to certain principles of conduct, which are assumed to exist in marriage. Often, the man's problems stem from his fondness for independence, and marriage, they naively assume, will force to abandon his previously callous demeanour. The logic that goes into this thinking is not better than that used to 'break in' a recalcitrant horse, a method of conditioning that involves putting the animal continually through the paces; pulling back on the reins, shouting, and the occasional use of the whip are part of the training. The reality is that human behaviour is difficult, although not impossible, to change, and certainly a person who has no regard for social convention before marriage is hardly going to have regard for such convention within marriage. Entrustment only works for people who respect it and fear social penalties for non-compliance. In present Western society, there is substantial lack of respect for contracts and expecting men to honour fully the marriage contract of obligations would be imprudent. We may safely say that women who marry men without certainty how they will regard a solemn oath could be confining themselves to years of misery.

Moreover, women wish to maintain the relationship or go forward into marriage for other reasons, equally ill-considered: it is easy keeping the status quo due to inertia; it is difficult to find another man; breaking up with potential marriage partners is embarrassing; having too many boyfriends makes one look cheap; there might not be another chance at marriage. Whatever the reasons for the push to marry, it is a matter of deduction to see that all of them are based on a lack of commitment and an absence of a substitute(s) for the marriage relationship. A life emphasising autonomy promotes such factors, and thus in a society where the average individual has strongly independent feelings, marriage is used to capture or 'nail down' the inconstant or mercurial man or woman. There is little doubt then that belief in the Hobson's choice concept of marriage will eventually become familiar.

In any case, as we can see in any higher-ranking area of life, *time* is the most important and yet least controlled resource. In order to do things properly, the individual must have enough time to learn about procedures, collect information, and make credible decisions. That being the case, clearly, everyone should plan for their marriage as early as possible. It is difficult, however, not to create idealised versions of one's potential mate. This overly explicit model can be a deterrent to settling for compromise situations; no one can be expected to fit perfectly into one's conceptions. Too many unrealistic requirements about the ideal spouse's personality will make difficult the marriage discovery process. However, there should never be any restriction on *logical* requirements about character, even if such requirements are constructed in such as way that one never makes a suitable match. Ignoring or denying key personal concepts could create a life that could very well be worse than that the one had by remaining single. Is it better to have no ideals but to be married, or to have strong ideals but to be alone? This is a question that can only be answered by the individual, as long as he or she has discounted the dangers of disregarding either marriage or idealism.

People will deepen a friendship, which is based on mutual enhancement, when they believe there is future entrustment and constancy. The process of courtship provides the path to taking this deepening to its logical conclusion, namely that of marriage, but it does not imply that the individual presently has the *capacity* to marry. Discovering whether a potential mate is willing to be committed to a relationship is not difficult, but might be time-consuming. However, to build a married life well into the future, many personal factors must be taken into account: Virtue, temperament, tastes, beliefs, finances, emotions; inevitably, the process of 'marriage' must be obeyed: exploring, evaluation, building, and execution. The reasons why someone would marry are many, yet they can be distilled into several all-important categories. In developing a successful relationship, it is essential to know one's own interests; to understand why one needs a companion to meet these goals; to know how to communicate one's desires effectively; and to have a willingness to sacrifice. These requirements might seem trite, but have yet to be proven wrong.

In developing a conspectus of marriage, there are considerations that operate for and against marriage which are of interest to us because they relate to the concept of independence. Four reasons potentially arise in encouraging marriage. Firstly, the emotional well-being and happiness of family life; secondly, the social prestige, acceptance and rank that marriage confers; thirdly, the satisfaction in having and raising children for economic and emotional reasons; finally, the maximisation of domestic, economic, financial and other pragmatic conditions. Obtaining reliable information about the first and second reasons is rather difficult. Little is known about the personal reasons why people married as there are no surveys of pre-20th century populations. We can establish the third and most easily the fourth reasons, as these have a largely utilitarian, and thus recordable, basis. Having children for economic reasons is apparent in societies where there is a place for them as a productive unit, and having them for emotional fulfilment is apparent when child mortality is an issue.

On the other hand, there are basically two obstacles to marriage. One is a lack of interest in and attraction to the opposite sex, a fundamental force that is not easily explained by environmental or sociological factors, with evidence to show that it is, to an extent, genetically determined. The other reason, of less but by no means trivial significance, is a lack of income and savings. In traditional societies where the pull is toward marriage, once the man has enough money saved and a good job, he will be ready for marriage. In modern society, the cultural pull is toward bachelorhood (where the individual maintains his freedom, easygoing lifestyle, youth and spontaneity), so a good salary would almost compel him to remain single.

It should be emphasised, that none of the above factors is necessarily positive or negative, for they can be either depending upon their interaction within a situation. One has to determine what combination of characteristics one actually has. Am I the gregarious type, honest, but possessive? Or am I well-off financially, self-centred to an extent, but still capable of empathy and change? Many factors influence the male-female relationship, and the axiomatic difficulty of reconciling them all produces the idea that successful marriages are more a case of *destiny* rather than *creation*. For all the pieces to fall into place must be great fortune indeed. However, that approach ignores the fact that people can and do change, so that earlier or later marriage (whatever is preferred) is made more likely. The multiplicity of considerations does not render the individual impotent in making decisions about his life. Somehow, some way, people do try to make sense out of all of these factors, and although it might be difficult, it is certainly not impossible to carefully assess all of them. As a way of assisting the individual, we shall be studying many of these factors throughout the rest of this book.

As men and women have been meeting, courting, marrying for many centuries, societies have collected and preserved these experiences in cultural norms. These norms can aid the individual in making a decision about marriage, removing part of the burden of processing information, but at the same time, not removing the responsibility of correct action. Thus, external factors often underlie the forces that stand in the way or catalyse the move to *connubium*. The most important of these might be the social pressure and cultural directives to marry. This often clears the way for one's experiences, necessitating major changes in one's life. Next, opportunities for marriage with a suitable partner within one's peer group must exist; this is often difficult to remedy. Easier to change is the allowance for a spouse in one's home environment and career. A practical or personal need to marry, through an intensification of feeling for love, companionship or marriage, is of course necessary as well, though such a need might be more externally determined than one realises.

Completing the search for a potential partner with desirable traits, a good disposition, constancy and commitment is relatively easy, when compared to the struggle to keep the sweet blend of manifold ingredients that make up a good marriage from turning into a farrago. It is little wonder that people might think it a 'miracle' of destiny or fate when the match is finally made and the glorious day of matrimony finally arrives. Many individuals can, nevertheless, assist a young man or woman in putting together a tangible scheme that would fulfill diverse personal needs, although there is only one person who ultimately has the final authority to render a decision, and consequently, only one who must take responsibility for that decision. 'We should marry to please ourselves, not other people', would be a good motto.[18] The community puts forward in its culture many suggestions that can often compensate for youthful ignorance. Hence, for many people, culture is an important, perhaps the most important, factor in resolving the competing ideas swirling about the issue of marriage. Cultures universally pull together several ideas that they all cite, but do not necessarily implement. We can say that, based on observation, nearly all people believe marriage should be delayed until economic matters have reached a minimal standard, but most are also willing to concede that it should take place upon reaching a certain age. Some people rigorously hold that marriage should not take place until certain economic conditions are fulfilled; some advocate marriage only when the couple is certain of emotional compatibility; and some maintain that marriage should be avoided whenever possible, with celibacy as a better form of life.

The forces that motivate one to hold these various attitudes vary in intensity, and are part of a complex mixture of temperament, history, and social necessity. Although the predisposition to fraternise with the opposite sex is certainly different from one person to the next, and varies in relation to the degree of extroversion, the culture might to a certain extent impose itself to form a false disposition, an 'innate' tendency. A culture is, of course, the composite of individual temperaments, and its rules and practices are normally consistent with consensus opinion. However, not *everyone* has the same temperament, and the culture might act to force those who deviate moderately to conform to larger practises. For example, it might make a moderately introverted person into a moderately extroverted one. We should understand, though, that the ultimate force that guides us is our free will. Everything else comes under the category of 'influence', and unless an influence cannot be refused, which is rare, the success or failure of an action is ultimately the individual's responsibility. Marriage is therefore a precarious adventure with great risks but also with tremendous rewards. Whenever human beings are faced with such a situation, the tendency is to either bear down and meet the challenge, or to retreat into over-simplifications and fantasies. Thus, we should ask the question: Do people in general take advantage of the physical resources at their disposal and the advice of more knowledgeable individuals, or do they leave the process of finding love to fate or chance?

TRADITION'S COMPROMISE: MARRY FOR MONEY, WORK FOR LOVE

The pursuit of material gain is probably the most noticeable factor in human existence. How to accomplish this is dependent on an individual's skills, ambitions, talent, as well on the social and natural environment. One person might be highly ambitious and highly motivated to work, but few opportunities might be available. Another person might be poorly motivated, yet have numerous opportunities opening up all around him. Obviously, motivation and occasion are not always related, but few would say that they have no intention or interest in gaining something socially tangible from life.

The means to this gain vary by time and place; however, most people in any society know what is required in order to obtain money, power, status, and, ultimately, gratification. It is a universal requirement that in order to make headway in life, a chain of events must be followed—education of some sort must come first in life, followed by gaining an occupation, then significant remuneration, followed by social status. Although it was only in the early 19th century that this chain of events became formalised, where 'institutions' arose to meet the need for clear fulfilment of each stage, the deliberate enactment of personal progress has been around probably since the beginning of the human race. We should not make the mistake of believing that people in the past simply moved to one household to another as part of a subsistence strategy. The farmer in Spain or Norway went through the same stages of development as the modern stock-broker in New York or London. Both cultures are linked in a very basic way by the desire to achieve contentment, a condition that is truly beyond 'culture'. The difference between these ages lies in the *intensity* of experience of each stage, not in *nature* of experience.

The final factor in the chain of life's milestones — contentment — could not and cannot be possible unless the full potential use is made of social engagement, education, and career in the establishment and maintenance of love. We should appreciate the fact that this linkage of the profoundly physical with the profoundly emotional has is buried deep in human history and psyche. In spite of the recent creation of support institutions, neither the desire for true love nor these factors leading to contentment is modern. What our generation might call 'quaint' or 'cherished and dear' feelings about one's spouse are neither recent 'romantic' ideas nor are they unattainable. For example, the ancient Romans unabashedly extolled the virtues of marriage, looking upon life-long union as indicative of stability and fidelity. The giving of life to such important concepts was rewarded by the community and even in some cases, by the gods, as in the myth of Philemon and Baucis. The Hebrews also knew about the importance of emotional attachment, as Ecclesiastes 9:9 (NIV) says to 'Enjoy life with your wife, whom you love, all the days of this meaningless life that God has given you under the sun'. Following Judaic traditions, the Christian Church from the beginning expected only the most caring and empathetic relationship between husbands and wives. Note that this expectation had nothing to do with material considerations, either before the fact or after the fact. Emotional fulfilment was openly promoted as the focus of marriage, as when St Paul, in Ephesians 5:28 (NIV), enjoins husbands to love their wives as 'their own bodies. He who loves his wife loves himself'. Traditional Christianity, despite its praise of celibacy, recognised that extraordinary happiness could be achieved in marriage as well, as we can see in the lives of many canonised men and women throughout the last two millennia. Some of the more major figures were Paula (347-404), Elizabeth of Hungary (1207-1231), Frances of Rome (1384-1440), Nicholas von Flüe (1417-1487), Joan de Lestonnac (1556-1640). Many intellectuals, poets, painters, musicians, composers also had happy marriages. John Donne (1572- 1631), whose poems and sermons are considered some of the best of the 17th century, openly credited his wife for his emotional strength and inspiration. One of the most charming descriptions of domestic tranquillity comes from the life of composer Heinrich Schütz (1585-1672). Although an author of exquisite sacred pieces, and totally imbued in mellifluity, it was said that he 'never knew or heard a more lovely sound or song than when he heard the voice or word of his precious wife'. '[S]he cared for him daily...when he came home from his work she was overjoyed to see him and ran with happiness to greet him'.[19] Both Donne and Schütz lost their wives tragically early and neither remarried, which as a pragmatic matter was rather unusual for their time. Fortunately, both used their respective losses as an inspiration to make the love they had felt resonate through the word, voice and instrument.

No one can regard the warm thoughts of literate people of the past without acknowledging that affection was common, and was not considered abnormal, unusual, or strange.[20] That these types of loving unions were praised by contemporaries shows both high regard for affection between spouses and the absence of concern about uxoriousness.[21] That we do not know more about such marriages is more attributable to the lack of detailed knowledge about the private lives of men and women of the past rather than some silent denigration of romance.

Ironically, the people that we know most about, the kings, queens, dukes, duchesses and other high-born nobility and aristocracy, often had the *worst* marriages, suffering through loveless relationships as the products of early and arranged marriage. Perhaps this is one reason why we think of the past as wrapped in such cold emotional desolation.

Academia has attained a fairly dichotomised view of society where the past is 'pragmatic', the present is 'romantic' when it comes to marriage.[22] The truth may be that it is precisely the other way around. Compared to the pre-industrial age, society of our time looks at the married couple not as a 'simple unit of production, but a focus of affection and solidarity'.[23] From the point of view of the 20th century, the history of the Western world could be reduced to simplistic metaphors of winter and summer: A cold, sterile pre-modern folk, marrying only for money; and passionate, steamy romantic modern people, where romance is by far the overriding factor. To look at marriage in merely economic terms grossly underestimates the value of affection in pre-modern times. It is true that material aspects were more of an anxious concern than in our day, but this does not mean that fondness and deep emotional satisfaction were irrelevant. Many today see the two issues as mutually exclusive: Either a couple is materially orientated or it is romantically orientated.[24] Our ancestors certainly did not view marriage as necessarily lacking in affection or thoughtfulness; most would certainly have been shocked if told that affection does not have to be at the centre of the ideal or proper marital relationship. Further, simply because they would have thought of a love-*only* relationship as reckless, they should not be condemned as unfeeling pragmatists. As respect, cooperation, consideration, all key ingredients of affection, were expected and experienced of and by family members, friends, and relatives, to have it lacking between a husband and wife would have been strange indeed.[25]

In the long history of Western civilisation, it is fair to say the themes of money, occupation, matching in personality, and opportunity have all played major roles in the decision to marry. Material concerns lay at the heart of previous generations' male-female relations though for very different reasons than the ones posited by historians. Status and occupation were often matched due to a conscious search for similarity and complementarity in background. Hence, in previous generations, greater *external* or public emphasis was put on material concerns than emotional compatibility. Perhaps the extent of dissimilarity between people in material factors was larger than in moral factors, thus the discussions to reconcile differences in status and not in personality. The demands of the economy inevitably impacted the decision to marry, and in turn affected relations between men and women. Although customs varied from one region to the next, and were sometimes quite untypical, there was enough similarity within and between regions so that a European set of 'norms' might be constructed. In understanding individual dynamics, whether a town, village, district or territory was part of this standard is largely irrelevant, as local norms are often the product of the universal disposition, character, or the 'spirit', of a people set to contend with specific social circumstances. Other customs, however, cannot be explained in such a way, and are likely the result of a greater than normal variation in inherent genetic disposition. Thus, the 'character' of a local ethnic group is due to influences that are part economic, part demographic, part organisational, part genetic and part undetermined.

We must therefore determine the extent to which human beings allow themselves to be influenced by external forces and the extent to which they freely and consciously choose their own course. If people largely allow external forces to shape their destiny, then our work in history, psychology and sociology should be edifying and fruitful; if not, then it will be impossible to predict behaviour, and the work of scholars is wasted. In studying the past, clear evidence of autonomous behaviour, whether by the individual or some social unit, is difficult to obtain, and so assumptions about 'similarity' and 'diversity' among cultures must be clarified. All science revolves around the simple fact that in order to establish dynamics, we need to see patterns in data. It is entirely appropriate, and indeed necessary, to carefully categorise the manifestations of a phenomenon, and thus note the apparent 'differences' between two regions or communities by putting them into two different 'categories'. But to reduce the number of categories, whether for the sake of expediency or following some partisan ideological programme, is a mistake. If one is trying to prove the existence of a phenomenon, say that economic activity has a decisive impact on human behaviour, then one might be tempted to categorise observations in such a way (by putting them into the 'same' category or two or more 'different' categories) so as to further a theory. The success in proving the decisive impact of any phenomenon necessarily attenuates the influence of that most basic, irreducible factor called *free will*. In studying any society, we must determine whether people make a choice due to an unquantifiable internal force (free will); due to identifiable internal forces, such as social concerns, ideology, apathy, habit; due to some other force external to the specific problem; due to a lack of an alternative, i.e. externally imposed 'choice'; due to ignorance about the alternatives. We touched upon this issue earlier in relation to the concept of whether a marital union was by fate or by choice. If people do act out of free will, then theories about the 'inevitability' of choice due to economics or culture are seriously jeopardised. For example, it is a well-known and consequently ubiquitous phenomenon that economic considerations in pre-modern agricultural areas prompt couples to have many children (high fertility). It would be a major mistake, though, to simply assume that whatever variations in fertility we see are due mainly to economic considerations, or even worse, to dismiss the fertility difference between two economically *identical* regions as 'negligible' when the percentage difference might in some other instance be called 'significant'. The fact is that a couple might *consciously* choose to have a large number of children and might *consciously* reject advanced procedures that would increase agricultural productivity, and thus their economic standing. Contemporary accounts sometimes make a point of saying that the squalor that was witnessed was as much the result of indolence of people as that of exploitation, inflation, unemployment or usury.[26] However, this is usually not stated explicitly, with the cause for the social situation being left open to interpretation.

We must make careful use of the information derived from various, though not necessarily competing, sources, such as census data, parish information, school curricula material, proverbs, legends, and personal testimony. Some are actual facts, some act as ideals, others as counter-ideals. We should bear in mind, that we cannot look at these observations with the same reliability as numerical evidence. What might be perceptible to the scientist in a statistical sense might not be so to an observer, even if trained. Further, the necessity to cite something in one's report depends on the object or event's moral quality. One describes a place or situation because something goes wrong, rather than when something goes right, and chances are that the authors of historical documents, on the whole, overemphasise the bad and neglect the good. Differences in the size of the community might engender different rules about interpretation of data; smaller communities might be held to different standards than larger ones, or rural versus urban. Also, the men who wrote the reports had to match the expectations of the time in order to maintain their social and governmental position—ideological 'purists' who might make accurate descriptions but only within a limited scope of observation. Defects in information might be attributed to the interviewee, as much as the interviewer. In addition, lying, boasting, exaggerations might have been prevalent, perhaps as a way to denigrate a culture or family and so elevating one's own.[27] Systematic analysis came slowly; observers converged their mental and physical resources on things that they understood, things that interested them, or things that they were assigned to view. The level of error can therefore be high in contemporary 'anthropological' reports, giving false impressions that can persist for many years.[28]

Thus, because of the emphasis on always separating free choice from forced choice, in considering the past we cannot overstress the importance of acknowledging the considerable *diversity* of family situations, whilst also paying attention to the *similarity* within a culture. However, human beings have a tendency to reduce diversity as a way of simplifying a problem. Although our ancestors in Europe shared fundamental moral precepts, to the point where we can confidently say that certain attitudes were universal, other beliefs were adiaphorous which varied according to processes of the natural environment, individual temperament, collective temperament, challenges external to the community. Yet one can read in many texts that 'wives were beasts of burden', 'girls were not wanted', 'clans had a strong, tight hold on their members'. These are powerful statements, and should not be made off-handedly as they sometimes are. Such factors might exist locally or regionally, but do not necessarily capture the deeper 'Spirit' of a people. Thus, one should exhibit the greatest care when making the assumption that any nation or region can be consolidated into one category. One can and *should* do so when required, but with the understanding that upon critical investigation, researchers usually find little justification for such a procedure.[29]

One of the most common errors made about the vitality of the human Will is in relation to marriage; did previous generations find the process for the most part *voluntary* or *involuntary*? The prevailing attitude among modern laypeople is that it was the latter, that men and especially women were forced to marry against their will, having to do so in order to meet society's expectations of fulfilment of mother or father roles, to provide children for society's well-being, to become a productive, and honourable member of the community. One wonders, in light of the evidence of history, whether this is not some sort of psychological projection of our *own* age on that of our ancestors. That some were forced, coerced or cajoled into matrimony is beyond question, but there is no evidence whatsoever that at least in post-conversion European civilisation, there was any long-term, widely-accepted 'duty' to marry, a breach of which carried serious penalties.

Most often, pressures to marry can be divided into four main categories: Economic rationality, pregnancy, family obligation, and cultural duty. The last is one of the easiest to ascertain, and it is the easiest to dismiss as a major factor. We know that traditionally the Roman Catholic Church and conservative Protestantism emphasised the absolute right of the individual to refuse marriage, and the absolute right to marry whomever he or she chose. The Council of Trent's Decree Concerning the Reform of Matrimony made a forceful statement about the illegitimate linkage of financial imperatives, social prestige and marriage:

Worldly inclinations and desires very often so blind the mental vision of temporal lords and magistrates, that by threats and ill usage they compel men and women who live under their jurisdiction, especially the rich or those who expect a large inheritance, to contract marriage against their will with those whom these lords or magistrates propose to them. Wherefore, since it is something singularly execrable to violate the freedom of matrimony, and equally execrable that injustice should come from those from whom justice is expected, the holy council commands all, of whatever rank, dignity and profession they may be, under penalty of anathema to be incurred ipso facto, that do in any manner whatever, directly or indirectly, compel their subjects or any others whomsoever in any way that will hinder them from contracting marriage freely.[30]

Not only does this restate long-standing Church moral tenets on marriage, it also indicates that there were serious enough lapses to justify issuing this statement. Of course, if such restrictions were promulgated for the high and mighty, then they would apply to all the lesser classes as well. The latest revision of Canon Law is also passionate in its condemnation of any kind of persuasion which 'boxes in' a person, altering a person's life negatively with the only option being to marry that person or someone else.

A marriage is invalid if it is entered into due to force or grave fear inflicted from outside the person, even when inflicted unintentionally, which is of such a type that the person is compelled to choose matrimony in order to be freed from it (Canon 1103).[31]

What exactly 'force' or 'grave fear' means is not specified, but one could read into this any kind of duress, including interminable nagging by a parent if it causes depression or other significant distress that can only be alleviated by giving in to the persistent demands. The validity of a marriage might therefore be a function of the subjective opinion as to the nature of the 'force'. Additionally, the Church is so concerned with the freedom to enter into marriage, that even *unintentional* coercion makes the union invalid. As marriage was one of the most important decisions one could make in one's life, if not the most important, and happiness within it of paramount importance, any kind of coercion was unconscionable. Thus, the cultures of Europe, as they are derived in large part from biblical teaching, the canons of the Roman Catholic Church, the catechism, and the writings of the early Church Fathers, must have had an unequivocal adherence to the principle of *free will* in matters matrimonial.

Besides the loud, unhesitant proclamations of the Church, which found their way into the parishes, the common sayings of European peoples about marriage, love, husband, wife, and children, as compiled by Meider (1986), betray a definite concern with wise deliberation. One hears very infrequently statements bemoaning the inevitably of marriage; in fact, there is quite commonly an urging to forestall or forego marriage. Why should anyone be urged to do something unless he or she maintained a clear *choice* in the matter? If pressure to marry had historically been great (or at least over the period from the 18th to 19th centuries, when these expressions were formed and most commonly used), then certainly the sayings of the plain folk would have informed us of them.

As for the pressure to marry due to economic reasons, here indeed there is evidence of conditions that non-facilitate early marriage and favour late marriage. When real wages in England are compared to crude marriage rates in the period 1551 to 1851, we find that the tendency to marry was predicated on changes in the economy.[32] France followed a similar pattern, where a negative correlation existed between grain prices and marriage rates in the 19th century.[33] However, in England there was a thirty-year lag on average between a change in wages and a change in marriage rate. This might be the result of a whole generation experiencing a declining economy, for example, and then entering this into the cultural 'record', where the next generation reacts to it. However, from this reliable data we do draw an important insight into the internal disposition of Western Europeans. As we do not see any evidence of *in*flexibility on the upward or downward side throughout this period, we conclude that people were not *innately* more inclined to marry or not to marry. Further, personal choice still prevailed in many cases. Although economic factors clearly influenced the decision to marry, there were many who went against the trend. In fact, during the steep declines in income of the period from about 1751 to about 1771, *most* people in England went ahead and married 'foolishly', and during the periods of improving economy of 1625 to 1671, and 1820 to 1840, *most* failed to react swiftly and forwent marriage 'unwisely'. These periods of counter-trend behaviour (the 'lag' mentioned above), when so many people quite deliberately married in the midst of a clearly slumping economy, is hard to understand, but does not diminish the strong larger conventional trend. Hence, although the economy had a major influence in the decision to marry, it was by no means absolute.

It is easy to say that pregnancy was not a factor in rushing marriage as illegitimacy rates, with some exceptions, were low until the 20th century, and pre-nuptially conceived births were also quite uncommon.[34] Finally, much more difficult to gauge is 'family pressure', but if folk sayings are an indication of family disposition, then we can say that family pressure was not overwhelming, although certainly was greater than that passed on by the community.

In toto, people of the past indeed had the ability to make up their own minds about marriage, based on cultural, religious, and economic decisions. There was an expectation that the individual would carefully deliberate this decision, not rush into it on account of the push from mother or father, or the pull of infatuation, status, sexuality or financial advancement. We might ask the question, why would some cultures have a low opinion of marriage, as preserved in their aphorisms, when they undoubtedly had periods when married life was quite *good*, that is during times of lower mortality, economic growth, older age of first marriage? We might say that most people had a good opinion of the *concept* of marriage, which they attempted to implement, but might have had a poor opinion of the marriages that they saw in their own communities. Perhaps it was this high valuation of the concept of 'Marriage' that made people react quite negatively to 'marriage' of everyday life when they witnessed *others* misuse this institution. Since a good marriage has always been difficult to come by, people might have been somewhat harsh about marriage in line with another very common saying, 'better safe than sorry'.

Let us now look in more detail at the reasons that specifically made it difficult for people to act freely. As we do not have any objective indicator of the willingness to marry, we must extract whatever information we can from the indicators that we do have. In research on the marital practises of the past, the emphasis is usually on two dependent variables: average age of marriage and celibacy rates. Age of marriage and celibacy rates are widely available, going back to at least the 17th century. These figures, in association with other social and economic statistics, can enlighten us as to what individuals thought of marriage.

The current model of marriage practises in the pre-modern period stems in part from the work of John Hajnal, beginning a debate in 1965,[35] which, in the years since, has forced this original model to be modified.[36] Building his theory on Malthusian ideas, he asserted that there is a zone of low nuptiality in Europe, northwest of a line drawn from Trieste, Italy to Leningrad (now St Petersburg), Russia. He believed that this division, which arose between the 16th and 17th centuries, was based on a tradition that required a newly married couple to form a separate independent household. The performance of the economy was a critical factor in determining the age of marriage, and the basis for a household, and in one sense for 'love', was financial. Europeans had become inured to achieving a certain lifestyle and were reluctant to fall below that standard; indeed, they wanted to progress to a higher level than the previous generation. People believed, paradoxically, in an 'American dream' long before there was an America.

'Low nuptiality' is a way of saying permanent celibacy and historical surveys show the persistent and widespread, though not constant, occurrence of celibacy throughout Europe. Because of this diversity of marriage patterns, scholars have been unable to cite some overriding cultural factor to explain low nuptiality. Instead, the economic situation, with similar diversity of local situations superimposed on regional and international trends, is often implicated in the propensity to marry. Economic developments affect occupations and living standards, which in turn affects the need and desire for marriage. For women, marriage conflicted with employment as a servant; for men, a greater involvement with their occupation, such as working long hours, travelling, and socialising, etiolated relations with women. Moreover, demographic factors are often a factor in keeping people from marriage; the cities provided diversions and entertainment for many people, whilst offering better living conditions and alternative family structures for many men and women of the lower classes. We can see these situations in an analysis of death records for a parish in Warsaw, Poland for the period of 1760 to 1801.[37] The percent who remained single until death increased during this period. For men, the percent single increased from about 8% to 24%; for women, the figures are more erratic, but rising from about 4% to 11%. These are high figures by our Western standards, especially for men.

Census records give us a similar picture that shows even higher rates of celibacy. However, the city was in the past a fairly volatile demographic entity and we should be careful in assessing census records as these point to a particular point in time. People can temporarily immigrate and reside, which might significantly change the balance of single to married. A 1791 census of the same parish found that about 22% of men and women over age 50 were single. However, this includes large numbers of tradesmen, senators, servants and so on who had come on the occasion of the debates in the Great Parliament held in 1788 to 1792. The death record analysis is somewhat more accurate in assessing proportions, and this underlines the difficulties inherent in obtaining accurate celibacy rates. In addition, other local conditions were in effect that might make the rates for one city very different from other similar sized cities. The rates for women in this parish resemble that of smaller towns in Western Europe, as higher proportions of women living in the larger towns and cities were permanently celibate.[38] Whatever social and economic factors could account for this are not clear, but it is intriguing to see the evidence of cultural segmentation emerge in the differences between urbanite and peasant at such an early stage in the 'miraculous' development of the Western world. What is even more interesting is that the first sign of this miracle is revealed in the *domestic* domain, where the demands of a complex economy, migration, and standard of living affected marriage age and married life.

Hence, economic conditions had a major role in facilitating or hindering marriage throughout early modern Europe. But we shall also see that conditions at home, especially when they interact with economic factors, contribute significant aspects to the concept of independence, which in turn has its own effects on marriage. We start by looking at nineteenth century Spain, as examined in REHER (1991), which exhibits practises and principles that were fairly typical and widespread across Europe in the pre-Industrial period. The main themes of traditional periods were elaborated in real terms; dependence on inheritance money, occupational limitations on female servants, marriage market inequalities, and opportunity effects through death were all priorities, and in that order. In general, these factors held better for females, and for celibacy rather than age of marriage. Male and female celibacy rates were geographically coincident, ranging from about 3% in the central portions, to highs of 15% and more in the northern coastal region, parts of the eastern coast, and the south. Inheritance practises also coincided with the propensity to marry: the more impartible the inheritance practise, the later the marriage age, and the greater percent who remain celibate. Unable to obtain the funds for married life, many had little choice but to remain celibate, either living with their families, with non- related housemates, or in a domestic service situation. In the last case, it is not surprising that the more girls who worked as servants, the later the marriage and more celibacy. As marriage between servants was often not possible, a person in such an occupation was limited in this regard relative to other occupations. Moreover, the lower the male-female ratio (marriage market), i.e. fewer males per females, the lower female nuptiality. Out-migration, from the region to other areas, resulted in many women being left without a match. There is a small but significant interaction between impartible inheritance and sex ratio, indicating men left the area if they could not inherit, a situation which created an imbalance in the sex-ratio.

Economic factors were also responsible to a large extent for the changes in the last theme mentioned above, that of mortality. Poor work conditions and high population density in cities were undoubtedly responsible for many unnecessary deaths. Thus, the toll that the new modern economy exacted on health and well-being must have dampened enthusiasm for life and love. Bearing this mind, it is puzzling, however, why people in Spain were *more* likely to marry if the incidence of mortality was *higher*. Clearly, something overrode the emotional reaction to social disruption. Possibly seeing an opportunity to marry when a husband or wife died, an individual could in this way raise his status and his financial position. A man might never have married, had not another man died and made 'available' his wife. However, this relationship between death rates and nuptiality might not entirely be based on personal financial considerations, but might be affected by an ethos of population control. Society has always been understandably sensitive to changes in its size and has found ways to control it. Before the use of artificial contraception, the only reliable way to control fertility was through marriage practise. Indeed, '[t]he classic regulatory mechanism among west European populations of the early modern period was marriage'.[39] The special demands of larger society were not lost on most individuals, as the economic welfare of the individual was consciously tied to the welfare of the whole society. When death rates declined, the annual increase in the population would be higher and the only way to stop the population from reaching unmanageable levels was by delaying marriage.

The evidence shows that mortality was connected to celibacy rates in early modern Europe, for we see that in the 18th century that an improvement in death rates was met by a delay in and abandonment of marriage. In the period from 1700 to 1880, the celibacy rate in France rose steadily and peaked for women at nearly 15% in 1820, and for men at around 10% in 1840. For women the low in 1700 was about 5%, and in 1880, it was 11%; for men the figures were respectively 5% and 8%. These changes could be attributed to a form of population control, lowering births through celibacy and late marriage to compensate for lower mortality. Thus, measures such as these served effectively to stabilise the population and the economy. Population growth was managed through various mechanisms as a way of avoiding overuse of resources including land, the most important of which was delaying marriage as a way of reducing the number of births per woman.

Thus, changes in marriage practise resulted from changes in living conditions. It would appear that such a limitation was imposed when people were very conscious that a rise in population would endanger the welfare of all, a situation present in late 19th century Ireland, France, and perhaps other parts of Western Europe. Even with impressive images of whole communities starving because of uncontrolled fertility, people were probably more conscious of the dangers of overpopulation at the far more relevant 'region' of the household. On this social scale, standard of living is more important than possible early death, which is seen only as the most dire consequence of unregulated population growth. Families were chiefly concerned with quality of life for themselves and their children than the possible dangers to the community of overpopulation. In cultures where opportunities for asset accumulation were limited, it is possible that there was greater emphasis on judicious expenditure planning *within* marriage. The poor accumulation of assets at the beginning of marriage is probably linked with having a lower echelon job (a job other than artisan or merchant, for example), which in turn makes current income meagre. Further, as savings were generally not available, the family had to be very parsimonious in its spending habits. But more than anything else, a married couple had to pay close attention to their reproductive activities. The principle involved, unlike others concerning trade or finance, was actually so simple that even the most uneducated could understand it. Every child required more food, and in order to avoid economic strain, that child should work to feed himself or herself. A very young child is obviously incapable of self-care, but once a child reached an age where he or she could help in the family enterprise, then income (of whatever form) would increase, and another child could be added to the household. A clearly defined period of separation between births is of critical importance, with the goal of never having more mouths to feed than could be provided for. Thus, a woman marrying later, but having the same interval between births and the same age of final birth would have, indeed must have, a *lower* fertility than a woman marrying early. In this case, the cultural factor of timing, or birth spacing, is more important than exogenous economic forces. Although no doubt couples practised various means of controlling fertility in marriage, including periodic abstinence, coitus interruptus, and infrequently abortion and infanticide, the most clear and reliable method was through the adjustment of the age of marriage.

Marriage age is a regulatory mechanism or fertility 'governor' preventing overpopulation that results in lower standard of living and, more uncommonly, higher death rates. The governor's viability is based, however, on two premisses. One is that men and women in times of potential or real material distress delay marriage because they do not have the financial means to establish a household. The other is that couples do not take measures to accelerate or decelerate the pace of births; that is, the spacing of children within marriage is the same, regardless of marriage age. The first premiss is very common throughout history, the second is more problematic. It is assumed in the latter premiss that people do not use any other form of contraception except abstinence, and that given a certain natural fecundity, babies 'come when they will come'.

Thus, the idea that marriage age strongly governs fertility is weakened by the observation that the equal spacing rule is subject to many exceptions, where couples do not leave to chance the number of children they eventually will, but have a specific target in mind. This target is based upon the minimal quality of life a child should have, the amount of emotional gratification each child brings, and the amount of additional income of each additional child. There might have been reasons why couples did purposefully abstain from sexual intercourse in order to reduce the possibility of pregnancy. For example, sometimes a rise in child mortality was met with a *decline* in fertility not a gain, demonstrating a definite control of fertility *within* marriage. This was the case in the English village of Colyton where childlessness for women marrying below age 35 went from 8% to about 20% in the period from 1560-1629 to 1647-1770.[40] It is plausible that couples might not have wanted children in high mortality periods in order to avoid the almost inevitable heartbreak of losing a child, even if it meant being deprived of valuable labour on the farm. Emotion, not economics or fecundity, had in this case a key role to play in controlling fertility.

Other anomalies occur. There are instances where, for example, marriage is *late*, yet where fertility is also *high*. In areas where men and women have adequate work before marriage, they might be able to *accumulate substantial savings*, so that if they were to marry late, their financial position would allow for more children than if they married early. Thus, an early marrying couple would have 100 units of currency saved, and a late marrying couple might have 200 units. If each want to spend the same amount per child, then the late marrying couple would have more children than the early marrying one, if nature cooperated. However, this would only apply if the woman in question did not work or worked little in outside employment after marriage. This is indeed the pattern for industrialised societies, where it was not uncommon for females to work full-time before marriage, but unusual after marriage and certainly rare before the youngest child was under age 8 or 9. If parents had the intention of having more children if their finances improved (an eminently logical course), then later marriage in this type economy would facilitate having a larger family, thus the equation of later marriage = more children (higher fertility).

Even where money could not be saved we might see a violation of the regulatory theory, and late marriage did not necessarily entail lower fertility. The pre-Industrial economic situation was such that people sometimes saved money only with great difficulty, and the focus lay on what one earned at the present time and what one could obtain from inheritance and borrowing. Further, if it was the people's custom to set aside a certain fixed amount of money per child, then wherever there was no significant difference in the amount of wealth that couples would have at the beginning of marriage, whatever the age of marriage, then there would be no difference in the number of children one eventually had. If inheritance of net worth from parents or attaining a dowry was *not* a factor, then marrying late or early in this situation made little difference. Creating a good current income basis for a household was the only important issue, but this income could only cover present expenses and little would be left over for savings. The financial position of a man marrying at 22 could only be a little worse than one marrying at 28, since the latter could have not added that much to his finances. In this case, marrying later does not mean marrying wealthier. Hence, if the early marrying couple and the late marrying couple each had saved little or no money, and each planned to set aside the same amount of money for the raising and care of each child, then both couples would have the same number of children, if nature allowed them this. The fertility rate in either case would be roughly the same, as the financial position and the amount that could be spent on each child would be little different. We would therefore see no correlation of any kind between age of marriage and fertility.

Because of situations like the ones above, in more recent years the fertility governor or regulatory theory has come under attack as not being applicable anywhere except the well-documented and well-studied country of England.[41] It appears that the theory is generally applicable, but with notable exceptions. Apparent contradictions might be explained by one or more models, which incorporate specific economic and cultural factors.

The interaction of employment, savings, living standards, inheritance and availability of marriage partners varied from one region to another, often due to exogenous factors, such as specific economic conditions. However, even when the end results are different between regions, based on an examination of existing evidence, the reasoning processes that people used were essentially the same.

Let us look at an interesting set of early 19th century customs as they existed in Nanterre, a town near Paris.[42] Firstly, the area's very high rate of return from the land made it possible for even small plots to produce an adequate living. Secondly, the fact that some of the children in a family could settle into work outside of agriculture reduced the likelihood of inordinate population pressure on the land. Further, due to the nature and demands of the agriculture and wine growing, Nanterre did not ordinarily have resident servants who worked the land, but day labourers who worked whenever there was a need for outside assistance. Because of this practise, children originally helped out on the farm, and then after marriage, they left the household and wage labour was brought in. This economic situation, where men and women could 'freelance' as labourers and where farmers did not have to depend on a family for production, produced opportunities for independent living, and a fairly large number of households being occupied by single adults: bachelors, widows and widowers, with or without children. Nearly two-thirds of the households in Nanterre were nuclear, but some 23% were solitaires. Many unmarried men could live as boarders, and about 5% of the nuclear households had boarders living with them, usually because they produced significant income. These arrangements lessened the pressure to marry.

If people had a desire to marry, an extensive kinship system facilitated the securement of a marriage partner, because farmers lived in areas where neighbours were often relatives. People in this social climate evidently felt confidant enough in their future that it became common for parents and children to reach an agreement known formally as a *demission de biens*, where the parents would retire early, giving land to all their children in return for a life income. This freed the children to marry without having to wait for an inheritance. Further facilitating marriage for the children of farmers was the practise of giving some land to children upon their marriage and the practise of furnishing a significant father's dowry. Daughters could save money in anticipation of marriage by working as laundresses or seamstresses. Artisans, on the other hand, who came to Nanterre and thus had to take time to establish themselves, married later. They had fewer family members to draw upon for assistance, as can be seen in the fact that often they had friends, instead of relatives, witness their weddings. This social class also had fewer financial resources, and had less of a chance to provide a dowry or land.

Not surprisingly, farmers' marriages were both socially and geographically endogamous; most people wed those in the same trade or occupation as themselves or their fathers'. Whereas the marriage practises of Nanterre were not particularly common elsewhere, the desirability of marrying someone from the same background as onself reflected a very common theme. For example, socially prestigious farmers/wine growers' daughters tended to marry sons from the same trade, although there was a tendency for daughters to marry sons from other trades. The social situation did not remain static, and following changes in the economic structure, artisans grew in status and become numerous after 1820. Although other trades were generally endogamous and people preferred similarity, there was a 'pull' to marry into the largest and most lucrative occupations.

Exogenous factors freed people to make decisions about their adult life and marriage without having to worry about future obligations, family duty to work on a farm, or possible financial problems due to overly large families, early marriage or waiting for an inheritance, especially for younger sons.Therefore, economics to a significant extent determined the nature of family relations in at least this part of France.

In the south and the more remote areas of France, a very different culture applied, but one that was still based on exogenous variables.[43] To put it succinctly, as the economy weakened so did family relationships. Without overgeneralising, we can say that people essentially lived in a closed, rather suspicious world, where people erected successive barriers around themselves as a form of protection. Living in small villages, farmers and their families were distrustful and sometimes hostile to outsiders. Within the household, fathers held nearly total control, with wives in secondary position and children even further subordinated. Families rarely had cordial relations with one another, even though they frequently had to work with one another. Children were used as farm labourers, and if a child worked somewhere else, he would be expected to give over his earnings to his family. We also see that respect for traditional parental functions was declining, with schools taking over many child-rearing tasks, including the daily supervision and education of children. Men and women were warned to refrain as much as possible from giving money and land to their children, because this would only put parents at the mercy of their offspring. Although families were usually restrained in speech, parents often did not hide their dislike for their own children, and parents in turn were also derided and maltreated, especially in old age. Distrust between parents and children was matched by distrust between the sexes, beginning in childhood, and then continuing into adulthood, where males became indifferent to females, thinking them to be responsible for man's downfall. Many regions had high rates of celibacy, which might partly explain the denigration of women. By the end of the 19th century, fertility was dropping considerably, not only because of celibacy, but also because married couples were limiting fertility. How else could couples save themselves from the potentially disastrous fate of raising children, only to have them selfishly and spitefully abandon them in old age for better opportunities elsewhere?

'Need and greed' kept families together, not mutual desire, affection or moral compunction. Companionate relationships were indeed difficult to come by, and people spent more time using psychological devices to distance themselves from each another, than pulling themselves toward one another. A simple device could be utilised in many different situations: If one devalues what one really desires, then one can convince oneself that one does not want it that badly. The social situation in the southern French countryside, especially when distilled into the simplified form as seen above, is manifestly contradictory. Why would parents maltreat their children if they expected to depend on them in old age? Were they surprised when their own children treated them like animals when they were treated the same way? Why would families live together with animosity and rancour when they needed each other for support? The only rational answer would be that people no longer thought they were able to obtain what they wanted from the family and thus disparaged it. What we see is a case of a *transient* culture, where the insufficiency and despair of the 19th century created a crisis situation of mutual vindictiveness. The adage that the worst of times brings out the best in people is fanciful at best, and here we see good evidence of insuperable human frailty. When put into difficult circumstances, instead of becoming even more promotive of honour, devotion, and respect, people degenerate to pettiness, aloofness, and generalisations, in essence causing them and the family to self-destruct. Perhaps the meanness stemmed from the realisation that a culture and a way of life were about to pass into history.

Also, in times of peril, individuals, without training or prior experience, tend to over-control their personal situation. An attempt was made to achieve intermediate goals against the strong crosswinds of financial expediency, but instead of using subtle movements that allow the various forces to fall into an equilibrium, many used their options rashly and crudely, making attaining a steady course a hopeless undertaking. In such a challenging scenario, with the knowledge always in mind of the dangerous consequences that come from error, one desires clear results quickly, with any delay being disturbing. One could gain control of even very difficult situations by simply allowing the various mechanisms to 'settle down' after initiating some kind of action. Raising children and dealing with a family in difficult material circumstances is sure to provoke people to take harsh measures for rapid, certain results, but by doing so, they sow the seeds of enmity that will come back to haunt them.

Reasons for this kind of social turmoil and poor economic situation are not impossible to find. A major contributor to the problems that families faced might have been one component of the Code Napoléon (1794), which forced landowners to divide their property equally among heirs. This made it difficult for farmers to resist the temptation to limit births so that the land would not be split up, causing hardship for future generations and destroying family power. Where property ownership was common, birthrates indeed fell. However, as many peasants did not own the land they farmed, the laws concerning inheritance had limited applicability, although at the time this reason was commonly given or assumed. More relevant, and perhaps more troubling, a factor, which explains declining birthrates, was an economic environment where children no longer had the monetary and pragmatic value they once did. Here, contraception, continence and late marriage combined to restrain fertility.

Still, the most important reason for the indigence of the peasantry might have been high taxes and rents. They laboured and struggled to survive under onerous burdens over which they had little control. Our sympathy for the peasants is however tempered by the knowledge that their plight was to some significant extent self-imposed as well. Country people, although regarded as simple in tastes, would often sell their best agricultural products in order to buy items that might be considered as distinctly frivolous.[44] By the late 19th century, most people in France had many options as to where they could work, what kind of work they could do, what productivity measures *they* could implement, how and what they could sell, and what they could buy. Thus, as personal choice played a role in determining living conditions, so did it, at the very least, *indirectly* affect marriage timing, family size and family structure.

The south of France was not alone in its economic deprivation nor in its reaction to it. Analysis of conditions in contemporaneous Ireland, although very different in history and politics, demonstrates that the Spirit of the people described above, far from being characterised as merely 'French', could justifiably be called 'European'. Before the Famine, in many parts of Ireland land was subdivided and given to sons as families relied on the labour of family members. Thus, what was the product of law in France was the product of culture in Ireland. Subsistence on these smaller holdings would not have been possible, however, without grain prices rising and the viability of cottage industries. After the Famine, however, the situation changed dramatically. The former land practises were no longer valid, and the room for error was perceived as being far smaller; now, the cultural Spirit is more visible and easily dissected. Land came to be poorly managed and yield declined, with the result that culture now demanded that inheritance be impartible. For this situation, many blamed the landlords, the English and the Protestants, but few blamed the peasants themselves who were evidently chiefly responsible. Factional fighting and age-old rivalries in the community probably made people reluctant to hire outside help, instead using more dependable family labour. Thus, when land inheritance and dowries did not materialise, the basis of married life was withdrawn, and many never married. Those who did marry did so with money as a prime consideration, although many marriages were arranged without much consent from the prospective bride. These changes exerted a major toll on relations within the household, causing dangerous centripetal forces to arise within the family. Women were frequently treated as units of production in loveless relationships, and often married considerably older men. In fact, it became common by the turn of the 20th century that half of married women were more than 10 years younger than their spouses. As parents did not wish to yield control and delegate authority in domestic matters to children, resentment tainted ordinary relationships, and even firstborn sons were kept in subordinate positions for many years into adulthood. We can see in these observations underlying dynamics, the most important of which, for our purposes, is the emphasis that people gave to the concept of an absolute minimal standard of living, that is, people put material independence over that of familial affection and sacrifice. Thus, the standard of living for each family member would *not* change in relation to changes in household size. In a society that was as materially minded as post-Famine Ireland, evaluation of people was often on the basis of economic 'worth'. For example, the main reason, we suspect, why the youngest sons were most condescendingly treated is because they threatened to make impossible everyone getting their legitimate slice of the pie, a portion that was theirs by 'right'. These individuals often threw the family into financial disarray, but they managed, however, to form close alliances with their mothers, who, probably because of their lower productivity during pregnancy, found themselves similarly deprecated. Not surprisingly, selfishness, distrust and feelings of inferiority abounded, but for those who wished a better life there were few options, as few urban areas required labour and servant status would bring even further disrepute. Thus, many who did not inherit land escaped to America, in the process breaking up families and creating yet more animosity and envy among those who remained.

People had to react in decisive ways to the crises and so marriage standards were raised, with the result that many men and women did not find each other sufficiently aesthetically, economically or romantically attractive. Men wanted to raise themselves above the ignominy of labourers and neglected sons. The common acceptance of the saying that 'the lucky man waits for prosperity', that is, waits for the propitious union with a well-to-do woman, resulted in fairly high rates of permanent celibacy in this period. About 25% of women never married in the period after the Famine, and the ones who did evidently had some difficulty in maintaining their rights and prerogatives in the matter of their prospective spouse. Some women went to work overseas in order to obtain enough money to lure prospective bridegrooms. The money would be used to buy better clothing and jewelry, creating the impression of some wealth,[45] indicating that appearances rather than real merit had already become the focus of courtship. Irish marriage rates and birth rates did not significantly change since 1864 when records began to be kept, until the 1960s. Other countries' rates declined over this period, eventually catching up with trend in Irish births, whereas Ireland's marriage rates are still considerably lower than that of other nations. Oddly, because of the above factors, Ireland was a 'modern' nation before any other in Europe,[46] and its patterns challenge Hajnal's theories about economic conditions being invariably linked to marriage patterns. Promoters of the theory of economic pragmatism ignore the importance of other *incentives* to marry; marriage is a whole 'package' of considerations, including appearance, personality, and deportment. *Pre-existing* compatibility between future spouses, at least in the area of manners, was now an issue. No matter how hard they tried to be 'pragmatic', the Irish could not countenance marrying a person still burdened with the 'rustic image'. In addition, incentives to *not* marry could be found by this time, such as support from siblings, surrogate heirs and the government.[47] It is probably from this period that many proverbs of distinctly negative cast were created, such as, 'beat a woman with a hammer and you'll have gold', 'it is difficult to trust a woman', 'there's only one thing in the world better than a good wife—no wife'. Some of these reflect the negativist thinking of the English, French and other cultures, but undoubtedly they had, and possibly still have, a poignant ring in Ireland.

Ireland was typical of all other pre-modern nations in depending on land as wealth, forestalling marriage when it was unavailable. But it was different from other countries in not having industry as compensation for high population density and very unwise subdivision practises. The lack of cooperation between family members and gross materialism we also see might be the product of a poor economy, and thus might very well occur anywhere in Europe under the same circumstances. This could indeed be a recipe for disaster: the mixture of early marriage age and the practise of partible inheritance produced many heirs with small plots of land, who found themselves backward and isolated in a land with only sluggish industrial growth. The result was enormous starvation when the land was pushed finally past its limit to produce. In the aftermath of the Famine, the family situation changed but apparently for the worse, where whatever civility was left was extinguished by the struggle for the remaining resources. It is true that famine can happen anywhere, and people can lose their heads in desperation. However, the famine in Ireland was much more disruptive due to the absence of economic collaboration, industriousness and progressivity, an unfortunate attitude that might be peculiarly Irish. Even as patriots might have us believe otherwise, characterisations of a people must also carry temporal limits, and so our observation might is appropriate for the people living on the island before the mid-1800s but perhaps not those living there in the present day.

Compared to the peasantry of France and Ireland, in social structure and lifestyle the nobility of Southwest Germany were very different indeed. However, they had a similar, albeit more consistent, long-term reaction to economic forces. The evidence, as presented in HURWICH (1993), shows that people did not divide estates among offspring during economic downturns mainly to preserve their prestigious way of life, and as a result, hardly half of the sons and daughters born in the 15th century married. Most of the unmarried sons, and nearly all the unmarried daughters entered the Church, this being especially true for lower-ranking noble families. Higher-ranking families placed sons in military careers. This pattern was similar in other Catholic parts of Europe: Florence before 1700, Milan before 1750, Toulouse before 1760; of 17th century French dukes and peers, half the sons and half the daughters did not marry. When Protestantism became the established religion in various regions, daughters were more likely to marry, since there were no convents in which to place them. However, in other Protestant parts of Europe, the older ways persisted, such as the Protestant part of Geneva, where a quarter of sons and daughters did not marry.

The reason why land was not divided among heirs rests primarily upon economics. In general, the eldest son did not necessarily inherit, and although there is a long-standing tradition for *all* brothers to inherit, this was done *only* when economic circumstances allowed. In the 15th century, during a period of agricultural depression and fewer options in secular careers, land division was avoided and more of the nobility's offspring entered the ranks of the Church. Conversely, the period of the 16th century and the early 17th century brought forth an expanding economy in agriculture and better occupational opportunities, with a concomitant policy amongst the nobility of subdividing estates. In this situation, fewer children remained unmarried and fewer entered the clergy. By the late 17th century, noblemen again refrained from dividing estates, a tendency that was an outgrowth of the effect of the Thirty Years' War on grain and land prices, as well as on tenant income. Again, a larger proportion of children remained unmarried, although this effect was more pronounced for females and in general was not nearly at the levels seen in the period before the 16th century. In spite of dour financial circumstances, the more favourable marital outcome occurred as a result of men being able to engage in alternate occupations and make honourable lives for themselves.

Economic and demographic upheavals leave deep marks on a culture, which revises its outlook and priorities according to the realities at hand. One does not quite know why Germans coined proverbs such as 'he who marries does well, but he who does not marry does better', or 'marriage is both heaven and hell'. They had a suspect view of marriage, but without the aspersions, or even misogyny of some other European cultures. The negative experiences of Germany in the Thirty Years War and its growing pains as a nation might have reflected adversely on many households. The unfortunate dispute between the social ideal of equanimity (all brothers inheriting) and of economic reality (only the eldest inherited in difficult times) made many cast a stern eye on marriage perhaps as psychological protection against the heartbreak of not being in a position to inherit. Marriage denied to a man or woman who was never attracted to it in the first place is no great hardship.

The invisible hand of fiscalism that pulled or pushed (or shoved?) people into marriage in Europe extended to regions more than three centuries and a continent away. People are indeed slow to transition into new lifestyles, and no matter where they lived, those raised within the culture of an agricultural community would as their forbears still consider land, and not only money, as necessary for marriage. The unique self-sufficiency of a farm has an enduring appeal even today. This is why we notice that whites who resided in the rural southern United States in the early 20th century would delay marriage if farmland was expensive and jobs outside of agriculture (i.e. manufacturing) were available.[48] As in Europe, land was king, and the difficulty in obtaining it significantly affected how and when a man could expect to begin a family. In the urban environment, where land for most people was an irrelevant factor, income became the main focus. Men working in factories could often only find a meagre basis for a living, with marriage a distant aim. Sometimes, however, the money from jobs in industry might be good enough to maintain a household, but country people living in the cities would still see this strategy, based as it was on nothing more than 'paper money', as bound for failure. Only if the rustic emigrants to the cities dispensed with their belief in older traditions could they utilise the savings from their work and marry early. This would, in essence, also nullify the influence of inheritance practices on marriage.[49] Such newfound freedom was indeed desirable, but it was tempered by the knowledge that modern city life did not offer the safety of family and land that people in the 'backward' countryside could fall back on.

We see that people in every country and situation had a definite idea of the 'proper' standard of living, and they could not easily envision a viable marriage that did not attain it. Although the private, innermost thoughts and attitudes of people on the matters we have covered in this section have not been preserved, some indicators that illuminate actual thought processes are available. One such source of evidence is the proceedings of marriage courts, which contain the views of ordinary people and persons in authority on the issue of courtship, marriage and family relationships. Unfortunately, there has not been a great deal of research on marriage contracts or litigation. An example of how the procedure might have changed is taken from research done on Neuchatel, a parish in Switzerland.[50] Cases where one party wished to annul a marriage were brought before a special court. In the period from the mid-16th century to the mid-17th century, promises of marriage were binding if made by persons at the age 20 or older and in front of two or more witnesses. The marriage contract and the agreement to marry were allowed to stand; whether the couple loved each other was *not* a pertinent concern. By the 18th century, the emphasis moved from a strict application of vows to a more flexible approach involving emotional and psychological compatibility. This is an attitudinal shift of great significance. All of the parties concerned had to be assured that the couple really *wanted* to live with each other; even if promises were made, they were not considered binding unless the woman was pregnant, in which case the interests of the child overrode the interests of the parents. The knowledge of a large increase in European premarital pregnancies and illegitimate births from before 1750 to the early 19th century no doubt forced the justices to declare the contract valid, thwarting the aim of a 'perfect' society built on harmonious households. Although we have no specific figures for Switzerland, we do have for neighbouring regions. For example, Germany on average experienced a rise of from 13% to 24%, France from 6% to 13%, England from 20% to 35%.[51] The illegitimacy rate was also alarming, with increases in Bavaria from about

3% in the mid-18th century to about 15% a century later. Other parts of Germany also experienced large increases from at least 1700 and peaking around 1850.[52]

Switzerland experienced changes in fertility patterns to a lesser extent than Germany, but the changes were still disturbing enough to instigate a change in juridical theory on marriage customs and practise. Persons in authority, charged with safeguarding not only traditions but the family, realised that people were becoming less serious and cautious in contracting a marriage, and they wanted to be as certain as possible that married life would remain viable. The same frivolity that attended the decision to marry also attended behaviours coincident with the relationship, which included premarital sex. Rising silently behind these official matters is the independence ethos, within whose form external factors seriously challenge the love or companionate relationship. It seems, however, that officials understood the changing morality, as intervention somewhat preceded the social change in fertility and sexual attitudes. The justices were aware of what was brewing in society before the changes actually occurred; men in power often have insight into what the future of the society in their care, though such information is not always wisely used, as in this case. Perhaps it would have been better to remain inflexible in marriage contracts as a warning not to enter engagement without giving careful thought to the feasibility of the relationship. The traditional structures of marriage should have been preserved as they functioned quite well. The insincerity and uncertainty behind the shaky vows of marriage would have disappeared after people understood the dire consequences that awaited the careless promise, but this could occur only during the period when the palpable virtues of devotion and integrity were still etched in living memory.

To summarise what has been said in this chapter, there is undeniable evidence that people have traditionally placed great emphasis on obtaining the time, money and other resources to find a suitable marriage partner and to establish a household. The formation of an independent household was a watershed event in the lives of most people. When resources could not be attained, due to poor employment prospects, no or little inheritance, or rising prices, people then delayed marriage. This did not mean that they did not wish to attain the ideal of love, but that it was put aside by pragmatic circumstances. Furthermore, when people were prevented from marrying, and when the economy was not faring well, then family members often became hostile, no doubt accusing one another, probably unfairly, of being at fault for this hindrance. This acted to destroy the bonds that might have been used precisely as substitutes for the marital bond. Where a son or daughter might have obtained satisfying emotional relationships from a father or mother instead of a spouse, this possibility was destroyed by arguments over money, inheritance, land-sharing and so on. Finally, we see in these changes the basis for the transformation of attitudes towards marriage, from one where economic considerations were uppermost in people's minds, although co-existing with their emotional needs for companionship, to one where financial aspects were not rejected, but the emotional aspect was neglected, looming like a tiger ready to pounce if not sated. Where before people could grow with one another into a mutual loving relationship, now they had to be compatible before the marriage, and even before courtship, took place. When the restrictions on marriage began to be lifted in the 18th century, due to conflicts between the calls of the new economy and married life, the emphasis shifted from marriage as a shelter of maturing and emotional deepening, to a venue where life as existed *before* marriage could continue and one where individuals had to share, perhaps guardedly, a house, bed and food with someone else. The fundamental, essential precepts of modern married life had been set, and the traditional conceptions were unobtrusively passing away.

Home life as we understand it is no more natural to us than a cage is natural to a cockatoo.
~George Bernard Shaw

To live with someone and to live in someone are two fundamentally different matters. There are people in whom one can live without living with them, and vice versa. To combine both requires the purest degree of love and friendship.
~Johann Wolfgang von Goethe

CHAPTER 3
EMANCIPATED CHILDREN

NOW A NEW PATTERN: GOOD FORTUNE GIVES WAY TO SKILL

Marriage has always been a confluence of various needs: Patronal, educational, occupational, emotional, financial, and communal. Thus, material issues are not the only considerations in the decision to marry, but psychological factors as well. We analysed in the last chapter how people dealt with the changing economy and only indirectly addressed the issues of personality and temperament. In this chapter, we look at the way people interrelate general psychological demands with economic and material conditions. In the next chapter, we will study a specific type of psychological requirement and see how this has been affected by modern demands of independence.

We should first understand that unlike economic factors, the mental aspects of human nature do not change very much over time. Even though a particular idea as to how to satisfy one of the above needs might be 'modern', it might nevertheless be of ancient origin. But short of using a time machine, we have no way of knowing with any great certainty how the general public looked at these issues in remote times. Today, we have far more information about individual attitudes, which gives us knowledge about the dynamics that influence people to marry. But this detailed information goes back only to the late 1800s. It is logical to assume that, if there is a period of time where the dynamics have not changed in three to five generations, from say the late 1800s to the mid-1900s, then they are part of a longer trend, probably much longer. We can safely apply these principles, within reason, to the cultures of the more distant past, from whom we are ultimately descended, not only physically but culturally and morally. This historical depth should lead us to appreciate the singularity, the unusual nature, of recent metamorphosis in attitudes concerning companionship and independence.

Drawing upon our own personal understanding of the universal need for 'fulfilment', that is, attaining all that one lacks, we discover this to be the unchanging, absolutely constant factor in human nature. Throughout the many centuries before the modern age, when life was otherwise tedious, bleak and threatening, one kept hope alive that one would eventually see the consummation of the material, intellectual and emotional; indeed, this prospect kept one from sliding into pessimism and cynicism. The individual sought the person, the romantic and virtuous 'beloved', who would balance out their own weaknesses, leading to psychological wholeness. Thus, *complementarity,* the dovetailing of differences between people, has always been a critical factor in reaching the ideal of love. However, history shows that beliefs about what was *possible* changed greatly. We will be discussing in detail these changes in subsequent secions, but suffice here to say that beliefs moved first from the idea of close complementarity to that of more distant complementarity, then reverting to a closer relationship, but one where similitude was more important than balance. This last phase seems to have been caused by more self-centeredness, greater intolerance of personality differences, and less necessity for complementarity due to changes in household function. Determining and handling similarity is more easy than dealing with the complexities of dissimilarity, and so when similarity became the focus of the search for a marriage partner, the belief developed that a love match could be easily made. Naturally, dealing with personality and background differences was still as important as ever but now neglected. Less time and effort were invested in ascertaining a person's acceptability as marriage partner. In addition, the 'popularisation' of the analytical and increasing education of the population, an outgrowth of the same forces that created the possibility of more similitude in marriage (as duties were transferred from mother and father to companies and schools), rendered a certain foreignness to deep positive emotion. This, combined with shorter courtship period, led to many foolish choices of marriage partner, with resulting problematic divorce rates.

The necessity of maximising the interrelationship between human similarities and differences in reaching personal fulfilment is quite important to our study, especially within the context of historical developments. This is the psychological requirement we spoke of earlier that will be examined more closely in the next chapter. However, we must first explore those general concepts about integrating personality and material concerns that have remained unscathed by the sharp sword of modernism, and then secondly, investigate those concepts that have become more relevant over time.

The most important aspect of the male-female relationship that has not been abandoned is the ideal of total mutual affection, since maximum contentment is gotten through an all-encompassing love with a person of the opposite sex. As in the past, men who remain single past the average marriage age generally have formed an ideal of the feminine in adolescence. They never find the woman that fits this ideal, and prefer to stay single rather than marry someone who does not meet their high standards.[53] In such men, the ideal burns strongly.

Preserving the ideal of affection becomes central to one's identity and existence, more so than gaining partial emotional fulfilment. Finding failure with ordinary women, the idealist draws energy from his concept of femininity, which exists as the imagination's 'perfect woman'. The ideal woman responds as an antipode to all the imperfect behaviour in the world, and a real wife would necessarily displace this Venus. Thus, people who marry late or never may have less interest in marriage precisely because they have very *high* standards. A fairly permanent standard is erected early in life, and efforts to dismantle it can lead to resistance if not hostility.

Individuals with high ideals about the role of love in marriage are clearly more interested in retaining the ideal rather than enjoying the benefits of marriage, although both areas are meaningful to them. Thinking of this kind often throws a spanner into the works of sociology, since it is not based on 'rational' considerations, easily measured factors such as income, status, education, but instead on soft 'irrational' notions. Yet, that this is an important facet of male-female relationships cannot be denied. Of course, men who do marry at the average or early age might have ideals as well, but they are not as lofty as the late or never-marrying. It is also possible that they have actually found their ideal women. Most men, though, who ardently value these precepts formed in childhood will be sadly disappointed.

Hence, men and women are still captivated by the ideal, and they seek to reach it, but due to the particular issues of modern existence, they fail. Perhaps this partially explains the paradox why modern people, who supposedly strongly believe in a romantic notion of marriage, are often unwilling to enter into stable relationships, unwilling to marry early, and indeed often unwilling to marry at all. They wish to preserve the ideal, and so they seek earnestly, as in past times, for the companion they imagine, but now the long road does not lead to triumph, but only to a sad comprehension about the contradictions present in many relationships. From observations of modern life, key questions arise that revolve around the issues of autonomy and love. How can one proclaim to be looking for a Mr Right or Miss Right, but yet marry someone that was clearly never 'right' to begin with? How can one be both consciously seeking that single 'true love', but yet have numerous sex partners? How can couples advocate marriage as the only place where the warmth of true companionship can occur, yet doggedly pursue a career, when it even threatens to dismiss love and affection?

In light of these competing factors and disappointments, it might be thought that the importance of marriage is dwindling, with a parallel rise in the satisfaction of being unmarried. In fact, this is not the case. More than ever, people want to marry. We find that the differences in well-being between married and unmarred are *increasing* not decreasing. Differences in happiness appear greatest in the most *modern* European cultures, whereas almost none exist in the traditional ones. Married persons are becoming more dependent on spouses, not less; overall happiness in life has become intimately tied with satisfaction in marriage. Not surprisingly, between 1950 to 1980 suicide rates rose far more for the unmarried than the married.[54] All of this points to the increasing isolation of marriage as providing gratification to the *exclusion* of other relationships and institutions, a critical fact we should not ignore.

It is possible to obtain satisfaction with ordinary friendships, but these relationships have become superficial. In the past, when people could get emotional satisfaction from a job, hobby, close relationships with a small circle of relatives and friends, there was no correlation between the number of one's friends and marital tendency. Today, *quantity* of friendship is a key factor, more so than quality, and such a dynamic takes the place of marriage. Perhaps if one has many more than the average number of friends, one can permanently delay marriage. In the past, in the absence of friends, people might not have married more quickly. Why have people become less dependent on non-marital relationships for emotional fulfilment? The reasons, as we shall determine in subsequent sections, are varied: Relationships are less stable and less homogeneous due to people coming from more diverse backgrounds and different geographical areas; there is a preoccupation with materialism, instead of aesthetics, people and spirituality; diversions in the form of mass entertainment make it less necessary to cultivate friendships.

Let us concentrate for the moment on how the continuing high importance placed on marriage affects modern living. Indeed, this emphasis creates an unsafe situation. The male-female intimate friendship is ostensibly critical to one's success in life, but many paradoxically spend little time working to achieve such a relationship. Moreover, in spite of attaining some security in one's life, the average individual too often relies on one person who clearly does not bring him the emotional satisfaction he wants. It is irrefutable that such a person was chosen rashly and heedlessly, and that older courtship principles were ignored. In a specific and fairly rigidly defined cultural context such as marriage, the contemporary 'match' often brings not peace but friction, especially when the relationship itself is based on physical factors, not spiritual or psychological ones. The streets of the modern life are filled with often troubled and struggling characters, not the joyous, secure people envisioned by our parents and grandparents. The yearning for love is still so great, yet the men and women who try to satisfy this yearning end up often dejected and lonely.

As relationship ideals are intensely personal, only the individual can have the ultimate responsibility in choosing the method to reach these ideals. However, traditions have laid out clear paths that will assist the individual in attaining psychological wholeness and fulfilment. In the modern Western world, the usual or typical route is for a man or woman is to finish education, then begin a full-time career, then marry, then have children. After this point, the sexes have somewhat different paths: women often must leave work for awhile, and then possibly return to full-time or part-time labour force participation. After the children have grown up and left home, the parents have an admittedly ambiguous role. The path of life as presented here does not merely end with the wedding, and the couple live 'happily ever after', but involves activities that are antecedent to marriage and activities that carry on well beyond the maturation of the youngest child in the family. Society understands that the ideal of love is not just reaching a place but continuing success in jointly overcoming the obstacles in life and enjoying its most profound spiritual, artistic and intellectual offerings. The recommended actions along the path prepare the individual financially, mentally and emotionally. Some might worry, however, that too much freedom might be lost by following this course. Schooling, in particular, appears to be critical in changing personality and establishing a career. Nonetheless, there does not appear to be any recurring conflict between educational experiences or educational attainment and acting out the traditional role in the family.[55] Each step in the process, when taken with deliberation and accepted on its own terms, does not necessarily negatively affect any other step.

There are, of course, restrictions in the life path we are discussing that create discernible patterns of behaviour. Women who marry late tend to be individuals who are in the process of acquiring higher education or pursuing careers and not surprisingly are often of conservative background, through which this traditional segmentation between roles can be transmitted. In the US, these women tend to be middle-class Roman Catholics, who marry outside of their class and work only until the first birth. Such a pattern is indicative of individuals who plan carefully by amassing greater economic resources.[56] Devout Catholics and others with traditional conceptions about family life, understand the need to *settle* into a role before moving on to the next stage. They first put aside marriage plans to concentrate on obtaining an education and then establishing themselves in a well- paying job. They then save money so as to establish themselves again, this time in the domestic role, which allows them to remain at home with their children. The weak link in the chain might be deciding on a marriage partner, who might very well be chosen hastily.[57]

A situation where the various strands of ideals, education, career and materialism are successfully woven together might be found in Madrid, Spain. In this fairly typical example of a contemporary Catholic and traditional, though urban, culture, dating begins at about age 16, serious dating by age 18, with the ideal marriage age being 23. There is fairly good agreement between theory and practise, with one-third marrying within one year of the marriage age ideal, and if outside of this range, the tendency is to marry later than the ideal age. Individuals have a relatively free hand in choosing a mate; indeed, many parents do not even personally know the person their son or daughter is seeing. Although persistent reinforcement of independence ideals, as would be found in more modern countries, is absent, the desire for self-sufficiency is nevertheless strong, and relatively few couples receive money from parents (25%) or share an apartment with their parents after marriage (33%). However, they maintain that economic considerations are not generally important in affecting the disposition to marry (37% say they are), but they are more important in affecting the length of courtship.

Couples desire to live in a well-furnished residence separate from the parental abodes, an arrangement which necessitates careful accumulation of domestic items and furniture whilst putting money aside. Thus, the period of steady dating and engagement is by Western European standards quite long, usually lasting nearly four years, with even longer courtships being acceptable. Specific economic factors which force sons or daughters to leave home in order to work might create unusually long courtships. They marry *later* because they give most of their income over to their families, without being able to save much for themselves. Leaving home to work is more a case of economic necessity to support the family rather than fulfilling a desire to be autonomous. Actually, it seems the opposite of the independence ideal, for they have less freedom as to when to marry.

Furthermore, long and short courtships are *both* associated with late marriage, thus forming a U-shaped curve with respect to length of courtship and marriage age. Long courtships are often expected for late marriers, who might spend years waiting for material circumstances to fall into place. On the other hand, the reasons for a short courtship are not immediately apparent. Such relatively brief courtships might be understandable for those who marry early, as they might not have much of a chance at courtship if the socially accepted age of dating is fairly high. Yet, short courtship can also be understandable in the lives of people who have already spent a number of years saving money *before* courtship; dating, engagement and marriage can all be temporally close together in these cases. In addition, because of their older age, they might wish to hasten the process before the 'door is closed'.

Of course, economic factors are not entirely responsible for decisions related to marriage. Siblings tend to affect one another in terms of marriage age, where if one marries late, they will all tend to do so. Such cross-influences operate within a neighbourhood community as well. Other factors that affect marriage age in other nations, such as education and income of parents and of the couple, seem to have little influence in Madrid.[58] Perhaps such absence of effect is due to the emphases on education and income being more a function of a modern lifestyle, and consequently they have little bearing in a culture based on traditional values, even though these factors are in the process of becoming important social components.

Here we see in operation a number of traditional, probably ancient, dynamics: the care in selecting a mate, the desire for an independent residence, the patient amassing of resources, the putting aside of marriage considerations in order to support the family, and perhaps a group dynamic effect on propensity to marry. There are some new considerations, however: the longer wait to have a 'modern' standard of living, the lower involvement of family members in the couple's relationship, the non-issue of the economic necessity of children. Hence, a compromise is reached, wherein people experience independence and gaiety during youth, but plan on having a comfortable home after marriage; these pursuits, however, are put aside or modified when other more important issues arise. They are willing to make sacrifices, balancing their own needs with the needs of others, be it family or friends. Thus, individuals ostensibly are committed for the good of themselves and the community to making the right decisions about choice of spouse, choice of residence, finances and material standards. This occurs without much cavilling, and individuals, even within the modern climate of independence, are prepared sometimes to go through long courtships to achieve the goals of minimising friction within the family by discharging their filial obligations, and at the same time live relatively well with a spouse that they truly respect.

Madrid is an example of a modern society being able to integrate traditional and modernistic demands. The discipline exists in a general population to rationally balance individual and group needs. Of course, this particular mix of ideas is more common in regions still accepting long-standing customs and Christian beliefs, and cannot be assumed to exist in the areas of Europe where there is only a tenuous attachment to the cautious, introverted temperament of forbears. Moreover, these changes seem to affect women more than men. The role of outside work in a woman's life is attached to a certain extent on supporting her family of origin, and also on saving for marriage. It is assumed that women will not have to work after children are born, but this depends on the material needs and expectations of the household.

In the 20th century, however, attachment to traditional values, religious belief and church attendance have declined significantly and are no longer relevant to many people. The path carefully laid out by Christian teaching, where different social roles are carefully treated individually, has given way in post-traditional times to a confusing array of choices. Thus, the rejection of traditional values, such as refusing to become a member of a church or refusing to believe in God, leads to a resistance to conventional family values and dependence on a man, which in turn spurs a desire for independence, and so necessitates participation in the work force. Further, as family life and the instruction of children often demand submitting oneself to a moral regimen derived from Christianity, there is even less desire for irreligious women to marry. Simply put, women with little or no religious belief are more likely to be in the labour force, and are more likely to never marry.[59] However, the lower the level of belief amongst men, the *less* their participation in the work force, a finding opposite to that for women.[60] In addition, the nonreligious were more likely to engage in uncommitted, sexually open relationships than the religious.[61]

Women now seem to have two courses laid out before them: married life or career. They feel they must fully and intensively pursue one or the other, but not together or even in sequence. In addition, blurring the boundaries of these roles appears to be acceptable. One could see this as a wholesale rejection of conventions about men's and women's roles, a choice to live without marriage, children or other commitments, in a free and easy Bohemian life, outside the social mainstream. But it is more likely that this is an attempt to *sever* the conventional links between home, business, moral values, spiritual belief and success in larger society. Each, it is believed, can now be achieved and savoured separately and in whatever combination or order one chooses. For example, one might have children out of wedlock, pursue a career for several years during which time one cohabitates, then returning to school, and then living alone again. There is no desire to leave society or to be marginalised, yet there is the desire to fulfill different roles at different times, thus leading to cohabitation and illegitimacy. Instead of finding fulfilment in these varied roles by experiencing them in a particular order, one can move freely in the material, external world of business and at the same time experience the various aspects of married life. In short, a major redefinition of roles has occurred.

These changes are, objectively speaking, not socially desirable. They encourage an abandonment of the ideals concerning home, marriage and the economic bases for the household. In the past, the expected timeline for life had benefits that were manifestly obvious; it was not mere custom that held people to a particular course. The heart of the confusion in modern times might very well be in calculating the overall value, the net worth after subtracting liabilities from the assets, of working outside the home. Traditional women and non- traditional women both see the necessity of being in the labour force, but clearly for different reasons. Whereas the nullifidian works as a way of achieving a highly personal, unique combination of standards, the religious person works because she wishes to attain *both* a traditional and modern set of values. Both types of women use a career in order to establish themselves materially, but each type also has another reason for doing so: one does so in order to attain a *juxtaposition* of 'custom-made' roles, whereas the other does so to avoid a *clash* between two traditionally defined roles. Very often, the irreligious want to create a life that is entirely suited to their desires, minimising restrictions and sacrifices; their motto might be 'I will do what I wish, when I wish, in whatever way I wish, and no one can tell me otherwise'. On the other hand, those who welcome secular and religious traditions for the invaluable assistance they offer in finding contentment will be careful to respect roles that come from these traditions. We should add that religious, traditionally minded women are bound to do better in life than the nullifidians, as they accept the discipline that comes from traditional wisdom. However, waiting for each role to occur in succession does produce certain problems. Marriage within their own socioeconomic class might not be possible for these women, as the choice of partner is relatively limited for those who wait until their 30s to find a husband, a situation which necessitates going outside of one's chosen familiar social groups. Such a marriage might not be ideal in terms of personality, but if the other aspects of this lifestyle are well- planned, then there are at least fewer grounds for spousal disputes.

We can understand that people might be reluctant to marry whilst they are still in college, as they do not have a stable career or good earnings. But why might individuals refrain from marriage when they are proceeding skilfully in well-paid careers? If you have the money, and a willing companion, why not go ahead and marry? People who put themselves into their careers might find that the exacting standards that they require for work do not translate well to home life. Although rigorous and demanding demeanour is an asset for success in work, it becomes a disaster when dealing with friendships. As men and women become closer, the demands that one makes on the other might become too onerous. It is not surprising to learn that individuals who have been unsuccessful in finding a marriage partner usually fail to form meaningful relationships because of great rigidity and low sociability.[62] Since women, in particular, feel they must compete and are often afraid of losing their position or power, they might *over*compensate by being rigid in instructions to co-workers, never satisfied with their work, or unrealistic in setting schedules. It is likely that this carries over into private life where living with someone else can become intolerable.

Hence, single people in high stress occupations are not unaware of the potential for 'contaminating' the home environment with the problems that arise at work. Dealing with difficult people in difficult situations all day induces a certain distaste for human relations in general. Unless one has a strong belief that one will have an especially sympathetic spouse and children, one is tempted to go on living alone. Stress contagion is a not uncommon occurrence many couples experience, where the conflicts and overload of work influences the occurrence of conflict in the home. Overemphasis on precision or unrealistic demands could precipitate quarrelling, with the tendency to focus dispute on a small number of areas. In reviewing a study of home life, males somewhat more than females transfer arguments from work to home, and the former much more than the latter shift conflict from home to work. We also find that major issues of contention arise in the married household fairly frequently. Men claimed they had arguments with the wife or a child about once every three weeks, whereas women (perhaps more accurately) reported conflict about once every two weeks.[63] Thus, the expansion of work responsibilities in the latter half of the 20th century might have contributed to the present difficult climate at home. Not only does work in general tend to bring familial disruption, but certain occupational duties might exacerbate the tensions. This is more of an issue for women, it would appear, whose roles have an effect on how much stress they experience. For example, although female clergy experience less stress than the general population, they are more likely to experience role overload than male clergy. The former perceive more stress and believe they have fewer personal resources than males.[64] In such circumstances, it becomes understandable why certain individuals might not wish to marry, when the unpleasant likelihood arises that struggles that originate in the office will continue at home, and that unresolved differences at home will exacerbate tensions at work. For the harried full-time worker, an empty home might become an oasis of peace, indeed, perhaps the only one.

From the evidence that is available, we can see that the demands of education and career have largely dissolved the long-standing organic associations between marriage, career, sexual intercourse, child-bearing and child-rearing. Yet in spite of these changes, there is still a link between two areas that many people believe *should* be maintained, namely that of marriage and child-rearing. Whether a person wants children or not continues to be an important factor in the decision to marry. People have pragmatic reasons as to why they would want children, as older men and woman without children and living alone are more likely to be socially isolated, i.e. without any face-to-face contact with others. The loss of essential links with the world is far more likely for people who do not have children than for people with children. Only about one in ten of the latter have not had any social contact in the last day or two, but about one in four of the former have not had such contact. Although childless individuals might fraternise with others as compensation, they do *not* see family, friends or neighbours more often. Such isolation is particularly strong for those in poor health, and from manual labour/working class backgrounds.[65] No matter how independent one might be at earlier ages, one cannot easily countenance such 'autonomy' in old age, when sympathetic support from others is imperative. Children provide special social and emotional benefits that cannot be fulfilled by others, apart perhaps from a spouse. Those in poor health and others with special needs are particularly dependent on close relatives, who, more than others, feel obligated to tolerate the emotional and physical strains. Being a member of a social class that is outside the mainstream economically and educationally makes it even more difficult to reach out; fear of ridicule and criticism makes for an insular mentality that limits social interaction to a small network of dependable kin. It is clear, that whether or not one likes to entertain the idea, isolation in old age is significantly more likely if one has no children. That isolation can even be nightmarish if one is childless *and* unmarried.

Companionship, however, is not the only reason that one has children, as many can expect a spouse to serve in this capacity well into old age. Children bring many rewards to couples, who fulfill their destiny as nurturers and contributors to mankind. Children have always satisfied deep emotional desires, by bringing a sense of purpose to life, by giving one the opportunity to impart guidance and knowledge, and by perpetuating the family name. In addition, children could serve to aid in occupational and household chores. Emotionally, the labours involved in raising children could expiate the moral offence of enjoying sexuality. But many nowadays seem to purposely ignore these facts and their potential needs in old age; children form an unnecessary adjunct in a society obsessed with superficial pursuits, autonomy and youth. Those couples without children, far from seeing children as a path to consummation of their roles, see children as *impediments* to self-actualisation; they instead look for fulfilment through education and career. In fact, such couples see children as creating nothing less than a threat to marital harmony.[66] No longer do children bring the kinds of rewards they did in the past and for those who desire to be childless, marital life has been transformed. Many couples see marriage only as a public certification of their relationship and little else. The growth of the self within marriage occurs through external factors, not necessarily through the activities within the household.

Actually, the pressure to have children, just as the pressure to marry, whether acknowledged or not, might be *more* extensive than in the past. Now, because of the demands of the industrial economy, many feel an obligation to contribute to society by providing new members. The insistence by the present culture on families and individuals to achieve the age's promise is great. Their child might be the researcher who discovers a cure for cancer, the astronaut who lands on Mars, the President that finally reduces the nuclear threat in the world, or the scientist who develops a cheap form of fuel. Married couples feel they must provide the human resources that will maintain and complete the arduous struggle for perfection begun in the 18th century. However, this duty does not exempt spouses from 'self-actualising' and they can only feel exasperated by costly and incongruous social requirements, without really knowing the source of those demands.

The modern person's lifestyle is still hardly 'free' from constraints or demands. Some demands, as in the case of having children, are relatively untouched by time, but other demands no longer exist, yet have been replaced by others. Key factors that encouraged or discouraged matrimony for our ancestors are no longer pertinent. Clearly, inheritance is no longer a major factor in acquiring the financial basis for a household or setting up a business. Few people are constrained by the terms of their employment, such as was the case with those in domestic service, apprenticeships or farm labour. Marriage markets are generally balanced, and few regions experience major in-migration or out- migration. In this improved social situation, ideals about companionship, married life and male-female intimacy are allowed to flourish and are thought much more attainable. The focus can now be more on personality factors in the search for a relationship, and a longer term view of the successful establishment of a household. There are more personal, and less pragmatic, factors being taken into account.

However, freedom from stringent material criteria does not mean that pragmatic factors are unimportant; economic conditions still strongly affect the age of marriage and the propensity to marry. Since the husband and wife are alone responsible in setting up a household, it would stand to reason that they would take the greatest care in assuring the continuing material viability of a family unit containing themselves and their children, who begin to arrive promptly one to four years after the wedding. Through long experience, mankind has come to understand that when financial troubles cloud the horizon, it is very difficult to have a happy marriage and such difficulties are usually one of the top reasons given for divorce.[67]

Marriage can act as a way of improving one's financial situation, by reducing expenses, reducing taxes, and pooling income. In the past, this desire for efficiency translated to a general inclination against division of wealth, households and property. Unless some overweening economic factor compensated for the inefficiency, splitting households was unquestionably imprudent,

...since it would be necessary to place two cloths on two tables, to burn two logs in two hearths, to hire two servants for two households, where only one is needed...[68]

The 15th century writer who wrote these words was expressing a contemporary though embattled idea. In contrast to the modern centrifugal forces, traditional society felt centripetal movement, towards collectivity, towards the centre, and towards cooperation. In this scenario, marriage was seen as a positive development in the economic sense. But the trend in Western culture has been towards forging a self-made course where privacy and self-dominion prevailed but only when the financial situation permitted. What seemed reasonable in the slowly unfolding societies of the Middle Ages and Renaissance did not seem reasonable in a strongly growing economy where producing the extra cloth, logs, servants, furniture that furnished the new households was no longer a problem. Flexibility and opportunity in the modern society have eradicated old problems but have produced new stresses and strains.

However, marriage was not the only manner in which the traditional ideal of economic efficiency could be accomplished, but through any one of a myriad of other forms of living arrangements that brought or kept people together. In the modern world, though, household fusion is common only through marriage. Any consideration of long-term money management must take into account marriage plans and tendency, and any decisions about marriage should take into account the effects of those decisions on personal expenses; the areas of finance and married life have become bound up with each other. A fuller appreciation of household financial management must be taken into account, as in any enterprise, all sources of revenues, or inflow of funds, as well as possible costs, or outflow of funds. Money quite simply brings independence in any society, at any time, and food, housing, clothing and other costs are important. Independence from economic burdens comes before independence from people, for relationship can be more easily modified than material matters. In modern society, inheritance is a non-issue, and any dowry is questionable.

Hence, how do we understand expenses, in addition to income, figure in the decision to marry? It is self-evident people will want to forestall marriage if they feel that their revenues (from work, inheritance, savings, and so on) will not be adequate for the life they have envisioned. But what about forestalling marriage because *expenses* are simply too high? It might also appear self-evident that people would also delay marriage if expenses are high. But clearly in this instance we are talking about factors outside the control of the individual, and a delay of marriage makes little sense, unless one expects expenses to decline in the near future. The specific monetary factors of conjugal life have been little researched and are thus difficult to follow. What we examine here is the question of whether analysis of international data tells us that the ability to obtain a car, furniture, or appliances affects the age of marriage. Data for such items is sparse, and we have only general categories to follow, i.e. food, durable goods, entertainment, personal items. Our analysis reveals that the *higher* the cost of domestic variables such as food, clothing, household durables, and the *lower* the cost of housing and recreation, the likelier that a woman will marry *early*.[69]

As a general principle, the establishment of a modern economy invariably involves the loss of time for household tasks, and so one of the first priorities of such an economy is to make available cheap goods and services. Food, clothing, domestic articles and durables are the basic items of any household and a higher cost for these items would entail marrying early as a way of reducing the costs of these items through various means. A man and woman might have a greater tendency to move directly to a marital abode from the parental home if living alone was simply too expensive. If people find that they are better off marrying early in order to reduce expenses, then they are more tied to a particular place and have less time to give for a career. One way to reduce costs is through consolidation of expenses; understandably, sharing the same furnishings would be less expensive than having the same kinds of items in two different households. Another way would be to take advantage of a woman's domestic skills and capabilities. Previous generations knew that women were invaluable in the household, for as the English used to say rather unrefinedly, 'the wife that expects to have a good name, is always at home as if she were lame'. She could knit or sew, reducing or eliminating the expense of buying clothes. A wife could also cook for both herself and her husband, freeing the latter from the bachelor's burden of having to cook for himself, or from taking the expensive route of dining out. Although the orientation to perform domestic duties is cultural, the high value of a wife who can perform these functions is universal. Such a woman would be quickly 'snapped up' by men who are concerned about living expenses.

As there is evidently a wider variation in food costs than in the past, the cost of such items is a major determining factor in the decision to marry. Where food is relatively expensive, fewer resources are available for other activities and the amount a household spends on food is positively related to the probability a woman will marry early. In the earlier history of domestic life, edibles were almost always prepared at home using basic ingredients, whereas in our day, food can be prepared easily in a restaurant, fast-food shop, or factory. It is expedient to have at least one family member manage provisions and cook in the household in nations where food is relatively expensive in order to preserve funds. Where food is efficiently grown and processed by companies, the extra amount added due to labour does not make the total cost exorbitant. Thus, the home budget in nations with relatively cheap food permits more dining out and the buying of mass-produced items requiring only simple processing.

Other costs can act to facilitate or non-facilitate marriage. As we discussed in relation to the pre-Industrial era when more money is available for entertainment expenses, young men and women will have numerous divertissements and amusements that act as suitable alternatives to married life, which in turn lowers the marriage age. One reason this money might become more available is on account of lower food expenses. Entertainment acts as an alternative to the gratification of married life, but only an approximate one since there can be no direct substitution of the quiddity of conjugal existence. Yet, if entertainment is cheaper, age of marriage is not increased but *lowered*. Although young single people in many cities still enjoy entertainment as an alternative to marriage,[70] and have satisfactory emotional outlets in this manner, it would appear that this activity is often used in service of a higher purpose: to date and to court. Thus, recreation does not really act as a *substitute* for married life in our day but as a means to getting married. Leisure activities are important components of a young person's budget, as often meeting friends and dating are tied together and indeed revolve around expensive diversions. If recreation is expensive, then the dating experience becomes more difficult, and this in turn makes it less likely that a person will marry early. This is perhaps in contrast with earlier periods where the enjoyment of cheap entertainment would *forestall* marriage (meaning a positive correlation between early marriage and recreation expenses).

Housing also has a positive correlation with marriage age, indicating that a lower cost of housing entails an earlier marriage, and a higher cost encourages later marriage. Lower residential expenses therefore facilitate the formation of a conjugal household. However, people can adjust to circumstances if the need for marriage is high and costs remain intractable. A couple might marry and then live with one spouse's parents because buying or renting a residence is simply too expensive, even if both husband and wife work full-time. If the costs are far too high, or availability is extremely limited, then they might actually forego the idea of creating their own separate household, and simply take over the running of the household when one or both parents die. We shall cover housing and various related issues in more detail later on.

Although the negative correlation between housing cost and marriage age is still traditional, the other relationships are not. A higher cost of food would ordinarily have meant a decrease in real income, followed by a *decline* in nuptiality.[71] Perhaps the modern household is able to save more money if married, but this thwarts the independence ethos as people decide to pursue love instead. Out of the three choices of living arrangement that people had in the past—live with own family, live alone, live with spouse—the cost of living with a spouse (and probably children) was highest, followed by living alone, and the cheapest was living with one's family. There was often no choice in the matter of food, clothing and furniture; most of it was made at home, borrowed or handed down. In whichever of the three living situations, it was a case of 'do it yourself' in order to survive. Thus, the question then became whether marriage was reasonable, as the three, four or more children that would be added to a couple's own household might be more than they could handle. In the present day, where people can make things at home or buy them ready made, clearly it is cheaper to share. Since the size of a married household does not have to grow by very much, if at all, (since fertility being much lower than in the past), then one would prefer to marry instead of staying at home, thus fulfilling the ideal of love, as well as effecting a sound financial design.

Taken together, we see how food and other items in the household budget could have an effect on the decision to marry. However, we might envision a situation reverse to that portrayed above: Instead of expenses affecting marriage age, marriage age affects the economy, and that in turn affects the household expenses. When it becomes general practise to marry early, young adults have their liberty limited, and the economy then becomes less flexible and less viable. Further, as more women marry young, their contribution to the work force declines, which in turn hinders the development of technology, and increases the cost of basic items, such as food. How might this happen? Such women might relinquish the idea of higher education and take jobs requiring lesser mental ability but greater physical effort. Companies will have this segment of the work force available for cheaper labour and eschew more advanced technology. Thus, the economy is forced to continue using expensive methods to produce food and other products instead of advancing in that field. To conclude this, however, seems premature, as the connections among women's age at marriage, work and production are not well-defined.

What apparently *is* well-defined is the way in which people still take economic factors into account, notwithstanding a commitment to personal freedom and, perhaps due to the pursuit of the ideal of love, the avowal that 'we can live on love alone'. Economics still maintains a critical influence on the decisions one makes in relation to love, and the individual's perceived level of freedom is probably not accurate. However, this lessening of independence has been allowed to occur by the individual himself, and has not been forced upon him. External variables continue to affect the decision to marry, especially a woman's assessment of the potential future earnings of her husband and the economic stability of a married household. Based upon an analysis of Western nations, multicorrelation reveals that the most important variables in association with late life celibacy are income per capita, concentration of wealth, and proportion of the male population in the workforce.[72]

Even though people might claim that there is no connection between material factors and the decision to marry, economic considerations continue to have a prominent role in the decision to marry, in a way consistent with the factors that have played a major role in the past. Further, specific economic aspects have a *very* important role. Whether a husband is firmly employed (whether he is a dedicated member of the labour force) is highly salient; his employment is undoubtedly critical in a functioning household and thus a happy marriage. Lack of employment and difficulty holding a job might be attributed to a variety of male figures a woman knows: father, brother, uncle, or some other relative. Recognising among family members limited career potential, few employment opportunities and/or a general indolence towards work might make a woman hold an unfavourable view of marriage. Although a single woman might make a good living by working within the female areas of the labour force, the significantly more complex enterprise of marriage, which involves higher material demands and children, must be supported for the most part by the earnings of the husband. Any interruptions in this most essential and irreplaceable cash flow might spell disaster; women would wisely wish to assure the dependability of this resource before embarking on an enterprise that operates so close to break-even.

For similar reasons, a lower income also prompts putting off marriage permanently, as women feel it difficult to come up to the standard of living they would like to see. Certain women, probably all up and down the socioeconomic scale, wish to reach a certain material level. This level has become, interestingly, an international standard, where years of cross influencing has created what could be called the prototypical household, containing, for example, a television, telephone, sofa set, washing machine, dishwasher, car, etc. This is applicable in poorer countries such as Portugal as well as wealthier ones such as Germany. This is a totally unresearched phenomenon, and conclusions can at this point only be conjectured.

A greater concentration of wealth, where income is in the hands of a few people in the upper echelons of society, also encourages celibacy. Women might see a clear disparity in earnings in the local environment, such as a divergence between upper management and everyone else in her department or company. One could achieve middle managerial status and still not achieve a significantly better income; earning power of a high calibre rests in the hands of the special class of executives and professionals. Such an observation might force the conclusion that the nation's business does not reward merit or hard work, but simply pulls people up through the ranks in an 'old boy network'. The expectation in the modern world is that advancement in position is met by a commensurate advancement in income, and if this is not the case, then, in the minds of some women, a future married household could not achieve the standard of living that was envisioned, no matter how hard working they are. If the expectation is for a husband and wife to have children, as it normally is, then they must assume that increased work will cause an expansion in income, covering the expenses incurred by all members of the family. If this expansion in income cannot occur because of a failure to reward merit, then marriage itself is considered to be not worthwhile, as the family would undergo a *reduction* in living standard after children are born; the parents have reached a ceiling in income, and every child that is added to the household can only bring down the standard of living per person. This would probably be more of a factor for women who are sensitive to issues of fairness and have faith in the merit-reward system, who are ambitious and work hard, who believe that living standards should only increase, and who believe that married life inevitably entails having children.

In the United States, the growing income *inequality* between households in recent years is attributed to a number of factors, including declining unionisation, paying premiums for skilled labour, a shift from goods-producing to service-producing industries (wherein a *greater* disparity in incomes exists) and a change in living arrangements, away from married couple households to single parent and other types of household.[73] This last aspect is especially relevant to our investigation, although the *direction* of causality is opposite to what we claim. There is no doubt that more people living alone or single causes greater inequality, since the earning power of a smaller household will usually be smaller than that of a larger household. However, we also have no doubt that the distribution of income influences the decision to marry. Thus, this variable is probably bidirectional, in that it is related to permanent celibacy as both a cause and an effect. It validates the belief that a woman living on her own would probably earn less income than if living in a two-person household. We would in this case be saying that the relationship is obverse to the one cited above, that nonmarriage leads to *more* inequality rather than the other way around.[74]

The material aspect of individual and family life, formerly largely dependent on luck and good fortune, is now more based on skill, education, ambition and connections. There is little doubt that a man or woman living in the modern industrial materialist society has future marital happiness resting precariously on career success. This success is inevitably the result of factors that are emphasised consistently across classes and cultures, including obtaining a college diploma, early work history, stability in occupations, seeking promotions, networking with capable and experienced people. The complex interaction of these forces, compared to a century ago, has a disproportionate share of impact on a couple's relationship. A man's or woman's success with people, money, career and so on are added to the list of important traits that need to be evaluated in order to make them 'lovable'. A failure in any one regard could be the kiss of death for the relationship; accomplishment in the outside world is confused and alloyed with proficiency in the inner world of domestic life.

We should ask whether it is fair or appropriate to evaluate a person's character on the basis of his success in a career or in education. Is there any reason to presume that a well-educated man in an executive position would be a better husband any more than a man well down the ladder in the same company? Those who have a high education have indeed relied upon persistence and discipline, as completion of a college degree requires success at every stage in the process. But studies show that early academic success does *not* assure later success, although early academic failure strongly predicts later failure. Still, even when experiencing early failures, some can attain a high level of education.[75] Further, high school students' hoped for or expected future earnings are very weakly correlated with actual earnings.[76] Consequently, if the individual is using success in education as a predictor of success in business, the chance of error is substantial. The use of education as one indicator of someone's suitability as a marriage partner is astute, but only when such a method is allied with knowledge of its limitations. Where complex economic factors merge with complex personal motivations in the modern world, there is no easy association between achievement in one area with achievement in another.

In discussing a person's likely future in a career, and thus his or her's marriageability, we are at base focussing on the *proficiency* in making friends, dealing with people, gaining academic credentials, attaining career prestige and earning a satisfactory income. It is widely thought that a socially capable individual will do well in a career through his ability to make profitable personal contacts, and a scholastically inclined person will also do well in a career by virtue of his academic credentials. Knowing the interaction between these factors would be of great help, yet the magnitude and sequence of causality of these factors is often difficult to determine. For example, does education determine marriage age or the other way around? Does education have a critical role to play in career, prestige or income? The multifarious interactions of these factors demand careful examination, and the best understanding is reached when individuals are followed over a period of time, preferably from teenage years to mid-life. We are fortunate in having such a longitudinal study, as described by WILLITS (1988). It is unusual for its size and span of time, thus giving us considerable insight into the personality, group, material and educational influences that go into decisions about marriage in the 20th century. More than 2800 sophomores, at 74 rural high schools, were given a questionnaire in 1947, followed by another questionnaire in 1984 (at around age 55), the latter being given to all former students who could be found. The number of people finally assessed was 1,650. We have developed our own chart summarising the data, presented in Figure 1.

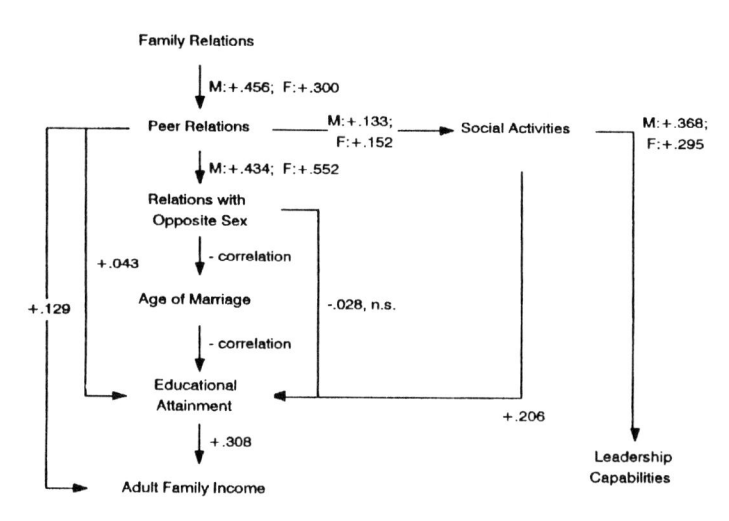

Figure 1

A number of points are evident from this study. Firstly, there is a fairly strong positive correlation between peer relations and family relations. Evidently the family prepares the individual for larger society. Where people learn how to deal with others cordially, intelligently and dependably at an early age, they are able to use these skills with non-family members later on. Not surprisingly, there is also an explicit positive correlation between peer relations and opposite sex relations. This would indicate that when one is able to deal with friends in general, one is able to enjoy good relations with a boyfriend or girlfriend;

learning to get along with people secures abilities that produce satisfying dating and courtship experiences.

However, aptitude with peers does not appear to link with an aptitude for education. Whereas good grades and participation in formal organizations tend to lead to higher educational attainment, good relations with peers had *no* significant correlation with attainment. Doing well with friends does little in the process of gaining an education, but extracurricular activities and certainly high grades have a definite influence on the way people progress through the layers of pedagogical experience. It is well known that school administrators and college admission boards often assess an individual by both grades and social activities, so it is not surprising that such a relationship exists. Further, success with peers has a positive effect on later family income and well-being, and popularity with members of the opposite sex generally has a *negative* correlation with education, though not with occupational prestige. The popular young man or woman who does well in dating will likely have many good prospects for marriage, leading to earlier matrimony with its associated adult responsibilities suspending or delaying higher college attendance. Hence, this situation does not bode well for one's educational course as plans might have to be put off or forgone if being married is of higher priority.

Thus, as we shall see recurrently in later sections, if there is the opportunity, concerns about companionship often come before concerns about education and income; some might find the fulfilment of spouse and family more important than external social considerations. There are those who seek a more secure and warm protector than knowledge, which is subject to constant revision and debate. Indeed, in the traditional conception of things, one puts one's faith in what one can see and touch. As Chaucer acknowledged, a wife is more important than wisdom, and a *good* wife is the greatest accomplishment a man can have. In this he echoes Proverbs 31:10 (NRSV), which states: 'A capable wife who can find? She is far more precious than jewels'. The results of the above study suggest that such a philosophy is not only sentimental but pragmatic as well, for popularity with the opposite sex (in addition to good relations with peers and academic performance) leads to *higher* family earnings and higher subjective well-being. This is rather curious to contemporary minds, since education is believed to have an important, indeed decisive, impact on later earning capacity and standard of living. However, it would seem that among the factors that govern well-being, education must stand along with choice of a spouse as consequential. The reason is this: A more popular young man might have his pick of girlfriends, and so enlarge his potential marriage partner pool, from which he would obviously choose the most resourceful, intelligent and capable woman. Clearly, such a wife might have a good earning capacity of her own, and she might find ways to save money on household expenses.

The most important, as well as the most puzzling, aspect of our analysis concerns the relationship between education, social activities and peer relations, since these three areas are so crucial to the conceptualisation of autonomy and independence. Educational achievement is positively correlated with school activities, whereas the former is not related to success with peer relations. If one is good at social activities, would one be good at peer relations? Evidently so, for school activities and peer relations *are* positively related. The individual might spend time with peers, which might increase his participation in activities, or the other way around. Whichever the case, his satisfying casual associations do not have an impact on his education, but do sometimes put him in the midst of constructive social activities of a more formal nature, which gives him the opportunity to display competence and leadership. This kind of social legitimacy does have a meaningful influence on his education and career, but not necessarily on finding a spouse.

These relationships are quite understandable. Yet, we wonder why peer relations are not related to educational attainment. Is it perhaps because each area requires different skills and techniques? And so here we come to the critical question: Can one realistically expect to attain just the right combination of education, social activity, career and companionship? In other words, can one have true social freedom and find true love as well, in essence 'having one's cake and eating it too'? By way of reference to common stereotypes, most people do not appear to believe that this is possible. It is often assumed that one must focus on the 'people' track and dispense with schooling, or focus on the 'academic' track and dispense with socialising, in order for each to fully yield its rewards. This, however, is flawed, as the evidence suggests that the putative connections within either 'track' might not exist at all. Thus, there is no guarantee that by following a track one will reach one's desired goals.

In an earlier section, we spoke about the ease with which one engages in social relations (extroversion), and the effect this has on the size of one's friendship circle and the desire to marry, mutual interactions that make up the outlines of 'autonomy'. People use peer relations to build companionate friendships which can lead to marriage or act as a substitute for marriage. Here we confront the issue again, but with the question of whether the track (education or career) that one is on is the result of innate temperament (as is the positive correlation between extroversion and close friendship) or whether it is a conscious choice. There is a definite dichotomy in the conventional thinking of young people about social roles, in that it is believed the average individual is forced to make an unequivocal *choice:* concentrate on forming good relations with peers, *or* concentrate on attaining a good education. To put it simply, one must either be a bon vivant or a bookworm; each obtains compensation and satisfaction in the long and short term, although each is treated differently within the peer group. Yet this kind of dichotomy does not really exist within typical youth social environments. One can be quite good at studies and still be congenial, or one can be academically inferior and also be unattractive to schoolmates.

In general, people hope that the individual is influenced by a predilection and is not a slave to an all-consuming lifestyle. In line with this, it is widely believed that in a democratic modern society one can freely *choose* either track without significant interference from the outside. In the study under discussion, there is no significant correlation between *peer relations* and *education*; grades and test scores still determine the lion's share of one's capabilities. This suggests that there are indeed no clear social or external impediments. However, impediments do exist, but they are for the most part innate or *internal*. It is true that many who have the potential to be bon vivants choose to be bookworms and then go on to college, and one can deduce from the facts of the above study that the very different courses of bon vivant -> lesser education, or bookworm -> higher education is not inevitable. Most young people wish to attain the combination of conviviality, study, social activity and education that is to their liking, but the theory that one should only or could only pour one's energies into either the 'social' track or the 'academic' track is erroneous. If many people were showing an unambiguous preference for one or the other, then there would be a *negative* association between peer relations and educational attainment, but this is not what we see.

Thus, based on our analysis of the above study, people possess the freedom to obtain the right mix of career, education and social activity, if they are able to live with or overcome innate limitations. Without making overly broad generalisations, it can be said that *success or failure in one course or the other is largely secured by natural aptitude, or the lack of it, and not by explicit choice*. For example, one might *wish* to converge one's attention on study and in the process forego peer relations, but college education might be elusive because one does not possess the required intelligence, interest or diligence. On the other hand, an absence of positive social qualities might make one a failure in cultivating friendships, but because of the right *inherent* traits one can direct one's energies through another legitimate and laudable channel, that of intellectual refinement. Further, the bookworm's college education might stand him in good stead when looking for work, but there are no assurances that his education will procure the income and prestige he wants. In any case, only a subgroup of socially dextrous individuals lacks the intellectual development to go on to college, and only a subgroup of socially limited individuals possess the acumen to go on higher education. Hence, individuals who conform to the stereotypes 'bookworm' or 'bon vivant', although socially obvious and the focus of attention, are not numerous enough for us to turn their life experiences into a general rule.

We also find that if one has success in *school social activities* then there is an increased chance of completing *higher education*. This must also be due to *nature* since if it were a matter of *choice* one could go directly to higher education without having to take the time and effort to become involved in extracurricular activities. Due to a fortuitous combination of looks, charm and various ineffable qualities, one is able to deepen friendships, have a good social life and become popular with the opposite sex. This could all take place in the life of someone dedicated to academic studies, but in reality it often leads to earlier marriage with little or no tertiary level education. For whatever innate reasons, the individual might have a good relationship with peers, teachers and others in a structured school environment, which translates to a good relationship with the opposite sex, which in turn has an effect on schooling. However, when these qualities are allied with leadership ability, then social activities can act as a powerful springboard to higher education. In this case, marriage might be put off in order to fulfill the potential for higher learning.

The often heard belief that those who marry early are socially competent but not well educated, and those who go on to college are socially awkward but obtain good qualifications and good jobs, appears to be incorrect. In reality, the former do have a path to a good living and prestige, not through education, but through likability and congeniality, in other words, through the force of *personality*. Sometimes, and rather unpredictably, they have additional characteristics that assist them in gaining a higher educational qualification. The latter might not be awkward at all; getting better education is not necessarily connected to being socially isolated. However, those who ignore social relations and activities are the most difficult for whom to make predictions as they do not have as estimable a course as the socially gregarious.

It should be stressed that the correlations between the variables cited from above study, though significant, were not especially forceful individually, demonstrating that other factors can certainly not be excluded. Thus, people have more freedom than believed in the sense that academics and social living are not mutually exclusive areas, but they also have less freedom than believed in that much is determined by natural or inherent proclivities and temperament. How much 'freedom' one has is determined to a large extent by how the indiviudal rates the difficulty of external constraints or internal constraints. For the person who has no problem modifying his own tendencies for the sake of achieving a goal, great personal freedom should be optimistically envisaged based on the scenario we have described here. Conventional wisdom about the modern person's total freedom and total control over his life are in this case not consistent with the facts and should be discarded. There is some relevance to the common assumption, but it lacks refinement to the point that the truth is obscured. This realisation could seriously damage the independence ethos upon which contemporary society has placed so many of its ideals.

These models concern people maturing earlier in this century when higher education was far more exclusive and so not part of the average individual's set of life goals. A person could marry early and relinquish further education without the fear of having compromised his reputation. However, attitudes to early marriage are not immutable. A recent study found that males who marry as adolescents tend to have fewer years of education, but earn less income and hold lower-status occupations. Considering the importance of high status, they predictably experience more marital disruption than other men.[77] In this case, it is the early marriage that might disrupt the possibility of education and a better career. This is at variance with the results from the study described by WILLITS (1988) cited earlier, where early marriage meant *higher* income, and so higher status. Cultural attitudes of young people in our generation might be distinctly different to those of a generation ago.

Matrimony early in life is now definitely looked down upon, and the ceremony is performed more as an 'emergency' operation than as the natural outcome of profitable peer interaction. A difficult home life or avoiding an even worse social disgrace, namely, the birth of an illegitimate child, might impel individuals to wed as soon as possible. Furthermore, disruption within the marriage might stem from the frustrations of being in a lower occupation and a lower social class, and the clash of educational and social expectations. The strong expectation is for young people to finish their education or become established in an occupation, then get married, and then have children. In the past, this sequence could be somewhat modified as people put human relations before that of career, but today, the succession of milestones is less amenable to change because the economy demands career be made as high a priority as possible.

For females, it is education, or the lack of it, that dictates marital considerations. The improvement in women's education, which brings better career opportunities, does give them the potential for greater economic independence, but this does not necessarily mean that they will greatly or permanently postpone marriage and childbearing, nor does it mean that the demands of education and career will unduly disrupt relations with a husband and children. Women might delay marriage only in the transitional phase from youth to adulthood.[78]

The modern simultaneous preoccupation with independence, standard of living and intimacy leads to sometimes unusual life plans. Nonetheless, it is at least possible in a modern economy to be able to attain goals relating to education, work, and family all within one lifetime, and even within a reasonable time scale. Eschewing such a pattern evidently has more to do with following personal conceptions and cultural values than being constrained by the rigid rules of peer group, school or business. Career or education becomes an impediment to satisfactory married life only if the individual *allows* such a condition to occur. However, people must show flexibility, since a highly specific life course might not be possible.

In this section, we have raised a number of important issues concerning the establishment and maintenance of the role of husband or wife. The success in achieving this role, it can be seen, is dependent on a number of important life decisions. Nevertheless, material factors in their pivotal relation to marriage are not discussed openly today, at the educational level, political level, or socio-religious level. Because of its relation to our study of independence, the decision to leave the household of childhood (household of origin), that is, the personal 'declaration of independence', is one of the most important of these decisions. The point in one's development cycle at which this occurs is possibly a critical factor in how one earns money, saves money, assumes roles, pursues education and builds a career. We shall therefore proceed to analysing these results by looking at the reasons why people would marry, based upon issues of home life, education, entitlement and economic rationale factors. As we examine this phenomenon, we should again return to address an important topic: Is the decision to leave home due to rigid social rules or personal choice?

THE FIRST STEP: LEAVING HOME

Lifestyle issues, centring around notions of adulthood, responsibility, and standard of living, are often the focus of social attention; the *way* one lives is a major concern for the modern man or woman. However, the actual accomplishment is less important than the appearance of accomplishing something *independently*. Similarly, how much pleasure one is receiving from an activity appears to be of secondary concern to how much pleasure one *appears* to be having. One wants swim 'effortlessly' through life, without major worries. In this scenario, the almost obsessive focus on external standards creates a habit of less flexibility that makes long-term relationships difficult. Fulfilling the long list of requirements, especially for the middle and upper classes, is exhausting and calls for more than a little sacrifice. As an outgrowth of social forces, and not individual deliberation, a nearly universally accepted preconceived plan, an 'independence ethos', is embraced.

What is this 'independence ethos'? It means the desire to engage in a challenge, and to win without major support from other people. To conquer this challenge requires drawing on personal resources and skills. To fail means either that the skills were not developed or that the individual did not draw upon them. By being in an accelerated academic course, attending an exclusive school, purchasing an expensive item, having a difficult mission-critical job, the individual calls attention to himself, and his successful handling of the situation, which others have not or have not had the opportunity, raises the individual in status, and thus earns him admiration.

One of the first steps the individual takes on the road to realising the ethos is to live in a 'special place', that is, to leave the family abode. Such a separation is difficult for both parents and their children, yet is usually inevitable. There are only two questions that need to be resolved: At what time should one leave home, and into what type of living environment one should enter. However, it is essential that we distinguish the objective of avoiding dependence on *parents* from the philosophy of withholding trust in and reliance on *anyone*. One could have nothing to do with one's parents and yet still be heavily dependent on someone else. Certain cultures emphasise leaving home as soon as possible as a way of showing initiative, fortitude, determination, a breaking away from an easy but controlled life. Those who do this might then either move in with friends or lovers, or they might just live on their own. Their choice might be out of financial considerations, or it might be that leaning on others in such a situation is not as obvious as depending on parents. When living at home, everyone knows the tendency is to depend on parents, but when living with others, the level of dependency is more private. Compared to living with one's parents, one can be just as much, if not more of a burden, on a friend, lover or spouse.

Hence, the meaningful cultural issue of claiming independence, the way that someone 'announces' their adulthood, is most visible in the act of departing from the household of origin, or as it simply known, 'leaving home'. If this age is too early, then the family appears unkind, if the age is seen as too late, then the individual appears immature and weak. Whatever the emotional consequences, in Western societies such as the United States, Germany, Denmark, Australia, and Britain, the age of leaving home is declining, although such an event is becoming increasingly a move to *independent* living, rather than marriage. In the period from the early 1950s to the late 1960s, the proportion of women leaving home for marriage was only about 50%, and for men about 45%.[79] The most recent developments in home-leaving can be attributed neither to marriage nor entry into work, school, parenthood, or military service roles. Many did not leave home despite entry into these roles, and many did leave without entering any of them.[80]

If marriage is not the specific impetus for leaving the family of childhood, why do people depart then? There are three groups that each have their own views about the reasons for leaving home, groups which are most noticeably distinguished by their phase of maturity. The first group are those who leave at around the legal age of majority of 18; the second are those who leave between majority age and mid-20; the third are those who leave as older adults, after their mid-20s.

The members of the first group were in earlier times motivated primarily by *practical* factors, but eventually based their decision to conform to a model emphasising social duty. The demands of home life were eclipsed by the call to adhere to a legalistic definition of 'adult'. Regardless of one's emotional, financial or psychological state, age 18, the 'magic number', became the time to cut loose, to 'individuate' both for the good of the individual and society. Yet the definition of what 'adult' actually means changes according to cultural and situational factors. In most countries, there is a dichotomy between the official majority age of 18 and the 'unofficial' majority age of 21, with no immediately clear rational basis as to why one or the other is used. When it comes to voting, driving a car, military service, sexual license (including marriage), 18 is usually the acceptable age; when it comes to drinking, attending nightclubs, viewing exotic or salacious entertainment, then 21 is the correct adult age. Those activities for which the age of 18 is appropriate revolve around productivity and positive contribution to society, whereas the activities approved for people 21 and over are more often than not superficial. Restriction on the latter activities carries an implicit sense of danger of succumbing to temptation, a weak threat in a society that has already given those under age 21 numerous licences. Having attained many serious responsibilities, the 18-year-old must wonder what unfathomable process takes several years to complete before he can taste the full plate of life's offerings. It is quite apparent that these are contradictory standards, and that there is a good chance that when it comes to the individual assessing his own feeling as to how 'adult' he is, he will be baffled.[81] This group is most likely to be insecure in its notions of independence.

The second group contains members with perhaps mixed intentions, people who do not yet know to which model of adult responsibilities should be accepted. They feel that 18 is too young, but 21 might be too old, although the departure by two or three years after the later age is certainly the very last chance to avoid being considered aberrant or a failure. These factors are undoubtedly tied into the process of college education. Since most people obtain an associate or bachelor's degree by age 21 or 22, thereby completing their education, the age of 21 would appear the right time to grant the individual full privileges and rights, since they then have full responsibility.

The third group contains individuals who still steadfastly cling to the traditional idea that it is prudent to *stay at home until marriage* or at least until they are well placed enough to establish their own household. Priveleges and rights are irrelevant unless one be certain one can fully utilise them. They seem to be fairly unconcerned about the 'decent' time to leave home and begin their own adult lives. Many of these might be immigrants or the children of immigrants from more traditional nations, where at the time of their emigration the modernist ethos had not yet found a comfortable dwelling place. Others might simply see the prudence in remaining at home, whilst finishing education, and saving money for marriage. Living at home is certainly the cheapest alternative, for it allows the individual to forego paying rent, food, clothing, and so on (or at least a large portion of these expenses) and instead putting them into savings accounts and investments. Proved by centuries of experience, this is the most rapid way to build a 'dowry' for women, and a capital investment for men.

Strong evidence exists that Western society has experienced a significant decline in the age of leaving the home of childhood, with this phenomenon being propelled by legalistic concepts. In the US in the period 1920-1979, there has been a dramatic drop in the percent of people who remain living with their parents as adults. During the 1950s, the decline was attributable to a drop in the age of marriage, but after this, the rising age in marriage has *not* resulted in a consistent increase in the proportion of adults living with their parents. Subsequent periods saw a consistent reduction in numbers living at home as adults, especially for older individuals. In the 1920-39 period, nearly 30% of males and females were still living at home with parents by age 30. Half of the males and 37% of females age 26 and over were still living at home in this period. The proportions age 26 and over still living at home declined to 20% and 13% respectively by 1965-69.[82]

The reluctance to remain living at home continued to become more prominent in the US and in other countries. In a study by YI ET AL. (1994), figures for the United States, France and Sweden point to a major change in concepts of independence in the West. In the US, the percent of males who were 25 and over when they left home for good was 21% in between 1950 and 1960, but this declined to only 14% by the period 1970-1980; the figures for females was 13% and 8%, respectively. In France, for males it was 38% and 24%, for females it was 32% and 19%, respectively. For Swedes, it was 38% and 15% for males, and 15% to 8% for females, respectively. Departing from one's family when well into adulthood has become a *minority* phenomenon, no doubt with all the attendant social disapproval that follows any minority action, regardless of the wisdom of that action.

What evidence do we have for the three categories discussed earlier? In order to determine this, we must look at patterns of home-leaving. If there is little outside influence to leave home, then we should see gradual changes in the tendency to leave home over the ages. There would be peaks, but not very strongly defined. We know in this case that there is little outside influence, since we would expect each individual to have myriad factors to determine that age at which he or she would desire to exit the current family situation. It would be highly unlikely that the exigencies of life for most people would all centre around 18 or 21. On the other hand, if there were sharp rises and strong peaks, then we could say there was an *externally* determined force that encouraged people to leave. Using the study mentioned above, we see that for both American males and females in the period 1970-80, compared to other ages, there was a sharp increase in the tendency to leave the family of origin between ages 17 and 18, and this drops off steeply until 21, then the decline is more gradual. It is a similar case for Sweden, although there is a more gradual decline from 19 to 23, then a sharp drop to 26, followed by a very gradual decline thereafter similar to that of the United States. The proportion of people departing in France peaks later than the other two countries at age 21, with a steep rise that begins at age 18. For ages 21 to 26, there is then an abrupt decline analogous to the one in the US, followed by a much more gradual decline. It appears, therefore, that externally derived ideas, such as the concept of executing a basic duty to society by becoming a worker and consumer, are indeed responsible for at least facilitating if not encouraging home-leaving. There is still a segment of the population that does place emphasis primarily on personal factors, however.

Further, the 'legal' or 'appropriate' age appears to have fallen over time. In Sweden, in the period 1960-80, the median age plunged from 24 to 21 for males, yet changed little for women, going from 21 to 20. France experienced a similar decrease in average age for males and females, from age 24 to 22, in the period 1962-1975. For American males and females, the median age for leaving home remained steady at about 20 over the period 1950-1980. Thus, in at least two countries, there was major change in views about leaving home in the period from the 1960s to the 1970s. The only reason for living with parents was to reach *minimal* mental and physical maturity, with other reasons, such as protection and security, becoming irrelevant.

What *personal* factors, in addition to external factors, can account for these trends? Within the household, attitudes of parents and children clearly are important in the satisfaction each member has with family life. Young adults more than their parents expect to depart home to live in a separate residence (with others or alone) before marriage. Stepparent families, more than other families, expect children to leave home early and to marry at the 'normal' age. In mother-only families, children expect to leave home early only because they want to delay marriage. A lower level of closeness in a family, as often seen in non-intact, non-traditional families, appears to precipitate expectations of earlier 'nest-leaving'.[83] Another factor is the inability of parents to organise activities within the household in consonance with their children's personality and temperament. Tensions arise whenever children feel they are not being treated equitably as a result of parenting resources being spread too thin. Consequently, women from large families have a lower probability of earlier marriage, and individuals who come from single-parent households are more likely to exit early for independent living, though again not for marriage.[84] The latter have formed a negative concept of marriage, both intellectually and as experience, and are eager to leave to form their own residence. People who come from households where an affectionate family situation is absent would want to avoid getting involved in marriage themselves, a form of life that seems little more than a distinctly offensive or insulting 'condition', and one that is regarded largely in ignorance and fear.

When negative factors of home life are felt in the aggregate, a concomitant change in behaviour patterns will occur. These households are characterised by distancing between parents and children, followed by a general breakdown in relations. That there is a disturbing rise in the incidence of these types of dysfunctional households is beyond dispute,[85] and it helps to explain the downward trend in the age of leaving home. Thus, a phenomenon that appears to be based solely on a social rule relating to economic productivity is in fact also based on a personal desire to leave, and the individual is caught in a push-pull phenomenon.

There are two distinct decisions made in reference to this critical choice of departure. One involves determining the appropriateness of continuing to live at home, the other involves determining the likelihood and means of obtaining the type of residence and social situation harmonious with one's personality and experiences. Certain environmental factors are involved in these decisions. For example, relatively high national, but not necessarily local, unemployment and lower population density *decrease* the probability of women departing for marriage or independent living. In addition, if the head of the household has a college degree, leaving for women, but not men, is less likely.[86] Those women living in less crowded areas, at a time when unemployment nationally is high, and where parents are well-educated, will find it less prudent to leave home. If presented with the choice of living with parents or living alone or with someone else, the individual might choose to simply remain at home if job opportunities are poor, outside social interaction is irregular, and parents can act as friends and respected authority figures, enlightened and competent in attitudes and behaviours.

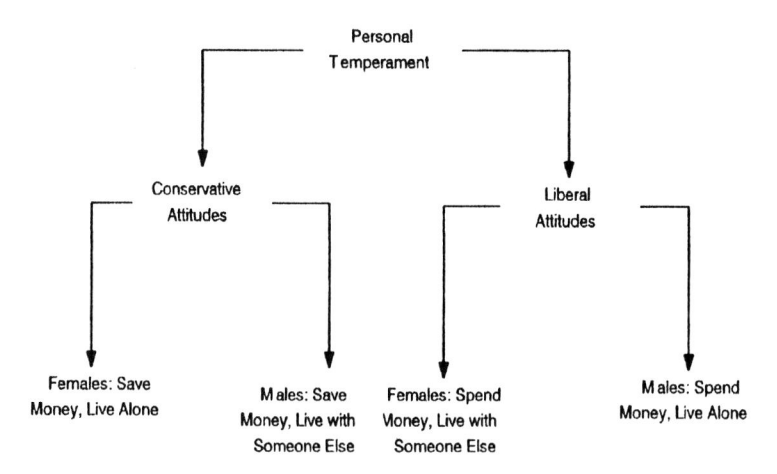

```
                        Personal
                       Temperament
                      /            \
                     /              \
              Conservative         Liberal
               Attitudes          Attitudes
              /        \         /        \
             /          \       /          \
   Females: Save   Males: Save   Females: Spend   Males: Spend
   Money, Live Alone   Money, Live with   Money, Live with   Money, Live Alone
                       Someone Else       Someone Else
```

Figure 2

The second decision includes a number of alternatives that must be scrutinised: one can depart to live alone, with one other person, with several other persons, or with a spouse. The choice of living arrangement is a function of one's attitudes and one's income; it is therefore a more complicated decision than the sole concern of the suitability of living with parents. Underlying the decision to live alone or with someone else are one's attitudes towards one's role in marriage and the symbolic expression of this. Temperament, desire for independence and conservative or liberal orientation towards marriage and companionship lie at the heart of these beliefs, and can be laid out in Figure 2.

Evidently, the desire for autonomy is largely independent of the above factors. The decision is based as much on a privately derived marriage intentions as on economic factors. The following is a summary concerning the probability of a person living with an unrelated individual as opposed to living alone, in terms of income and sex:[87]

Table 2

Probability of living with an unrelated individual and age of marriage, by income and sex.	
	Income level high	**Income level low**
Females	with others[L]/marry later[L]	alone[C,L]/ marry earlier[C]
Males	alone[L]/marry earlier[C]	with others[C,L]/ marry later[C,L]

C-Conservative in social orientation, L-Liberal in social orientation

Thus, women with higher incomes tend to live with someone but marry *later*, whilst males with higher income tend to live alone but marry *earlier*. Clearly, men and women have two *different* dynamics in operation in their choice of lifestyle. At base, the large majority of each sex desires *some* level of companionship by living with people of similar backgrounds, which would include age, class, education and, perhaps most importantly, income.[88] But there is also a segment of each population that for innate reasons (temperament) desires independence, however, possibly in association with some kind of steady companionship. These desires play out around financial factors.

Having high income, conservative men can almost immediately realise their marriage goals (if a woman is willing to wed), and liberal men can immediately realise their goal of being independent by acquiring their own residence. Men of conservative orientation might have the same needs as women for intimate friendship, but being the traditional providers for the family, they would desire *both* to bring in abundance as well as obtain companionship. However, for a time these men might live alone, economic conditions permitting, in order to show that they can achieve the independence ethos. With lower income, those men who foresee marriage at some point must almost certainly live with others in order to conserve funds; those men who want to be perpetually independent must delay their independence and *also* live with others until they too have adequate savings. In this category, the independent group is 'swallowed up' and is no longer noticeable by itself the way it was in the high income category (the ones who live alone). Men who both love autonomy and those who hate it might very well be sharing lodgings with at least the same short term goal: to save money.

The conservative woman might wish to marry early when she is not earning much money, and the liberal woman might live alone out of a strong desire for independence. In addition, there might be some conservative women who for a time will live alone as well, out of a desire to achieve a modicum of independence. Women might feel that they do not need to save as much money as men since the latter are the traditional economic providers and would probably take the lead in savings. This would explain why women with lower incomes might not have a need to save money by sharing a residence. But why would they then share a residence and defer marriage when earning a *higher* income?

One reason might be that women who have high-paying and thus career-demanding lives are more likely to have greater difficulty making sacrifices in marriage relationships. We have already mentioned the difficulties caused by the 'importing' of stress into the household from the office. Perhaps possessing and/or wanting to maintain higher ideals about marriage, women might see this kind of friction as the major contributing factor to the alarmingly high divorce rates; they wonder whether they themselves will ever be secure in a marriage. Fully maintaining the two different spheres of work and home is perceived as taxing intellectual and emotional resources. As a result, career women set up their lives in such a way, so that conflict in either sphere can be met with routes that afford protection and escape. Thus, if a woman is earning a low income, living with a man whom she feels might eventually withdraw his affections would make her dependent and vulnerable, whereas living by herself gives her more control over her destiny. A low income often means few savings and few alternatives; conflict in this 'marriage' would entail meagre choices for such a woman, who does not have the money to relocate elsewhere, at least not in the near future. On the other hand, if she is earning a high income, then she might cohabitate with a man, forming a close approximation of a marital relationship, in the knowledge that it can be broken off relatively easily. Her 'partner' will have less of an opportunity to exploit her, as the woman has enough resources to keep her own life secure. She is not dependent on a man for her residence, her possessions, or her livelihood; her only weakness is her emotional dependence, something far more difficult to remedy than any material circumstance.

If a woman with a complex but financially rewarding occupation often experiences problems with relationships, and if she can live comfortably on her own income, then why not avoid these problems of companionship altogether by living alone? Why does our table above show a tendency to live with others? One reason might be that women in these positions are lonely and insecure and desire companionship as compensation. This insecurity might not be from the rigours of the job itself but from her social position. A woman with a good salary clearly has power and prerogatives that a poorer woman does not. However, the benefits of such propitious remuneration create problems on their own. Women earning high income are a definite oddity by traditional standards, and this group might largely be populated by individuals who are not interested in such standards, that is, individuals considered social liberals. Whereas it was not unusual in the past to see both high- and low-earning men, it was highly exceptional to come across high-earning women. Thus, well-paid women are likely to see themselves even today as belonging to a different social category from other women, being called 'contemporary', 'stylish', or 'modish' by virtue of their occupation alone. Perhaps because of this, women may be more *model* conscious than men, understanding the world in terms of explicit 'right' and 'wrong' life courses and using moral factors more readily when making major decisions. Women, desiring independence and privacy as much or more than men, evidently can use the companionship of a roommate as a proxy for that of a husband's. Especially if a career-orientated woman is liberal in her social views, a possibility we alluded to earlier, she might feel she is 'not the marrying type' but still live with someone anyway. A woman who cohabitates with a man might use, as a shield against community criticism, the respectability gained from higher occupational status. In these situations, women would obviously place more emphasis on income as a status marker. Low income marks a woman as 'traditional' even if she is not actually so, and she might shy away from sharing a residence with a man, especially in a sexual relationship. Women who have lower status occupations could not use their status as protection from communal and family criticism. They would be more likely to view marriage as the only respectable context of a physically intimate relationship.

Overall, we find that the departure from home involves both cultural and personal influences. There are those who, because of their temperament, wish to leave home by age 18, others because they feel that the community expects them to do so, others because they do not feel comfortable with life at home, and yet others because they are attracted to the advantages of the independent life. It is interesting to note that conservative values *still* hold sway in a modern society that has ostensibly 'liberated' itself from them. Some are trying to fulfill them, whilst others are reacting against them. Those who wish to save money could marry as soon as possible, and form a considerate, cooperative relationship, could be called conservative. Those who cultivate their independence in pursuit of a gay life, with a practicable escape route from misfortunate emotional relationships, could justifiably be called liberals.

It would appear that age of marriage, type of work, income and savings no longer have a major role to play in the decision to leave home. This important determination is now dependent on a standardised/idealised dynamic of home life, namely, one that integrates how one should associate with parents, siblings, neighbours, and peers. Thus, the important life event of 'leaving home' has gone from being contingent on immediate material pragmatic concerns, to being driven by larger social concerns. As such, this event is now a function of external and not necessarily advantageous factors. Such an attitude not only presents a threat to the future, but also presents a disturbing picture of present life, when external demands, some quite intangible, begin to contaminate a decision that will profoundly affect the individual for possibly many years into the future. However, this is not exclusively a phenomenon of the modern age, for our ancestors might in some cases have also been reacting to the quality of their family life in their decision to marry. In any case, the importance of building a mature personality, as well as adequate financial resources, in preparation for marriage cannot be overemphasised. How the individual begins his life often determines how well he will live it; limit the growth of resources early on, and you reduce the range of choices you have in a marriage partner, timing of marriage, and lifestyle. This tendency to leave home early, when not solely based on thorough objective evaluation of the facts, can imperil the welfare not only of one person but of a whole family.

ALONE BUT NOT ALONE

One could easily assume 'leaving home' is an unequivocal avowal of autonomy, a firm personal statement about one's confidence in the ability to tackle any and all of life's problems without the protection, support or safety net of parents. However, the evidence from Western societies shows that young people are not quite saying this; they often trying to attain *both* standards of independence and dependence. This should not deceive us into thinking that all people desire equally independence and companionship. Notwithstanding what kind of living arrangement people will eventually settle upon in a new household, there is always an innate desire for a certain type. Of course, everyone would like the freedom to choose friends and residence with a 'backup' of mother and father's resources when required, but some people desire more support than others, and some people desire to be left alone. Clearly, a number of factors affect the decision to leave home, and a number of factors affect the kind of household one would prefer to set up.

Therefore, what are the reasons for leaving the household of origin and moving in with someone else? It is entirely probable that one or both partners have at least some significant dislike of living with their families. They might not get along because parents are overly demanding or critical, children might be obstreperous. Moving in with someone else is an escape that gives the individual a freedom to do what he or she pleases, things that they could not do at home. Further, life at home might be cramped, uncomfortable, and unstable. Such vicissitudes might be elemental in forming the dream of a new life outside on one's own, where one has privacy and latitude in behaviour. Indeed, it might be a form of emancipation, of being set free from familial 'bondage', and for some it cannot come too soon. It would be short-sighted to suggest, however, that such individuals want to be all *alone*; they wish companionship, but on different terms. And so moving out from the family household undoubtedly relates, though indirectly, to the subject of marriage and cohabitation.

On the other hand, those who have no great love of familial 'emancipation' are characterised by certain factors as well. Women and especially men who live with parents well into adulthood, that is, those over age 30 who either never left home, or left and then returned, are different in personality and temperament than those who left at the average age. These individuals tend to be disproportionately widowed, separated, or divorced, of lower education, and not in the labour force. They have average or above average incomes, if working, but are less likely to have attended college. Persons who still live at home at this age are basically individuals who are less capable of independent living, who have a lower capacity for work, or better paying jobs; males in particular could be unmarriageable.[89] Some return home after divorce, or unemployment to regain some confidence and then remarry or get another job, leaving home once again. Others might become permanent dependents because of mental or physical disability. In a certain sense, this conforms to traditional patterns, of men and women who became comfortable with living at home, of parents who liked having one child live with them, and of children who never much liked competitive positions, work, or education. In this way, the household of origin provides a life-long refuge, and if recognised as such, and legitimated by society, individuals would not necessarily feel the need to move out from their parents' abode if they felt more comfortable living there. As long as people follow all important moral conventions, it is self-evident that they should not be forced to become something they are not. The conflict in modern society could theoretically be lowered if people set up a lifestyle more in keeping with their personalities. If an individual is inclined to develop a *companionate* relationship *external* to the family, and this is by no means a universal need, a delay in leaving home might give him or her more time to find someone of compatible temperament, and their ideal of love might substantively be reached.

By studying the succession of living arrangements a person follows in early life, we might be able to understand what it is that people really desire in the modern world. A pattern indeed emerges when comparing the tendency to marry early or late with the individual's residential status as age 21. Those unmarried who were living *alone* at the average age of 21 had the clearest relationship to marriage inclination, with the propensity to marry *late*.[90] Living away from home *increases* the likelihood of marrying *early*, and conversely lowers the chance of marrying late, when the proportion is of the whole youth population, not just unmarried.[91] Further, those who lived with friends, acquaintances or roommates were *more* likely to marry early.[92] Women who are moderately to strongly 'marriage-avoidant' (percent not married by age of 45 as well as those marrying at 30 or above) tend *not* to have lived with parents or other family members in early adulthood.[93] GOLDSCHEIDER & WAITE (1987), in an American study, found that living independently *delays* marriage, especially for younger adults and women, although it is less of an influence when living in group quarters.

The information above can be condensed into a table, where the increasing desire for independence is seen going from top to bottom and left to right (figures in parentheses indicate statistical significance not reached):

Table 3

	Marry 19 and under, males and females	Marry 19 and under, males	Marry 30 and over, females	Marry 30 and over, males	Not married by age 45, females
Living with parents	+			-	(-)
Living with family			(-)	(-)	(-)
Living with friends	+	+			(-)
Living alone	-		+	+	(+)

We see in this analysis the existence of two population segments, one that greatly desires *freedom* and independence, and who are most likely to be seen living alone in apartments and marrying late; the other segment greatly desires *companionship*, if not at home then with friends as roommates, with a concomitant tendency to marry earlier. The former might become bachelors of long standing, clearly independent minded, who are often characterised as being 'set in their ways'. They like peace, quiet, having things in life arranged to their taste and expectations; they would detest the disruption brought on by the activities of a wife and children. For the latter, they like to live with others, and are willing to leave the parental abode, but do not wish to live alone. They then live with one or more other persons, and then also tend to marry at some point in their lives. Wishing to achieve some kind of 'in-between' compromise situation, they were not so intent on living independently, but yet could not continue residing with their parents.

Thus, the decision to leave one's home of origin is usually predicated on a number of considerations. One has to ask oneself a number of questions. Am I happy living with my parents and siblings? Would I be happier living by myself, or with someone else? Could I support myself and still save money when living on my own? Would I be secure and content overall living alone, perhaps for many years? In spite of this social network one might construct, living by oneself does not meet the needs of intimacy, and residing in a city creates an even greater distance between oneself and the social environment. The negative psychological effects that arise from these deficiencies during adverse and stressful periods might be serious.[94] But many would rather face this prospect than endure perhaps even more serious problems living at home with dysfunctional parents and siblings, where solutions to one's problems might be almost entirely outside of one's grasp. Clearly, in most cases there are factors that push people out the door and pull them to a new situation; it is very easy to confuse the two. When one decides to marry or move in with someone else, the ostensible reason might be that one has fallen in love with that person, although the 'love' that one speaks of is a love of the freedom that awaits in a new living situation.

Because of this emphasis on the 'new living situation' possibly without adequately analysing the material aspects, we should examine the basic nature of housing. Out of a desire for privacy or seclusion comes the requirement for physical space, and housing is therefore a fundamental factor in human existance. The critical need for openness around one's person is intrinsic to all people, and indeed even other mammals. Not surprisingly, a serious unsolicited intrusion into one's space can be taken as a threat of violence, with a preemptive attack as justified. These desires vary according to culture, with European, especially Western European, cultures requiring more privacy than others. The type of family structure commonly seen in our history, that is, the nuclear household, and the kind of physical partitioning commonly seen in better homes, demonstrate a deep-seated requirement for retreat and seclusion, by oneself or with a loved one. One must be able to have quiet for rest or reflection and a freedom to live out one's vocation or avocations without interruption or encroachment.

We know that the availability of housing, of private space, is a crucial factor in determining the appropriateness of marriage. Housing costs are a critical yet underrated factor, ignored by individual and social planner alike. The first domain supplies a crucial initial context of marriage, for it is the physical space in which intellectual and emotional development will occur. Evidence exists for the deleterious effects of residential living space shortages and how much space is allotted to each partner can often have significant consequences. Although psychological well-being is not necessarily an effect of crowding, it often does result in lower marital well-being.[95] Marital happiness is a function of factors related to the couple's dwelling, which makes it imperative that housing is acceptable since it threatens the marriage directly. However, the acceptability of the situation is not immediately obvious, since a subjective assessment of adequacy of space is a better predictor of satisfaction than an objective assessment. Cooperation and elucidation of standards are critical to companionate relationships.

Thus, to wed or cohabitate without surveying the housing market first is careless to say the least, as the relationship between husband and wife can be severely strained if space requirements are not met. An appropriate strategy would be to assess one's housing preferences, to assess the housing situation and then to make suitable plans for how much of the household income is to be used in this fashion. As with any item in the budget, it must be evaluated in light of the constraints imposed by other items. Hence, a couple's requirements about the 'proper residence', in terms of accessibility, size, conveniences, age of structure, and aesthetic considerations, must be reconciled with their plans for schooling, employment, children, possessions and savings.

Marriages are weakest when external factors frustratingly dictate compromise in key areas. Such a feeling arises when prices of residences rise more rapidly than income, as then high prices mean high mortgage payments and high rents. During a critical period of social change, single family, apartment, condominium and cooperative prices had all risen to levels that make housing expenses difficult to support in a middle-class budget. Between 1970 and 1987, personal income per capita in the United States increased from $4,056 to $15,495 (3.8x)[96] yet the average new privately owned one family house (the 'ideal' for most people) price rose from $23,400 to $104,500, a four-and-a-half fold increase,[97] but existing house prices rose somewhat in tandem with income, from $23,000 to $85,600 (3.7x). The magnitude of change was greater than the national average in the Northeast (5.3x), and in the West (4.7x), but was lower than average in the Midwest (3.3x).[98] Thus, prices of new houses, and, in certain regions of the country older houses, outstripped the growth of personal income, causing an increase in the size of this item in the household budget. In addition, in certain regions of the country, the growth in house prices was far more than the increase in income, a fact not expressed in the above statistics.

Many other countries, including the United Kingdom, Germany, Australia, Belgium, Denmark and Sweden suffer from high housing costs, but this exorbitance might apply to different types of housing. For example, rental housing in one nation might be very expensive, and in another, it might be smaller first houses that are difficult to obtain, and yet in another nation, it might be a larger second or third house. Still, this situation is preferable to nations where housing of many types is virtually unavailable at any price. During the Communist regimes in Eastern Europe, housing, like other markets, was centrally controlled so that prices were kept within the range of affordability; the problem was availability. Often the situation was so bleak that the only residence a young couple could afford during their early years was sharing one with one or other set of parents. Ironically, they considered the death of a relative as one of the only opportunities to gain control of their own household. Many couples might not be so fortunate, and have to spend their entire married lives in the same household, essentially moving to their parent's bedroom once they die, and then having their own children and their spouses live with them, repeating the cycle once again.

We should point out, though, that the desire to live with relations might be more a function of culture than finances. In the United States, married couples of Russian origin are inclined more than other groups to have elderly parents living with them, whereas Italian-Americans tend to have married children living in their homes, but German-Americans were least likely to have either older or younger relatives living with them.[99] These ethnic groups are not very different from each other in average income, occupations, or social class, and so differences in living arrangements can probably be attributed to temperamental factors. Germans might very well have a more independent persona than Italians or Russians, an outlook which would affect their housing requirements. Thus, if temperamental factors were allowed to flourish, instead of being overawed by 'Anglo-Saxon' ideas, then there would be less pressure on housing in America and the economy could be organised in such a way that housing was made affordable.[100]

When someone is unable to immediately buy or rent what he or she considers a sufficiently large residence, patiently waiting for such an opportunity can be difficult when holding in abeyance other considerations. Fulfilling goals relating to housing often is viewed as vitiating both the independence ethos and marriage ethos, and other, perhaps quite inadvisable, methods might be pursued to find housing quickly, such as working longer hours, changing jobs, borrowing or even malappropriation. Thus, the proportion of the family budget that is made up by housing expenses is an influence that increases or decreases marriage age, as higher income and greater savings are necessary before a couple can live comfortably. In many cases where people marry young, they must live with the husband or wife's parents for awhile until circumstances improve. In most Western cultures this is considered undesirable as the couple expects privacy and control over the affairs of their household.[101] Thus, as the costs related to housing ascend as a percent of a household budget, the *less* the chance of a woman marrying young.[102] The option of living with one's spouse as well as with relatives and/or in a small residence, is generally less attractive than living on one's own or with a roommate, other things being the same.

Instead of the availability of housing determining marriage age, there is an alternative model we might consider: Lower housing costs are associated with lower age of marriage because younger married couples spend *less* on housing. Young couples have fewer resources, and so they cannot spend much on housing, instead preferring to concentrate on other expense areas, including clothing, entertainment, food, and transportation. It is questionable, however, whether these couples have much control over the housing expense item in their budget. The choice of housing is often the product of location and cultural pressure to attain an appropriate status. How can people of middle class and upper class backgrounds choose smaller units, with inferior amenities, perhaps in poorer neighbourhoods, without experiencing some kind of disapproval from colleagues and friends? Hence, the scaling of costs relating to housing and rentals is determined by a variety of factors, economic and social, whereas other portions of a household budget are more amenable to a couple's control than housing. A couple's greatest asset in this regard is the ability to migrate to an area with housing on a different scale, yet this is difficult to accomplish when the character, location and features of one's residence currently confer prestige.

The reality is that individuals must find some kind of balance between their spatial needs, their emotional desires, their income, and housing costs. We have discussed in this section the ways in which people attempt to approach this problem, and have found that whilst people still depend on one another, and there is no monolithic need for total freedom (solitary living), external factors still make people less free in their choice of living arrangement than they would like. Let us now look at how the concept of autonomy is affected by cultural factors that interact with a person's need for privacy.

The Perception of Privacy

What mediates the reaction an individual will have to the change between his current housing situation and the one he and his spouse will face in the future? Clearly, the average individual assesses the potential for housing using experiences gained from his own circumstances. Living in cramped quarters indicates that in general people in that country have less space, whereas living in a spacious residence betokens more space available to the average person. If we determine the average space available to the individual, we are not only establishing the parameters of his living environment, but also his capacity for finding private residential space of a predetermined size.

There are however factors which alter the importance of personal space. Space is seen at two levels, at the level of fundamental need, and at the level of status marker. Since having space is an advantage, the more space one has, the higher one's social status. As a result, a superfluity of space can bring haughtiness and disregard for others. Further, if the concept of personal freedom, obviously critical in our discussions, is propagated most effectively through media and education sources, then these factors must mediate or modify the individual's responses to his persent and future housing situation.

Education and advanced communications put the need for space at or near the top of one's list of priorities. Both education and communication can be called part of an 'information culture', which has a critical effect on how space is perceived as a personal issue and as a status issue. The educated hold that space and privacy are primary matters and see leaving a small residence as a short-term solution, offering escape from a difficult household. The undereducated put such matters further down on the list, they see longer-term solutions, and wish to conserve resources by staying at home and not moving out. We can thus put forward two models, one that involves less education and one that involves more eduation.

In the less education scenario, seen in Figure 3, the individual must forbear, wait for adequate space to become available; even though he might not like living alone in cramped quarters, he knows he stands a good chance of eventually finding better accommodations. His worldview values privacy, but not necessarily leisure or independence. By living at home in small quarters he loses privacy, but will hopefully gain it later, and in doing this he does not feel he has violated a major social ethic. Living in larger quarters means he has a better chance of attaining privacy in the household of origin than in some other household, his own or sharing it with someone. Further, this abundance then means more space is available elsewhere, *ceteris paribus*, and so he will feel more confident seeking a spouse.

The more education model, seen in Figure 4, finds the individual wishing to move out of a smaller home environment into one more fitting his preferences. He has based his worldview on certain unalterable premisses, specifically that independence, privacy and leisure are essential for a successful life. It is, however, very difficult to achieve all three simultaneously as most living arrangements involve sacrificing at least one. Living at home in smaller quarters denies him independence and privacy, but allows him leisure; living alone or with someone else in a smaller residence, whilst working to support himself, denies him leisure and privacy but allows him greater independence; living at home in larger quarters gives him privacy and ease but he lacks independence. The third situation would be the one most preferable until the desire for true autonomy becomes overwhelming.

Because culture influences ideas about independence, there are vectors that condition the impact of space on the individual's attitudes. These vectors are visible in two consistent, internationally available major indicators:

(1) the level of communications
(2) the level of education

People strive for differentiation and status in reaction to what they see and hear in the media. A greater level of communication by definition reveals more than the individual knew previously about the behaviour, attitudes and mores of others; this provides the information necessary for individuation. A greater level of education also gives individuals more information on how others live. By education we are not only talking about the highest level reached in formal education, but rather its quality and breadth, and the extent to which the desire for knowledge is met, such as can be measured by pupils per teacher and frequency of loans of library books. Individuals with extended or more intensive education infuse artificial concepts about the need for space into their worldview, seeing it in philosophical terms, not merely pragmatic ones. These requirements, coupled with an inclination for 'aristocratic' separateness, institute a collective demand for an above average amount of personal space, that is, society fosters an economic programme of building relatively large residential structures. Most importantly, key ideas about autonomy are given by education which alter the purpose of this space, for the emphasis narrows from two or more people to basically only one, the individual. Thus, a higher level of education, as measured by proxies, produces higher intellectual requirements, which in turn produces an increased need for privacy, study, reading, etc. Overall, concentrated education produces quite a different perspective on living arrangements compared to that produced by a more restricted schooling.

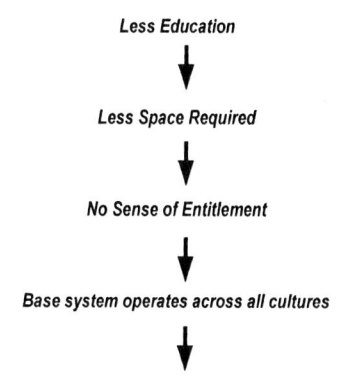

Less Education
↓
Less Space Required
↓
No Sense of Entitlement
↓
Base system operates across all cultures
↓
Negative correlation between space and later marriage, positive correlation between space and early marriage; less space: more later marriage, less early marriage

Figure 3

The living environment of the household of origin inspires a view of oneself vis-à-vis others, which is often not in relation to any specific individual, but is an overarching theme about social relations that colours one's life. When one is raised in a large house, one feels a sense of *entitlement*, of getting what one wants, and ultimately of supremacy over social rules. Where this sense of entitlement ultimately comes from is hard to determine, but probably arises from a collective temperament, economic structure, and history, influences that are facilitated by the media. One's house or room, bigger than that of others, is a sign of affluence and independence; this is especially true if one can have a room to oneself while others of the same social class must share. However, this can only function as such if it is agreed upon in a larger social context as being a *marker* of status. In other more traditional nations, where education and mass media are not as important, living space, although it does confer some status, is not a major determinant of power and reinforcer of preeminence, as the individual has other, more socially constructive ways, of obtaining respect. The educated person has these ways available to him as well, but they are inadequate in filling his need for differentiation brought about by the intense competition not only with actual persons but with myriad 'virtual' peers who can materialise through the various organs of the media.

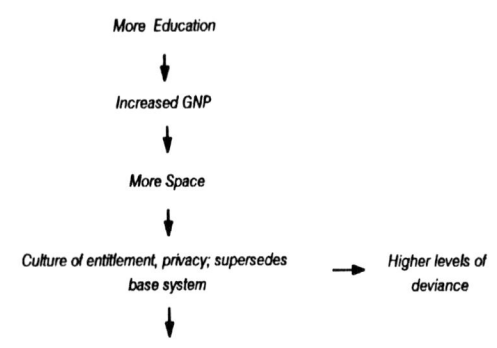

More Education
↓
Increased GNP
↓
More Space
↓
Culture of entitlement, privacy; supersedes base system → Higher levels of deviance
↓
Negative correlation between space and early marriage, positive correlation between space and later marriage; less space means more early marriage, less later marraige

Figure 4

Consequently, in engineering a visibly autonomous life, the individual separates himself from his peers by seeking higher status, and greater personal living space, if available, provides the symbol necessary for expressing such status. Marriage itself will be used as an instrument for independence if it means giving the individual his cherished liberty from a too-small home. Obviously, seeking egress from the family household is not the only consideration in marrying, but it is a highly significant factor when the concept of freedom has been cultivated. Thus, *the independence ethos, entitlement ethos and the marriage ethos are all closely related.*

It should be realised that although well-off people have more privacy, they can also develop self-centred attitudes. The lack of this cardinal resource can be frustrating and can result in aberrant reactions; however, an abundance of space gives one all the *more* reason to feel entitled and feel that one is not under society's laws. The distinction between oneself and others in such a culturally important aspect, to rise above the rest, can be easily translated to an unwarranted general feeling of superiority. We have said that educated and media orientated societies strive to increase space, as smart, learned, and enlightened individuals demand privacy. More privacy, however, often means more social deviance, as pro-social ideas are often squeezed out by self-centred notions in the information conduits. It might be that having too much space overall is *worse* than having too little.

Let us now see whether our hypotheses are correct. We must first define the expression 'personal space'. This is specifically the floor space in a residence on which a person can use for his own purposes, be it walking, sleeping, exercising, storage, and so on. Space might or might not be for one's exclusive use, as it might be part of one's room, or it might be a shared area. Furthermore, the space might be walled in, or some other divider, permanent or temporary, might be emplaced to create privacy. Because of the psychological importance of spreading out one's domain, the greater amount of space available, of whatever type, for one's private use, the greater the amount of 'living space' or 'personal space', and the greater the satisfaction with life. Indicators of personal space do not always conform to a priori assumptions. We find that in European nations, persons per room is not correlated with square metres per person or with other indicators. Nevertheless, square metres per person is significantly correlated with various indicators, as we shall see below. From this we can determine that not having one's own *room* is of less significance compared to the *size* of one's personal space. The indicator of persons per dwelling is negatively but non- significantly correlated to square metres per person, a weakness that is also surprising, since one would assume that with relatively few exceptions, the more persons per house, the less space each person would have. Evidently, house size and persons per unit fluctuate separately. Per capita income shows a correlation with space only when controls are used, it being positively correlated when the ratio of students per teacher is below average, and the ratio of persons per television is also below average (i.e. better education and communications). Thus, the ideas engendered and propagated by good education and communications cause financial resources, where available, to be directed toward construction in order to increase living space, but when education and communications are not as effective, then funds are used for other purposes. More frequent and broad use of information tends to increase the amount of space available by encouraging a higher standard of living.

Measuring educational attainment is fairly straightforward, but how do we measure the level of information flow? The conventional means of 'broadcasting' ideas in a modern Western society is through various diverse means including teachers, newspapers, television, books, magazines, films, plays and radio.[103] Generally, higher news circulation, fewer students per teacher, more loans from the library and fewer persons per television signify increasing circulation of information. Furthermore, the variables of persons per television set and borrowing library books can act as proxies for higher education. News circulation is correlated in the opposite direction one would expect, with fewer persons reading newspapers being related to a higher prevalence of tertiary education. This does not mean that educated people obtain less information than others, it might mean that they obtain it from sources other than newspapers, such as magazines, television, radio and libraries, where they might use an 'all-in- one' reference containing current events, entertainment and commentary. Further, it is possible that those who are educated, and presumably versed in the ways of academia, will prefer sources that are less-biassed. The frequently partisan or sensational reportage by certain segments of the media can make finding objective information difficult. They may still read certain newspapers of better reputation, but might read them more infrequently than less-educated individuals.

There is little question, however, that people with higher education have a greater exposure to various media which contain references directly or indirectly to the issue of autonomy. Although how many regularly gather news stories from whatever source is not known, there is little doubt that the wealthy do so far more often than the working and lower classes.[104] Certainly, for the better off there is a greater interest in the broadcast or televised word, sound and picture.

Families of different income levels do not apportion their funds that differently from one another among expense categories, as in the amounts spent (as a percent of total expenditures) on housing, transportation, apparel, health care, and other expenditures,[105] or on entertainment and reading.[106] But there is a great contrast in how socioeconomic categories allocate their resources (time and money) among certain specific forms of *art* and *media*. Of those with incomes under $5000 in 1985, less than 10% saw jazz performances, classical music, opera, musical plays, plays, ballet performances; fewer than 20% visited a museum or art gallery, and only 44% read a novel, short story, poetry or play. There are not many differences between the lowest category and those making $15,000-25,000. Above a household income of $25,000, however, there is a major departure in spending. Whereas of those making $15-$25,000, only 12% saw musical plays, of those making $25-$50,000, 22% did, and of those making over $50,000, 37% did. Of the first category, 9% saw plays, of the second, 14% did, and of the third, 28% did. Less difference is found in the reading of novels, essays or works of fiction: 53% of the first category read one, 63% of the level above it, and 77% of the highest income level. Perhaps most significantly, because of the cultural importance of the medium, we find that only 19% of the first category visited an exposition of art and culture such as a gallery or museum in the previous year, as opposed to 28% of the second and an impressive 45% of the third.[107] Finally, those making over $40,000 spent on average nearly $700 for television, radio and sound equipment, compared to only about $290 for those in the $15-19,999 bracket.[108]

A similar dynamic prevails for differences in education, as, for example, 80% of those who have graduate school education read a work of fiction in the last year, as opposed to only 52% of high-school graduates.[109] Those who have a graduate school education see musical plays, jazz performances, or visit museums or art galleries at least *three* times more frequently than those with only high school education. The ratio between the two groups rises to at least six to one when the media are classical music, opera, plays, or ballet performances.[110] Clearly, there is far more exposure to ideas, whether intellectual, academic, fictional, dramatic, when income and educational categories are above middle- range.

In our analysis of Western nations, we see that age of marriage, and so the value of marriage, is affected by the amount of residential space available, with the influence varying by level of education: For well-educated males and females, more space means *later* marriage, and fewer not marrying; for moderately educated males and females, more space means *earlier* marriage. We should add that greater use of information in a nation is also associated with having more personal space.[111] The tendency to remain permanently single is affected by space parameters, with more space per person *reducing* the proportion of women who never marry. It should be emphasised that besides the people who are persuaded by privacy and information dynamics, there is a proportion of the population which is *not* affected and which is dependent in large part on pragmatic, material factors. Then there is also a small segment that is not affected by space, material, economic or educational factors and would therefore not marry for any reason. Hence, evidence exists of two main groups who are in the marriage market: Those who have a strong tendency to marry and can use marriage for important status reasons and higher level personal needs (moderately pro-marriage), and those who have a weak tendency to marry because they do not see the point in cohabitation apart from satisfying very fundamental personal needs (anti- marriage). Our interest here is in the first group, especially in their interpretation of the concepts 'status' and 'personal need'.

Since we have statistical evidence that education and the media affect the importance of space, what other proof do we have that ideas transmitted through these vectors encourage people to believe in entitlement and to seek greater independence? We know that the 'independence ethos' covers several main areas: Satisfaction with home life, general attitudes, work practises, earnings/money, social rank, and concern with general welfare of the nation. In other words, a person's attitude towards independence is tied to his beliefs about family, community, government, and economy. If a higher transfer of information can be associated with opinions that clearly reveal a desire for freedom or independence, then the association is largely proven.

A study we have carried out of attitudes in the Western world show that the social vectors mentioned above — newspapers, books, college education, television, and teachers — have an influence in affecting attitudes on questions of social position and home life.[112] Each of these elements has a role to play in describing and analysing society, each has a different level of depth and scope. In order of approximately increasing scope and depth, we can list: television, newspapers, books, high school, college. We should also bear in mind that what is being analysed are measures of the flow of information, *not* of standard of living or economics.

Thus, people are reacting not necessarily to a better economy, but perhaps the *perception* that such an economy is present or in the near future. We should stress it is not necessarily true that a culture is really less rank or status orientated in well-educated or high information societies. Theoretically, it is possible that in a well-educated society, rank is no longer relevant as people become autonomous and reach a ceiling of ability; but the problem lies in belief, as the ideal is not a reality. In fact, there is an absence of strong correlations between a measure of social division (percent of total national income earned by households comprising the highest 10% of wage earners) and other indicators; there is no significant correlation with student/teacher ratio; a very weak positive correlation with over 25 with college education (r=.1888); a stronger correlation with persons per television (r=.3920); and a negative correlation with library loans of books (r=-.3018). We are not seeing a *real* eradication of rank and status in society through higher education and flow of information. These larger beliefs are not realistic assessments, but are nonetheless instrumental in gaining the confidence the individual needs to get what he really wants from life, that is, to be respected, to be in control, and to gain gratification from his social position.

The study of nations alluded to above shows that when information and education are increased, young people and older people see many things comparably. This increase in attitudinal homogeneity between age groups might be due to the same factors that increase similarity in opinions between people of higher education. When the information culture becomes prominent, one way to describe the overall effect on society is that of thoroughgoing optimism. People believe that society is fair-minded, it is not rank or class orientated, and it has a good future. They are also more satisfied with living at home, but sensitive to privacy and space issues, and less content with income.

Specifically, young adults like to be unconstrained by family imposition, rank, status, yet believe they do not have the means to express their individuality. An exception to this general view would be their greater concern with morals, which would work against the independence ethos. Older adults similarly have a desire for independence and entitlement which necessitate a stable social and political environment (domestic and international), where the current system is endorsed (if it were not then personal aims would be frustrated), and extreme measures are rejected. People are happier with individual, national and international affairs, feel closer to the political process, but less committed to others.

These opinions are not determined by all vectors working together with equal strength, but rather some appear stronger than others. Each element covers a certain set of social factors at a particular level of detail; opinions then arise that are commensurate with this purview and level of specificity. For example, the efficacy of the secondary school environment (as measured by students per teacher) has a fairly sizable influence on the things that young people will seek in life, in particular whether independence, pride in one's country, social position and wealth are important. These complex personal goals are formed in the teenage period, when the school environment provides many thought-provoking ideas about situations which directly impinge on social structure. Television, on the other hand, deals with a wide range of general factors, which impact views relating to reciprocal duties of individual and society (such as on fighting for country, morality and future potential). Newspapers are a major source of details about work, politics, labour and business, and so give people ideas on the issues and social interactions in these areas. Books, with their detailed, often historical themes, focus on things not related to the external structures such as work, politics, and economics. They influence how people feel about family relations, ambition, social connections and status usage. College education is quite specific in its influence, and such training gives people the power to say 'rank does not mean everything' because it bestows sophistication, erudition and discipline—aspects which when used properly can outweigh social status and family connections. Indeed, college education is unique in that it gives recognisable power that the other elements considered here cannot.

It can be stated unequivocally that in the highest sphere of social interaction, for people to feel independent, they cannot believe that they are constrained to follow social convention, such as delineated by rank, occupation, or profession. People have a vested interest in believing that there are no barriers to success, such as rank, position or wealth. Increased information spreads the 'gospel' that anything is possible in the modern age, and that there is usually good potential for success in the future. The result is that when relatively high levels of communications and education are enjoyed by a nation, social rank and wealth are not very significant as openly discussed social concepts, but independence is still crucially important. In the scenario, you must believe that you are free to live as you like, and that you and other people do not have to attain rank neither to succeed materially in life nor to be happy.

The achievement of social freedom is the raison d'etre for all education, to promote individualistic thought and action, to break the bonds of reliance on other people and on ideas that putatively hold no value. Therefore, autonomy is the keystone idea of education, which is dependent upon the collection of knowledge and is the means for the ultimate utilitarian conclusion of that knowledge. Well-educated people also might understand that higher rank is one way of getting ahead, but they do not see it as a problem or a goal for *themselves*. We might ask: Does indifference to rank and social position issues also mean not seeking *status?* Not necessarily, as long as independence and self- satisfaction are the main goals; if goals can be attained through means other than resorting to the complexities and the commitments that formal social rank brings, then so be it. However, unofficial status, as gotten through personal possessions and residential space, and as recognised between two people rather than in some collective way, will always be something that is sought after. 'Status' is unimportant for many as in the sense of official status, gotten through job titles, but *un*official status as obtained through space and personal possessions is still critical.

Hence, the observation that the increase in education and communication brings some kind of laxity to the social structure does not weaken our contention that the idea of autonomy is spread with information. People are not any less desirous of raising themselves above their peers and our study shows that people still want to have power over others. They want to live life as they like, and are not likely to believe that work is mechanical, meaning that the individual, as far as they are concerned, does matter. On the other side of the coin, when the individual is not 'I' and is someone else, the importance of humanitarianism is lessened. That is why there is less national pride, less desire to fight for one's country, and more social distancing in general. Democracy is believed to work because the individual thinks he has the *personal* power to influence the rest of society, to get his way and effect major changes, regardless of how others feel about these changes.

Rank and position still possess high value in that they reward accomplishment, reputation, credentials, diplomas, determination, and work history. Although symbols are meagre items in themselves, without reserving the pedestal and the laurel-wreath as privilege markers for the winners, there is little reason to exceed one's own or others' expectations. Society must have ways of giving individuals recognition that they have 'beat' others in an endeavour, and even such minor aspects as courteous forms of address or special seats at a table are coveted. Of course, there are dangers, social position can be twisted so that people gain unfair advantage, but it would be foolish to believe that social position ever ceases to be important.

Every individual has to compare himself to others in order to understand how he fits in with larger society.

These attitudes betray a certain selfishness. From self-centeredness stems a cynicism about one's fellow citizen, such as is shown in a reluctance to defend one's land even though one putatively endorses the national culture. Logically, one does not have to defend one's land if one envisions a good future for the nation. If one believes one 'deserves' a good future, then is it not likely that one would *predict* a good future as well? In addition, to say you are proud of your nation because you *believe* there will be a good future is more than a little disingenuous. It appears people confuse imagination with reality as the ideas of entitlement spread throughout society. Consequently, entitlement is present where opinions form a nexus: people believe rank is irrelevant, people predict a good future for the nation, and the primary goal of the individual is easy enactment of personal plans.

If one really *believes* one is free, then one cannot tolerate any restraints, one can simply not be pigeonholed or boxed-in. However, never is there any social situation in which every desire can be easily and legitimately satisfied; thus, logically we can maintain that entitlement, as a product of the desire for independence, creates some level of presumptuousness and arrogance. If you have a long list of 'things I deserve to get and am expecting', you will certainly have to compile a shorter list of 'things I deserved but did not get'. It is how aggressively the average individual pursues in fulfilling the latter list that establishes the country's reputation for level of pugnaciousness. Nevertheless, we know from ordinary observation, that bullies often seem indifferent in regards to their prey. The elementary reason for seeming unconcerned about the means to obtain the 'deserved' items on the list might be that such sentiments are signs of *weakness* and/or failure and so are considered inappropriate. To say one is dissatisfied implies subordination to a person or institution or system, and this clashes with the modern ethos of independence. When people complain too much, they seem under threat and not free. Thus, if one is to appear 'free' one must be accepting of the status quo, see society as full of potential to serve one's own ends, and see few obstacles or hindrances on one's path. This then produces a sense that one deserves to get what one wants; if this were uncertain, then one would not be truly independent.

We can see that behind the issues presented in education and media, there is an overarching theme of man attaining *total* freedom. If we can agree that these media, directly or indirectly, consciously or unconsciously, invariably favour the theme of man being independent, free, in liberty and without fetter, man living up to the great Western Enlightenment expectation of being a truly sovereign entity, then we can see how such exposure to communications and education can produce the sense of entitlement. The ideas that permeate fictional, news and academic works, undoubtedly affect the attitudes of consumers. One's personal space is rarely the main theme, yet it is often treated symbolically. In fiction, main characters often live alone, are under threat at home from outside intruders, have parties whilst parents are away, move out to live in small apartments in big cities. Although they serve the telling of a story, all of these plot devices are treated rather indifferently by the producers. They do not explicitly approve or disapprove of the concepts but simply weave them into the story, making autonomy a common background. It would therefore be difficult to find unequivocal examples where education, communications, living space, and marriage are all tied together into one dynamic. Nonetheless, it is apparent that by their ubiquitousness, a clear endorsement of entitlement, of freedom and privacy is present in all forms of the media.[113]

The findings presented above are consistent with each other and our major postulates. To summarise, space and privacy can be interpreted differently in reference to marriage depending on the outlook of the individual, his or her education, and standard of living. For a society with modern concepts, well-educated and affluent, *independence* is the almost sacred life-principle of the individual, and a lack of space is a challenge to ideas of self-government. However, this in no way means that the ideal of love is negated, but it is reduced in priority. In this situation:

• The tendency is to be independent and focus on the *present* living situation.
• The individual seeks egress if living space is small in general throughout society and in his own home. It is possible the individual might move in with friends as roommates, but it is likely that quarters would be cramped. The individual might prefer moving in with a love interest, since he would be living with someone more amenable. Parents in this society might also be able to afford getting a son or daughter plus a spouse an apartment of their own. In either case, the marriage is *hastened*. Thus, when space is lacking, the individual can share space with roommates but uneasily; it is better for him if he marries, since then he will be with someone more acceptable to him.
• The tendency is to remain at home if living space is ample. The individual has enough space and sees no reason to marry, thus marriage is *delayed*. The individual can remain with parents at home, or move in with roommates, since any residence will likely have adequate

living space for each person. Marriage in either case is not necessary.

Young people in this society are antagonised and threatened by the lack of personal space; to marry early would mean an escape from a too-constricted family household. Their new life might begin in an even smaller place than with the family of origin, but at least it would be with only one other person. Unlike one's parents and siblings, one can freely choose one's spouse, a person one could presumably tolerate much better. If space is available at home, where each child has his or her own sizable room, then the impetus for moving out to a solitary or shared residence might be eliminated.

In traditional, less-educated and moderately-educated, and less-affluent societies, *marriage* is the main aim. The ability to procure living space can mean early marriage, as couples can obtain their own private residence, producing a more harmonious relationship. Further, when housing is a critical factor, living in a city especially makes leaving home for marriage less likely.[114] In this situation:

• The tendency is to build up resources in preparation for marriage and focus on the *future* living situation

• If living quarters are inadequate in general and at home, then wait for opportunities and options to arise for adequate living space; parents might not be able to assist in purchase of a residence. All of this *delays* marriage. A limitation of space can mean delaying marriage until space currently occupied by a family member becomes available due to death or departure, or until the couple can save enough money to buy or rent a larger residence.

• There is a *hastening* of marriage if larger places are available, because one can leave home. Thus, with more space, earlier marriage occurs because of a better housing market (space is cheap) and/or space in the parents' house can be utilised.

The first situation acts as an inducement for early marriage, the second as either a barrier to or facilitator of marriage. Where space is available, it is a sign of opulency, and the academic and scholarly 'brain trust', mediated by an extended communications systems, will bring out and reinforce ideas about rights, privileges, social relations and material values. The less-educated and moderately-educated and moderate income people do not have the urge to 'escape' in order to conform to independence ideals elicited by education and communications. There is also no competition within one's extended or virtual peer group that forces them to develop a sense of entitlement or to seek higher status. In fact, people in the high-education and communications society will demand that not only a few of their ideals be met, but the whole set, often in disregard of what the economy and government can efficiently deliver. When counter-examples to the housing ideal are present, distressed individuals tend to take the quickest solution, namely to relinquish the companionship of family at an early age. By having a place of his or her own, the individual has the freedom to say and do what he or she pleases without having to answer to parents.[115]

We may add that studies show that interference with the need for space used for seclusion and temporary isolation, to relax, think, reflect, sleep, can create mental and familial havoc. A lack of privacy in general results in lower mental ability, impaired mental functioning, and greater deviance. This is evidently true of all Western cultures, regardless of income, government spending, and other forms of compensation. However, in societies with higher education and communication, the availability of space, although relieving the above problems, releases latent attitudes of defiance and hostility. The perspective is something like this: I have a large house, large rooms, many possessions, I have power over my environment, and people must find me attractive, intelligent, powerful.

It should finally be noted that it is easy to envision how arrogance can lead to hurt feelings, arguments, rejection of traditional norms and self-indulgence. These new difficulties are so strong that they not only negate the positive effects of personal space, but create additional substantial effects on their own. Traditional and modern societies lie in two 'bands', with the former below that of the latter; the two bands begin with about the same space per person, at about the same level of deviance. The two sets eventually part company, however, and although traditional cultures manage to reduce deviance in relation to more space, modern cultures at the upper end of the range are in a *worse* position. Therefore, the tendency to marry, thus the tendency to 'fall in love', is formed to a substantial extent by the complex interaction between two seemingly romantically barren factors: housing and social status needs. This is possible because the most pliable factor of all, mass communication, has become so powerful as to twist any concept from its original meaning.

HOUSEHOLD SIZE AND LESSONS LEARNED

Perceptions of privacy, and the subsequent need for departure, might very well be affected by factors *internal* to the household. It might appear that living in a large family is the same as in a smaller residence with reduced privacy. This is not so. A person might live in a large house, yet still have little room of his own if he has numerous siblings. The effect of being fenced in by four walls is not the same as the presence of four brothers or sisters. Thus, growing up in a large household presents some of the more complex forms of interactions and often the individual has to deal with conflicting forces in his social surroundings that eventually have an effect on his desire for opposite sex relations and marriage. Complexity in the family of origin, primarily due to a large number of siblings, prompts an individual response that is directed towards *or* away from marriage.

Logically, we can foresee two types of marital results for the individual coming from a populous household. A large family might *discourage* marriage, if children perceive that they must, if married, also have a large family, and endure the various problems that are caused by it. This is especially true if the culture of the time encourages large families, but does not provide adequate resources to deal with the burden of the household it advocates. If there is animosity between siblings, people could be induced to stave off marriage as a way of ensuring peace in their own future household. Seeing one's mother having to clean and cook for a large family, in addition to perhaps working a part-time job, makes it easy to understand some of the bitterness she can feel at times. Realising that one's father works two jobs, sometimes twelve hours a day, coming home exhausted, annoyed and sometimes injured, is just as disturbing. These observations certainly do not paint a rosy, delightful picture of married life.

The size of one's family does not only affect one's perceptions of family life, but also affects the development of one's personality. Constantly encountering people within one's living space, sharing resources and negotiating compromises, can create psychological damage. Verbal and emotional expression can be restricted in order to hide vulnerability and protect oneself from unjustified attack. The lack of privacy, the absence of warmth and closeness from parents, the incapacity to articulate one's feelings, the barely contained vexation and anger, all might cause especially the younger members of the family to feel frustrated, isolated and insecure. Not surprisingly, research demonstrates that in families where discord and verbal abuse are common, men from such households are more likely to avoid female contact.[116] How can one suddenly become open and congenial to women when for years such attributes would have meant exploitation?

In spite of these dire scenarios that are fairly common today, and seen personally and in the media, we should not expect only one type of result from living in a large family. The dynamics of a large household can create not a dislike of marriage but may facilitate it, although it should be understood that one may not actually greatly admire this lifestyle.

Although constant contact with other members of a household can prevent the formation of constructive self-initiated activities, it does contribute to one's knowledge of the complexities of social relations. Such 'schooling' can be valuable in dealing with the opposite sex in the difficult milieu of puberty and school. In large families, individuals are always dealing with others' problems, helping and interacting. Experience with extensive and varied social interaction is gained, whether one desires to have it or not. Those growing up in smaller families have more time for themselves, but a lack of variety of contacts and situations may cause social skills deficits, and thus anxiety in dealing with the opposite sex.

Thus, we can see why people from large families would want to or would be able to marry *early*. They are not afraid of the opposite sex; larger families usually contain at least one sibling of the opposite sex, thus allowing the individual to have dealings with them on a personal level. Thus, the more children per women, the greater the probability of having both sexes among offspring. Men especially seem to need early exposure to females to be confident in courtship. Love-shy (or female avoidant) males are five times more likely to have grown up without sisters, and in homes that were isolated from the kin family network.[117] Males from large families, presumably well informed about the differences between the sexes, would have few qualms or little nervousness about asking girls out for dates, and so the road to marriage might be short.

Further, whilst growing up, an individual from a large family might have little opportunity for private activities, and might become, as compensation, more gregarious or socially-orientated. People from families of only one to three children have more free time for leisure and developing avocations than individuals from larger households, who are often deprived of the opportunity for hobbies, either because their parents did not have the money to supply each child with what he wanted, or due to continual interference from other family members. By the age of 18 or 21, such men do not have pre-existing personal or career interests that consume most of their time and resources. Thus, little substantively stands in the way of becoming a marriage partner and they might marry early, not wishing to move away from family life.

In contrast, hobbies and other self-based interests give the individual the potential to create something entirely of his own, reducing the need for dependence on another, thus facilitating the bachelor's life and delaying marriage. Such activities can lead to *less* of a desire to marry; indeed, marriage might be seen as standing in the way of such enjoyment. If high fertility is actually a factor in *prompting* early marriage, a man coming from a very large family will be *strongly* influenced to marry early as a way of keeping the closeness of family going. There would be little or no hiatus between the domestic life of childhood and that of adulthood, as both would be governed to a large extent by considerations about the welfare of others, not simply oneself. In this sense of foregoing the extended single life, the offspring of large families see the 'traditional' and the 'modern' dynamic as not very different from one another.

We can deduce that the overall opinion of one's home life has a rather peculiar non-linear relationship to marriage tendency. There is an inverted N-shaped relationship between the presence of problems at home and the desire to marry. When experiences are good (problems are few), people would want to repeat them, and so they would strongly desire to marry some day. As experiences become more negative, the desire fades. However, as experiences continue to worsen, people will increase the desire again in order to make up for neglect at home. The individual might nevertheless seek companionship that he did not receive at home, and this would *increase* the likelihood of cohabitation and marriage. Finally, as experiences become very bad, the individual completely puts off marriage.

We should make clear that problems with child-rearing might occur in a family of any size. But if larger families have certain characteristic aspects about them, then the effects on marriage patterns of these attributes should be easier to track when fertility is used; there are no generally available direct indicators of 'family goodness'. In short, people living in circumstances of crowding experience a complex variety of emotions that point to what happens in the household: dismay about married life; hopefulness about married life; closeness to one or more siblings; aggravation at the behaviour of siblings; happiness in having people to talk to; a certain emptiness; anxiety or anger. A wider variety of experiences lead the individual to become more socialised, creating a greater receptivity to married life, but also inspiring a cynicism about marriage and people in general. Moreover, culture makes its own contribution in determining how well a person from a large family turns out and his or her views on married life.

Three models can describe the interaction between family size and marriage behaviour. If the situation of a large family is handled well and/or turns out well, then an individual from such circumstances will be more likely to marry, based on a positive view of family and good social skills. However, if the *opposite* occurs and the individual feels neglected by siblings and parents, he might *also* be more eager to marry in order to finally get the satisfaction from the much vaunted promises of hearth and home. This tendency to be attracted to family life we call the *Profamilial Model* of family experience. If family life is perceived as unrelentingly negative, with his skills at interpersonal relations also being negatively affected, the individual would assuredly not want to repeat the experience; even if he did wish to marry, he could not do so easily in any case. The likelihood of such a person marrying early would be small, and the chance would be higher he or she marries late or not at all. This pattern could be called the *Antifamilial Model*. Further, if marriage age is *not* determined by the size of the family of origin, but to a large extent determines the size of the individual's own family (that is, the direction of causality being the reverse of the other two models), then this could be called the *Fertility Model*.

The three models are equally likely to occur in a population, given the same background factors. They are also equally logical and appear to be supported by research evidence. Studies show that in contemporary Western civilisations, children in large families are raised with less investment by parents, more adherence to rules, less individual attention, and a greater use of corporal punishment. These families produce individuals with lower IQ, lower academic achievement, and lower occupational status; they also produce an overabundance of antisocials and alcoholics.[118] The individual might prefer to sort out his problems alone, mistaking his own experiences with that of the typical family, confusing his Father and Mother with fatherhood and motherhood. Further, the presence of antisocial tendencies is what one would expect as the most negative consequence of social constriction in early life. The various social deficits contained in persons who fit the above profile would in many circumstances minimise choice of desirable and potential mates and thus delay marriage. If this is true, then we would expect to see across European civilisation evidence of the Antifamilial Model, where higher fertility produces later marriage. However, studies also show that the larger the family of origin, the greater the likelihood of *early* marriage, and that having more siblings increases expectations for early childbearing (which would concomitantly increase the probability of early marriage, *ceteris paribus*).[119] If a large family produces a dearth of affection in a culture that otherwise encourages emotional closeness, then clearly the offspring from large families would rush into marriage to obtain what they lacked at home. They would make a special effort to find someone that they think they could love, and marry them as soon as possible as a way of maintaining that love. Earlier marriage would ensue if the desire for companionship overrides all other considerations, and such a situation would be consistent with the Profamilial Model. Finally, the Fertility Model also cannot be dismissed, as we find that women who marry early are more likely to end up having higher fertility, that is, a large family of their own.[120]

Our own analysis of European cultures[121] shows that there is a *positive* correlation between fertility (family size) and marrying young, and a *negative* correlation between family size and marrying later in life. At the very least, this would appear to refute the Antifamilial model, and the Fertility and Profamilial Models are not to be discounted. We must at least allow for the possibility that the emotional and intellectual effects produced by a large family encourage marriage. However, as we are concerned here with causal direction, we might use a technique where statistical significance is derived from robust regression.[122] The results of this analysis suggest that *higher* fertility (and by implication a larger family of origin) induces men to marry *early*, and induces men and women to *not* marry late. It also demonstrates that early age of marriage for *women* subsequently affects fertility (presumably their own). To put it another way, *the tendency for males to marry early and to avoid late marriage, and the tendency for females to avoid late marriage, are both driven to a significant extent by the interactions brought about by the size of their childhood family*. It would appear that whatever reservations about domestic life people from large families might have are put aside. They seek companionship and closeness, possibly overcoming psychological problems that had developed in that home life with an attractive, smooth spontaneity in social relations, a facility learned from living with opposite sex siblings. The Profamilial model now seems supported.

Since the Fertility Model is still also valid to an extent, we should point to the fact that in order to derive significant results linking females and early marriage, the highest fertility rate country in the set (Ireland) must be removed; to obtain significant results for males (both early and late marriage), and females (late marriage), all countries must be left intact. The common factor for both men and women is early marriage, which prompts us first to ask: Why would the dynamic of early marriage for women be weakened when Ireland, with its relatively high fertility rate, is left in the set? Whilst it is somewhat risky basing our observations on only one country, because the country in question is so distinctly different from others, we can make some conclusions. Ireland is known to be a traditional country by virtue of its social standards, that is, at the time the data were collected, it had no legal divorce, no legal induced abortion, low overall crime rates, and, last but not least, a considerably higher than average fertility.[123] What distinguishes Ireland from other traditionalist countries in the set (such as Spain, Greece and Italy) is its high fertility and its only average figure for percent of brides who are 19 and under. The people of Ireland do not seem to connect marriage age and fertility in the same way as do people in other countries. If we assume that early marriage determines fertility (Fertility Model), then for all countries in our database except Ireland, there is a lower cap or limit to the contemporary potential for births compared to the past. The dynamics of *strongly* traditional nations might be well outside the ambit of contemporary standards, and fertility above a certain level is determined by other cultural factors.[124] In other words, Ireland's set of social standards is different from that of other nations, even traditional ones, causing it not to associate marriage age and fertility the way other countries do.

However, in the case of men this limit is higher, approaching standards that might have prevailed more than a hundred years ago. If men marry young, they can be expected (or allowed) to have large numbers of children. If we were to assume that early marriage for *men* results in higher fertility (Fertility Model), then traditionalist nations with high fertility do not disrupt this dynamic and should be left in the set. This is precisely what we see in our data. It is possible to integrate high fertility into a contemporary context but only from a masculine perspective, that is, matching a high proportion of grooms under 19 with a high number of births. Early marriage for women does not require very traditional standards and mores, but early marriage for a man does require such an outlook. Evidently, when men marry early, they are necessarily more traditional in their approach to family life than women and do not dismiss the idea of very large families. The rules governing the links between marriage age and births have changed for women, but not for men. Women can partially preserve traditional values in marrying young, but society and/or the individual does not tolerate the high fertility that typically used to go along with the early establishment of a married household. Because it is highly unusual for men to marry before age 20, people might think that such individuals are dedicated 'family men' and so are allowed more children. Early marriage for women is not nearly as extraordinary and thus such marriage is no compelling indication of family devotedness.

Similarly, high fertility nations must be included in the data for both men and women when considering *late* marriage. Traditional standards, as represented most strongly by nations that differ significantly from the modern average, make a difference when it comes to marrying late; larger families for men and women *do* prompt them to *avoid* marrying late. In general, it appears that in line with the Profamilial Model of the individual seeing family as an excellent source of satisfying social relations, extreme fertility values (large families) help *establish* the dynamic for late marriage (that delaying marriage is not a good idea), but these same values somewhat obfuscate the reasoning for early marriage because the Fertility Model appears to intervene.[125]

If having large families, or high fertility, is an older traditional pattern (as embodied, for example, in Irish culture), then perhaps the dynamic for relatively very large families is drawn from the past, whereas the pattern for early marriage, more from this century. Having numerous children is very rarely nowadays a pivotal factor in married life, as many of the variables that warranted it (such as using family members on the farm or in the shop, avoiding social isolation, economic support in old age) are no longer relevant, and other factors work against having many children (female careers, busy schedules, maintaining a slim, robust physical appearance). However, a large family of origin is still a factor in determining why men will leave home to marry early. The conditions that arise because of the presence of many children in the household are still as valid now as in the past, and economic and other modern circumstances appear not to have eradicated the distress caused by emotional compaction and a lack of privacy.

We thus have competing evidence for all three models, but each seems valid in different circumstances. On the whole, the evidence seems to point to the Profamilial Model, however, being most common: A movement *away* from forming one's own family due to an unpleasant home life is unlikely; people still have a strong *desire* to marry, regardless of home circumstances; men and women are *more* likely to marry when families of origin are *large*. Because of the frequent but shallow interactions in a large family, the individual might both desire and receive a relatively rapid union. Companionship that was denied in the family might be found in marital life, whereas the communications proficiency gained in that same emotionally lacklustre environment might expedite relations with the opposite sex. Thus, an extraordinarily 'active' home life no doubt often produces extraordinary individuals, who by their very 'extraordinary' nature are the subject of interest. However, such people are considered attractive not in respect to any great personal moral advantage, but in relation to an odd combination of characteristics which eventually end up granting no advantage. The individual uses the asset of skilful social intercourse to gain a certain freedom, but then tends to lose it in a bad marriage, a marriage undertaken in a rush to feed that major liability in his personality, his emotional starvation.

The ignorance of the family ideal that is central to the Antifamilial model is evidently refuted. People generally understand that the experiences in their family of childhood do not have to be the experiences of the family of adulthood. Nonetheless, it is important to remember that this analysis pertains to people who have great knowledge of other families and who have freedom in establishing their own lives. They were born in a period when smaller families, strongly growing economies, improving standard of living, increasing life expectancy and better health were emerging as ingredients of a 'normal' society. It is quite possible, however, that our ancestors would have avoided marriage if they themselves had come from large families, as a negative stereotype of the 'tribe-family' had been ingrained in the social consciousness of Western Europeans by the 19th century. The 'duty' to continue family traditions of occupation, family size, inheritance and so forth would have made many large- family individuals quite unwilling to marry, if that is the only way that the 'duty' could have been avoided. Consequently, the social factors that might *discourage* matrimony for a young person coming fresh out of a large household are not prevalent today. Even if people in our day are raised in a large family, prone to numerous disruptions, they might still have good reasons to marry anyway. Children, although still considered a necessary 'ingredient' to the ideal family, are no longer considered desirable in large numbers, as both parents and their offspring operate under different material and psychological principles. The necessity of intellect rather than brawn for completion of tasks, the availability of pensions and savings for retirement, careers outside the home—all have served to reduce the economic value of a child, and thus the necessity of high fertility. Moreover, society has come to emphasise the individual, and greater attention and time is now expected in educating and nurturing each child. A large number of children would make the attainment of this new social requirement nearly impossible. Further, the concept of family life might not be as tainted by the presence of numerous siblings as it was in the past. Larger houses, more privacy and activities outside the home can now defuse tense family relationships. Even if his own household did not possess the benefits of a well-functioning family, a modern 'mega-family' child could see in his environment examples of families who did. A wider purview is possible because the higher population density and media exposure of our day allows the average individual to come into contact with other households, no doubt many will be bad, but almost as surely, at least one good, and that is the critical paradigm that our more isolate forbears might have lacked. These windows on alternate forms of family life make it less likely that men and women who are the products of large families would feel badly about their upbringing; married life, even with many members in the household, does not necessarily have to be a horror, and ways could be found to cope. Therefore, the traditional patterns and constraints of married life have given way to modern lifestyles that allow for privacy, space, material wealth, more direct child-rearing, and quality of child care.

Antifamilial ideas, which are not borne out in the above studies and analyses, might have been more common in times past for these reasons.

To summarise, our analysis concurs with the argument that social conditions in the home have an influence on an individual's psyche, which in turn influences the decision to seek independence by moving out and marrying. A large family, like everything in life, has its advantages and disadvantages, but here the drawbacks might distinctly outweigh the benefits. It is indisputable that a large family can give warmth, support and security, which create a sense of solidity and predictability in life. On the other hand, greater crowding in the household is often associated with greater *loneliness*, which in turn increases the likelihood of depression and suicidal ideation. Both the *quality* and *quantity* of social interactions are actually pivotal in the individual's life, and congestion, lack of privacy, and lack of separation, can aggravate the tendency to inflict social or psychic damage.[126] If people intelligently used the resources life gives to them with a long-term view, except in the most crowded households, large families would present a uniquely rewarding experience. Unfortunately, zealous intelligent use of resources, for whatever reason, is not common in man, and a combination of the use and abuse of resources is more typical. The superficial short-sighted reaction to this family situation is most typical; although you feel close to one or more of your brothers or sisters, you also argue with them about the sharing of items, use of facilities, their prying and spying and so on; you feel entitled to a larger room or your own room, but there is no way you can obtain one. A viable solution out of this predicament is to marry as soon as you can, even before you have reached full maturity and are financially secure. The concept of love and the concept of autonomy are thus both put in significant jeopardy.

Thus, we find a violation of a seemingly fundamental premiss. The presence of more people around the home does *not* reduce loneliness but *increases* it when there is not adequate separation. There is little doubt that this is a significant factor when parents, children, and siblings suffer from a major inability to compromise. Ironically, the culture of today seems to emphasise companionship (marriage or pseudo-marriage) at all costs, even where there are major personality or psychological complications. In the next section we will examine a phenomenon where the focus is not on the use of marriage to facilitate an escape from the household for a fast solution to basic emotional wants, but rather using marriage in a more advanced attempt to manufacture emotional wholeness.

SUBSTITUTES

The way one's parents deal with each other and their children affects the way that one will appraise married life. Hence, attitudes about marriage undoubtedly form early within the family. If parents quarrel with each other, with relatives, with children, then one might see marriage as a battleground. Every child's life needs to be cultivated to a certain extent, which entails providing guidance, supervision, nurturance, protection, moral instruction, leadership, and material well-being. When this encouragement and promotion are missing, the child has fewer mental resources, and views married life as less satisfactory, useful and instrumental. The most distressing result of all is that such a child is made uncomfortable by social relations and sees himself as a stranger in his own culture and community. To such a person 'marriage' is a terrible strain; even if a man tries his best to find a good wife, the chances are small that he will succeed. It would make sense for him to put off marriage, and live life his own way for as long as possible in order to forestall the 'dreaded' life. Commentary about the joys of bachelorhood and the terrors of married life become common in such a society. Because of the embarrassment of having parents who failed to provide critical emotional and intellectual enrichment, feeble witticisms often taking the place of informative discussion.

If this attitude towards marriage were common, then there must be an easily perceptible cause within family life that affects communal life. It would stand to reason that *social disruption is an extension of disorder and instability in the household*. Simply put, disorder in the household produces disorder on the streets. In the modern age, there are a number of major event periods that have weakened the family bond. The effects of two World Wars and the Great Depression caused many families to split, because of migration, death or divorce.[127] Fathers were lost on the battlefield and the ones who came back were often disabled or had to search for work wherever they could find it. Movement to the cities from the countryside also divided families, and occupational routine changes, technological advancement and labour actions caused fundamental shifts in belief and attitudes. Moreover, the loss of children to war or disease can devastate the remaining family members. The surviving children, seeing this suffering in a unique way, with an understanding not easily available to outsiders, would want to avoid this themselves. Their reasoning is quite simple: If I never have children, then there is nothing to lose, no pain to suffer, no regrets or emotional turmoil.[128] In such a milieu, where parents struggle to keep the family afloat and deal with the exigencies of the workplace, the children very often receive poor guidance and attention. Individuals from families that witness privation and failure naturally intend to avoid such episodes in their own lives.

Absence or loss of a parent can occur even in the best of times, and does not have to be due to large-scale events such as war, economic depression, or occupational restructuring. The macrosocial situation is merely a multiplication of many similar private family situations. Friction in families based on selfishness and ignorance causes just as much if not more damage to a child's life than economic depression or migration. The increase in household disturbances, as fomented by divorce, domestic violence and the dislocations mentioned above, has been tied to a swelling of criminal activity. Clearly the result of antisocial feelings, the disturbing presence of youth-related crime is indicated by the significant increase in under age 18 arrests since 1950. Homicide, the most antisocial act of all, sharply increased in the United States in the first quarter of this century, reaching a peak in the 1930s, declining, then returning to its former peak by the 1970s.[129] Visible in research and anecdotal evidence, the effects of home life are indeed far reaching.

Thus, although the child of a seriously disrupted household might not see his situation duplicated on a large scale, his personal experience is nonetheless painful enough for him to seek amelioration. He might be all that much more eager to marry as a way of finding compensation for his loss, a way of obtaining the family life and the love he never had. Perhaps through their own marriage such people would attempt in adulthood to find the missing pieces of the mental structure that grants emotional independence, a project begun but not completed at home. An additional factor that might propel them into marriage might be an immature outlook, gained precisely from the same poor parental guidance and absence of nurturance that caused the problems originally at home. Thus, a poor and disrupted family life could lead to either delaying marriage or rushing into it, that is, late marriage or early marriage. Such a decision depends to a large extent on an individual's level of maturity, innate disposition to work, level of risk tolerance, ability to plan ahead and impose self-discipline, desire for companionship, ideas about love, and general expectations about what life has to offer.

However, there is undoubtedly a *mutual* relationship between society and family, where one affects the other at different times and places. Not only do events in the home influence the behaviour of individuals in the community, but events in the community affect the dynamics of marriages and families. This forms a pitiless cycle, where unsettled conditions in the community cause disruption in the home, which in turn produces even more societal turmoil. As we saw earlier, the stresses of modern life can 'contaminate' the household and induce many to refrain from marriage as a way of preventing such 'contamination'. However, as observation of our times can attest, government can only with difficulty prevent the stresses that originate in the household from contaminating society. The onus clearly rests with the individual to keep his home protected, a 'sacred' area of peace and tranquillity, safe from mental intrusions. With responsibility over social problems being constantly passed around, the 'buck' stops at one's own home.

Hence, one of the most important reasons why one would start courting or dating is to bring serenity to one's mind, through finding a substitute who can complete unfulfilled aspects of guidance, affection and support. Studies show that where a parent is absent, and a household is 'non-intact', dating starts earlier compared to an intact household.[130] The conditions at home often can be strenuous, with a single parent unable to keep harmony without a spouse. Such parents might be unable to make proper decisions without a consort; they might also, albeit unconsciously, push their children to marry as convenient way of removing them from the roster of household members. Arguments and contentiousness could easily break out as individuals compete for limited resources, against a background of financial uncertainty.

The individual, deprived of a sound intellectual disposition, might easily lose interest in a job or hobby. Fulfilling activities are no longer present, and to occupy this void he might turn to doing things that include other people. The need for companionship in a marriage could spontaneously result from the loss of friends, family or others who were close, and afforded emotional and material comfort, advice and protection. This loss typically occurs when the providers of the support or the one who is supported undergoes a change in schedule, a different job, or moves away. Such losses could prompt a search for other means of emotional gratification, which might include a romantic or companionate relationship.

In relation to individual mental development, often the worst disruption in the family, going beyond separation or divorce, is the actual death of a parent. There are obvious similarities between the life of a person coming from a family where there was little privacy, due to many children or little space, and a person who loses a parent or other loved one. As we have seen in the last section, the former experience less attention and affection than people in other family situations, and so do the latter, but with special difficulties. One can possibly repair relationships with parents in a household with structural limitations on affection but one has little recourse about actual physical removal of a parent. Therefore, the most critical of losses is that through *death or departure* of a mother and father. Not surprisingly, the loss of a parent can potentially instigate the strongest effects on the propensity to marry.

A parent can function as a *friend* and/or *mentor*. The loss of parent can thus entail losing both someone who provides companionship as well as someone who educates and edifies. The natural response to losing something is to find a replacement as good as if not better than the original. After the death or departure of a parent, grandparent, friend, or teacher, an intimate partner or spouse can function legitimately as a substitute. On the other hand, without an appropriate instructor in morals, ethics, and social behaviour, the individual might feel very unprepared to deal with life and close relationships. He might refrain from marriage out of fear of being unable to cope with a spouse and children and all of the responsibilities that that brings. Our examination here is similar to the one undertaken in the previous section, with people becoming broadly pro- or anti-family; however, we refrain from using these terms since 'family' as a whole is not the influence, but only one or two members who act as individual forces.

In pursuing an investigation of how people react to the loss of a parent, we must differentiate between different kinds of mortality because they impose different kinds of psychological harm. 'Death rate', meaning deaths as a proportion of the whole population, is an indicator of *general* loss, of people of any age group who might therefore represent any role in the family. Because each death in a person's social circle or community might affect a different area of life, it betokens indefinite feelings of disorientation and pessimism. The death of someone linked to an age category, on the other hand, signifies the loss of a *specific* role model. Since every age group brings different responsibilities, and since these responsibilities can be grouped into 'role' categories, such as student, bachelor, apprentice, nurturer, confidante, teacher, patriarch and so on, age of death is connected to a particular form of social disruption. Two or more deaths within a particular age category indicates a more intense or pointed loss of a role model. A deprivation of overall guidance from one or more persons often follows the demise of an older person and can engender a retreat, especially when the death is of a father figure. Hence, the impact that death has on the individual is direct and not merely abstract. We can see that in a country where the death rate is higher than average, marriage age and tendency would also be untypical.[131]

Thus, psychological injury in childhood and adolescence influences at what point in their life development people marry. Wholeness in family life comprises moral and ethical support and instruction in cooperative living. The loss of these components could produce an inadequate or dysfunctional model of marital life and parenthood. Cessation of support and instruction about the socially correct way to deal with a family results in one of two possible attitudes:

(A) A reluctance to marry out of fear of committing errors because of inadequate upbringing, or
(B) A reckless rush into marriage out of ignorance of the pitfalls, because of a desire to finish one's personality development through deep personal involvement.

We should first point out that, in studying any changes in death rates, the two effects might be masked by an opportunism effect, that is, people marry because death presents a chance for marriage that did not exist before. For example, if there is an increase in the number of deaths in a community, the marriage rate increases because the newly widowed, with good financial resources, are attractive to people who have been delaying marriage precisely in order to build up their assets. The rush into marriage is not because people want to make up for losses in their own families, but because they are taking advantage of losses in someone *else's* family. If society puts much emphasis on inherited wealth and savings, and not on earned income, then this phenomenon would be expected to occur. In earlier times, when death rates increased, celibacy and marriage age *decreased*, that is, when more people died, more were willing to marry.[132] This fact would appear to support (B) above. However, more people married possibly because a larger pool of available people became present when the death rate rose, thus facilitating matrimony, especially for individuals with high standards concerning financial status and personality. For some, it was not a case of marrying to compensate for deficiencies in the family, but simply a seizing of opportunity that the large pool of 'single' men and women (widowers and widows) offered. This dynamic would not really apply in our day, as the death rates are far lower than in the past, and there are relatively fewer widows or widowers looking to remarry. More importantly, the belief in opportunism in marriage is less prevalent because of the increased emphasis on the individual's money-making ability. Getting rich through marriage is seen as an activity distinctly lacking in altruism. If the belief is present at all, it has taken the form of a 'gold-digging' mentality that has little room for contemplating marriage unless there are substantial returns from the committal.

Another factor might also mask the effect that emotional and intellectual relations within the family of origin have on the choice of spouse and timing of matrimony. In a time of increasing deaths, whatever disorders are killing people are causing others to fall ill and require assistance, giving individuals more of a reason to seek the support of a spouse. The underlying social phenomenon of this factor would likely be based on a *fear* of sickness and death, which could arise in times of plague or famine, that is, in times of a sharp rise in the death rate. This could work in conjunction with the phenomenon mentioned above, that as more marriages are dissolved due to the death of one member, more people are eligible for marriage. Both dynamics can force an increase in the marriage rate when the death rate increases. However, as the year to year fluctuations in death rates are small in modern industrialised nations, it is not likely that more than a very small number of people will take these actions. When the death rate rises, not many men and women will marry early as a result of increased opportunity for wealth (availability of widows or widowers). Likewise, few will marry in order to use companionship as a proactive means of dealing with future or present ailments. A death appears to influence the behaviour of more than one person (a potential spouse looking for material gain or health provision); mortality carries an emotional impact where the loss of one person is leveraged, so that the lives of two or more people are touched. A change results in the operational patterns in the household of origin, or a household socially near the individual (for example, an uncle or grandparents).

After accounting for these two exceptional situations, we might pose the following question in relation to contemporary standards: Does a relatively high *death rate* in Western cultures entail *late or early* marriage for men and/or women? Based on the previous section's finding of more stability in late marriage results, we should see if analyses of modern data reveal whether high death rates and low life expectancy or whether low death rates and high life expectancy are associated with late marriage and permanent celibacy.

The results from an analysis of Western nations can be summarised as follows (dynamics apply about equally well for both men and women, except for the propensity to never marry, which only applies for women):

Table 4

Effect of mortality on marriage age and propensity to never marry.		
Mortality	Effect on marriage age	Effect on propensity to never marry (females)
+death rate, general	later marriage (weak)	less likely
-death rate, general	earlier marriage (weak)	more likely
+death rate, age specific	earlier marriage	more likely
-death rate, age specific	later marriage	less likely
-life expectancy	earlier marriage	more likely
+life expectancy	later marriage	less likely

Our research shows that people understandably react quite strongly to the loss of a parent or parental figure, more so than when reacting to family size, which was discussed in the previous section. A higher general death rate induces men and women to eschew marriage in their 20s, and encourages later marriage.[133] However, using age-specific death rates is more instructive than the general death rate, as they provide stronger correlations.[134] Males and females respond more explicitly to *specific* loss than general loss, but females react less strongly than males in reference to late marriage but as strongly to early marriage.[135] Thus, when it comes to the decision to marry late (over 30), men and women both respond, albeit rather weakly, to general loss of the 'significant others' around them, of whatever age. Not only do many men and women avoid putting off marriage after experiencing a specific loss, but they also show a tendency to rush to form a companionate relationship (marry at age 19 and under), an effect that is equally significant for both males and females.[136]

Another way to measure the loss of significant figures is through the use of life expectancy, specifically for men. The results are similar as those for age- specific death rates. Keeping in mind that the age for fathers that would be critical in raising a family would be between the ages of 35 to 50, a *longer* life leads to *later* marriage, and *lessens* the likelihood of not marrying at all,[137] that is, a negative impact by a family member on one's early life makes one less likely to marry early whilst not rejecting it altogether. Other things being the same, the *shorter* life-span implies a higher death rate, which means that fathers, mothers or a similar authority figure would die relatively young. This loss stimulates a tendency for some sons and daughters to avoid marrying late, and some daughters to never marry or marry very late (past age 45).

Since age-specific correlations are all positive with early marriage and negative with late marriage, and the general death rates are positive with late marriage, the two types of indicators cannot both be describing the same phenomenon. It is logical to assume that if a single death in any age group causes the individual to delay marriage, then a single age-specific death cannot *also* hasten marriage. Thus, a *single* death's effect on perceptions might not be that significant, but more consistency is obtained when a person experiences *multiple* deaths. More than one death, but in different age groups, would cause the individual to perhaps pursue (A); he has the ability to deal with life but not with close, intimate relationships. Some disruption has occurred in personal intellectual and emotional growth, but not enough to cause dependence on someone else for completion of 'training'. It appears probable that experiencing more than one death in an age group *reverses* this tendency, and impels people to marry. The age-specific death rate represents a multiplier in an age group and general death rate a singularity since it is not likely people lose more than one person in the same age group over a period of a few years. The connections between marriage age and general death rates can be explained by considering the links between age and social roles: the general death rate could indicate the death of a person from any social group, but the age-specific death rate refers to individuals within certain social categories.[138] As the general death rate can be for any age, it is *inclusive* of the specific age groups. By 'any age' we mean any status or role, and so a wider range of possible disruptions can occur, in one case a cousin, another an uncle, another a parent, another a friend, and so on. Modern people, being socially adept, are quite resourceful in gaining knowledge, succour and advice; they can employ people from different age groups, and thus different *social roles*. The loss of someone from one age group can be compensated for by becoming close to someone else, from the same age group. But a loss of two or more people in the *same* age group is more disruptive.

The particular roles of people lost within the individual's social circle can be discerned by seeing that males and females both peak in correlation (significance) in the same age groups, namely: deaths in the age group 55 to 59 and the age group 70 to 74. These groups would represent, for people in their 20s, the roles of parent and grandparent respectively. Further, robust regression shows that the age of greatest impact on late marriage is 45 to 49, which if a father, would affect a son or daughter as a teenager. We can see that loss can have its greatest power when it occurs at critical points in a person's life. The 55 to 59 age group incorporates parents, and the group 70 to 74 incorporates grandparents. The individual who was the child and grandchild, respectively, of the deceased would be around 22 at the time of death, that is, the beginning of a career and independent life. If the parent were in their late 40s, then the affected child would be in puberty. Thus, the loss of a parent or grandparent would most clearly be felt on children who are 15 to 25, and would create the most significant impact on the value of companionship.

We should add that although people would most naturally form close associations with parents, it is not uncommon for individuals to have warm relationships with a grandparent, who can be more of a friend than a parental figure, since there is often no necessity for the older person to maintain a higher rank or position of authority. The removal of either figure might make the individual search for emotional counterparts, and this increases the likelihood of early marriage. When figures from *both* generations, such as a parent and grandparent, are lost and in a relatively short period of time, the individual is presumably even more impelled to marry quickly. Hence, a person is most impacted by major loss around the time when major concepts of the world are in formation and around the time when marriage is being seriously considered. Two or more such tragedies exact a disproportionate reaction, where the total loss is perceived as greater than the sum of the individual losses. Such disruptions in ideas and mental development cause people to seek a companionate relationship for comfort, maintenance and as a framework for a personal evolutionary process that was arrested earlier in life.

Besides attitudes (A) and (B) described above, a number of other, less likely reasons could account for the observation that the premature death of a parent leads to a greater likelihood of *earlier* marriage. We know that children rely on parents, but it is quite possible that parents can rely on children. Such reliance might be so great that matrimony is degraded or discouraged, as it would seriously hinder the friendship that has arisen. In fact, a parent might look to a child as a spousal replacement, who can provide the loyalty that was not forthcoming in marriage. Such closeness can encourage a protective (or a 'caged') atmosphere, where in older age, sons and daughters may see themselves as guardians of their mothers (especially if her husband is no longer there), feeling that for the time being, they must sacrifice emotional gratification for the sake of filial duty. When a parent dies in such a close relationship, then the individual would desire a replacement in order to continue to experience close supportive relations, this time with a new, though not necessarily similar, personality. In addition, as an incentive to stay with a parent, the substantial part of an inheritance might be promised to the child who remains as guardian, providing them with a good material foundation for their own life. At the death of both parents, the individual is 'set free' and left with a desire to continue a close guardian relationship with someone else, a relationship built on a significant monetary foundation. This dynamic was more common in past times, and it is not particularly relevant in our century, where the savings of one generation have not made for that much of an addition to the living standard of the following generation.

Each generation enjoys a large improvement in income that makes it easier for the individual to save or borrow enough money on his own to form an independent household. However, this might change.

Further, the death of a parent can produce a need not only for emotional support but also for *physical* support. People generally put great store in patterns of activity, no less so than in the area of health. A son or daughter is the carrier of the genetic material of both parents, and so episodes of physical weakness in either might well be repeated in the offspring. Thus, grave illness in one or both parents in mid-life spurs unfortunate predictions about one's *own* future health. In many such cases, there is a dreadful anticipation that the same pattern of illness, with small variations, will befall oneself. In the case of precocious invalidism, marriage becomes an extension of the idea specified in (B) above, where 'love' must include critical care during sickness. Hence, the fear of a shorter life span with poor health (either real or imagined) might encourage them to seek companionship as the most important goal in life. The spouse then on many occasions acts as a type of health attendant, in addition to having other functions and playing other roles. Marriage in this case becomes an extremely meaningful life concept, as one's very physical well-being depends on someone else. However, other people, with similarly high concepts about marriage, especially when it comes to physical care, might never find a spouse because it is difficult to fulfill the requirements. Even with the fear of illness, they prefer to wait, thinking being saddled with a spouse and children as well as one's own infirmities is worse than only having to take care of oneself, an overwhelming task only in the worst circumstances.

If life expectancy is longer, however, then such emotional concerns might not be important; a devoted partner is not a necessity when one feels one will 'live forever', and so one could be more assertively independent. Marriage is relegated to a secondary, though still meaningful, role, and the individual might marry late simply due to a lack of a good reason to marry earlier. Health is therefore a major concept that can significantly enslave or empower.

We can say that in some cases the *supportive* function of a spouse is eclipsed by what he or she might bring *materially* to the marriage. In essence, the nursemaid is then less important than the business partner. Marriage is not held in such high esteem; one does not have to put off marriage forever because a person cannot be found that aptly fills all personality departments. As in any 'business' enterprise, partners fundamentally operate not on a psychological, emotional or intellectual level, but on a simple material level, and people can therefore be moulded and shaped, they can change to meet the demands of the situation. Thus, the range of choice for potential partners is much greater. On the other hand, some in the same situation might marry late, being too buried in the demands of their life. A spouse might have some attractive qualities, but these are in competition with career, leisure pursuits and revelry. The larger implications of our discussion are explored later in our investigation into how society's attempts to deal with the conflict between love and independence have made personality and habit differences between spouses a burden.

In conclusion, to answer the main question posed earlier, it would appear that men and women respond, although somewhat weakly, to loss of emotionally significant figures, of whatever age, by putting off marriage. It is likely that more than one figure must be lost to have a consistent impact on marriage propensity. Since the general death rate captures losses from different age groups, the effect of loss is 'spread around', so the person does not feel incapacitated. Development, however, is hindered to the extent that relationship might be kept at a distance. When *specific* role models are taken into consideration, as in the reaction to multiple deaths within key age groups, such as that of parent or grandparent, the direction changes. At around the time of average or expected marriage age, a loss of a parent or grandparent would make both men and women want to marry earlier, not later. We can see that disruption of key personal relationships have a measurable impact on how people appraise connubial life. Other factors that lead to affiliation with the opposite sex are either ignored or trivialised. Whilst other issues are not to be discounted, there is little doubt that the loss of a parent or other authority figure has a significant effect on the decision to marry.[139]

Hence, considerations about space, privacy, family size, living outside the family, the loss of important family members, seem to have profound effects on the urge for 'romantic' involvement. The conclusion to be drawn from the preceding discussions is that men and women obtain highly significant assistance from each another on a wide variety of matters. But this assistance is not necessarily exclusively obtained from the opposite sex, much less a love interest. One can obtain help from family members, relatives and friends, regardless of sex. The most close relationship, and thus the context in which assistance can best be used, is between a man and woman connected by entrustment. People ultimately rank emotional satisfaction over that of intellectual or pragmatic interest. What lies at the nexus of all human activity is what one most desires in life, and that is to be loved, and to be loved means to have another pair of hands help in reigning in the volatile, ever-changing forces of the world. If one does not obtain this protection at home, because of the confusion that arises out of a large, crowded household, or the death or departure of parents and relatives, then one will seek it in others, even offering the wedding ring as a means of securing it. Such desire overcomes many obstacles, even the obstacles of doubt based on troubling personal family experiences, which by themselves would otherwise effectively hinder marriage.

THE WEIGHT OF MANY INFLUENCES

In this chapter we have analysed a number of material and psychological factors that are critical in the planning process for marriage. These factors were family size, expenses related to courtship and marriage, living arrangements in early adulthood, amount of privacy at home, death of a parent and/or other emotionally significant relative.

We would now like to know how these factors work together. It should be borne in mind that putting variables which otherwise are significant in bivariate combinations do not necessarily work when together into one equation. The effect of, for example, two variables acting independently on my behaviour might be well established. I might have two friends, John and Simon, each of whom exerts a significant influence on my purchase decisions. The more either of my friends insists on buying something, the more likely will it be that I actually buy it. However, if we *combine* the influences of these two friends on my thinking, we find that my decisions then become more unpredictable. If both friends are highly insistent on the appropriateness of a purchase I have in mind, I might become *less* likely to buy it, simply to show that they 'can't push me around'. For the same reason, if both John and Simon are very much against my purchase, I might also resist their opinions. I might then turn to a third friend, whose influence is not recorded, and ask for his advice. Whatever the case, the independent influence of the two friends is not doubted: each can definitely sway my opinion. But the joint influence of their opinions, if and when it does arise, holds to a different dynamic. Hence, the interaction of social forces, predictable under certain circumstances, is not predictable in others.

In the case of influences on the decision to marry, similar motivations might be found. For example, a small amount of privacy (space) and a large family size each separately might induce a desire to 'break-out' and to marry early; however, when the effects of both factors are combined, a desire to *not* marry early might be become manifest. One might be overtaken by a 'smothering effect' that makes one desperate to reach out into the resource pool of the immediate social environment in order to find solutions beyond the simple or obvious. Thus, marriage and family might be seen as overly taxing, and some temporary companionship might be sought. The resources which they call upon could be numerous and quite varied, and cannot easily be captured within a single analysis.

At the risk of oversimplification, but for the sake of comprehensibility and cogency, we attempt to combine as many as possible of the variables mentioned in this chapter into one 'grand' equation. This will allow us to visualise how these influences might operate and coalesce to affect age of marriage. We find that not all can be combined, but good results can still be derived which can be made understandable at the personal level.

The influences that make people marry young (age 19 and under) and those that make people marry late (30 and over) appear to affect two different segments of the population. The former segment might be more immature by nature, less desirous of independence, and the latter might be more developed intellectually and introspective. This is underscored by the fact that there are fewer variables impinging on the decision to marry early than on the decision to marry late. One would suspect that more mature and intelligent people would take into account more variables in their decision than people not so endowed.

In the case of early marriage for men, family size and death of a parent are significant.[140] We might say: If you belong to this segment, if you came from a relatively large family and experienced the death of a father you would have a tendency to marry early. Cordial relations with people are placed higher in priority than social status, and the loss of such a distinguished person in your life makes you seek a substitute, even if this person is not a distinct parental-figure. As your family was larger than usual, you are accustomed to dealing with people, which might facilitate your desire to start your own home as soon as possible, as a way of making up for the lack of affection in childhood.

In the case of early marriage for women, family size, recreation expenses, and privacy are significant variables.[141] We must note that in the case of women, large family size might be the result of early marriage rather than the cause. If you are in this segment, if you came from a large family where there was little privacy, but you had the means to enjoy leisure activities and recreation at relatively low cost, you would experience a tendency towards early marriage. Thus, like men, you desire to break out and start your own family, to make up for the dearth of affection and attention whilst growing up. The fact that women in this position might have had little privacy, being pushed into close living quarters for many years, also contributes to the feeling that in order to become 'adult' they must obtain their own residence and furnishings. However, this must be shared with someone else in order to make it meaningful and to make it stable. Interestingly, the death of a father does not contribute one way or the other to the decision to marry early.

Late marriage for both men and women is influenced by family size, privacy, the death of a parent, and recreation expenses.[142] Thus, the segment involved, more refined and intelligent, would marry late. The following scenario might be present: you grew up in a small family, with lots of private space for yourself, but you suffered the death of a father at some point as a teenager, and you find that recreation expenses are high. You feel that, as do certain men, status is highly important, and that you are privileged in this regard because you enjoy great privacy and have a small family with good interaction, but are hindered to an extent in meeting the opposite sex because of the high cost of socialising. You have the opportunity to develop your own rewarding activities, whilst still feeling that others respect you. The death of your father or father-figure definitely makes you feel more isolated because this has not happened to your peers; you feel different from them and thus less involved in peer relationships. Also, this loss makes you feel that you have not obtained as much instruction about life and people, making you reluctant to start intimate relationships out of fear that you will do something wrong. This attitude fits in with the rest of your personality, which demands refinement, solitude, and adequate preparation.

We note that the variable we use as a proxy for death of a father can either have a negative or a positive influence on late marriage, depending on whether this variable is used by itself or in conjunction with other variables. It would appear that two different segments of the population interpret this differently. For those who are not status-orientated, and thus who do not take privacy, family size, and expenses simultaneously into account in their lives (that is, they are not using multiple variables as described above), but who are still people- orientated, the death of a father clearly means desiring that a substitute be found, and so marriage is hastened. The loss of one relationship demands the setting up of a similar or replacement relationship. But for those who are more status- orientated, more sensitive to external judgements, the loss of a father means to delay, not hasten, marriage. In this case, the loss of the father, when taken in conjunction with other factors of import to the individual, creates the sense of delayed maturity, of an incomplete up-bringing. Consistent with this outlook is the belief that small families and privacy are part of a superior lifestyle.

Before we finish this section, it behoves us to make two points about the applicability of the above analyses. We have already suggested that it is likely that the type of person we have been discussing in this section, especially the late marrier who takes several variables together in evaluating their lives, is not entirely ordinary. They are more likely to be deep thinkers with a penchant for unconventional solutions to problems. For imaginative, perhaps introverted, people, a rich inner world can be constructed if enough personal space and privacy are available. Through books, television and other media, situations pictured in the mind provide contact with imagined friends from other times and places, who can become substitutes for the inadequate social relations of the external world. The loss of a parent, and the reduced social interaction in the household, might actually necessitate such a construction. Far from being pathological or strange, such mental fabrications can vastly improve a person's life, and just as importantly, prevent imprudent involvement with the opposite sex. Thoughtful people, who take into account a multiplicity of variables, are also more likely to build such an inner world, more so after the loss of a parent. This world creates a refuge, thus delaying or largely obviating marriage.

Moreover, although many in a modern population have experienced one or more of the negative living situations described above (large families with four or more children, the death of a parent, very small living space), there are many others who have not. However, there is little doubt that the *elementary* factors of attention, advice, privacy and support have, when held back, to some extent an effect on *all* people. These underlying forces can only be observed manifesting themselves in certain ways, putting limitations on the analysis of international data. The limitations are not necessarily applicable in real life; we should whenever possible focus on basic dynamics not on the manifestations. Further, we should not think that the factors that constrain our analysis also limit the ambit and expression of that factor in everyday life. For example, the death of a parent produces problems similar to the experiences caused by the abandonment by a parent, divorce, separation, or excessive overtime and travelling. The tendency to seek alternative means of support outside the home might be, in these cases, significantly increased, although not as much as if that father had died. All situations, however, relate to the *same* basic underlying factors which then affect the child: loss of support and advice. Consequently, he or she evacuates to alternative relationships earlier in life, abandoning family relationships, when the home situation is not supportive enough, whatever the actual reason. The small numbers of people who are affected directly by the phenomena under study should not make us think that these factors influence only a minority of a country. The same factors exist in some quantity in the lives of all people. Thus, the factors studied here apply to everyone, or potentially to everyone, and cannot be ignored.

As the contours of the present time resolve into shape, often we find distinguishing features that separate it from the past. We ask: What new world have we discovered on our adventure, to what land has the ship of modernism sailed? As long as the new country provides plentiful harvests, the people have seen fit to leave the problems of love and marriage to the individual. Our attitude, of course, is not so indifferent. We note that the children born in this new land treat socialising, courtship and recreation differently; they are insistent on early departure from the home of childhood; they are more arrogant and materialistic about life expectations; they have more unattainable ideals; and they have less virtue. What still remains from the country of forbears are the immutable ideals of love and emotional fulfilment, the importance of parental companionship in childhood, the critical need for both similarities and differences between spouses, and the centrality of economics in married life. However, the long-term viability of modern marriages, based as they are, at least in part, on factors totally unrelated to the background and concerns of the spouse, is much in doubt. Since the part of the relationship that delivers affection and fulfilment is now potentially disturbed by thoughtlessness and opportunism, we are compelled to examine the most basic aspects of relationships and how they have been impacted by the source of this selfishness, namely the modern desire for independence. In the next chapter, we shall discuss the underlying personality factors that contribute to creating a bond between a man and a woman, some of which, whilst remaining unchanged in their effectiveness, have been unwisely re- prioritised or ignored altogether. It will be apparent that over the last two centuries, the parameters of male-female relationship, usually discreet in nature and only infrequently of interest to national leaders, have undergone such a transformation that the modern materialistic society, which spurred these basic changes, can no longer claim that they are beyond serious public concern.

He was reputed one of the wise men that made answer to the question, when a man should marry?
'A young man not yet; an elder man not at all'.
~Francis Bacon (1561-1626)

For every marriage then is best in tune
When that the wife is May, the husband June
~Rowland Watkyns (fl. 1660)

Chapter 4
A Search for Simplicity

Don't Waste Time: Think Alike

Although economic and material issues are important in the decision to marry, the desire to have emotional contact with someone else, the need for compassion and companionship has always been and always will be a preeminent factor. In the last chapter, we have seen how factors unrelated to the pertinent aspects of the relationship can become the motivating factors for marriage. In the lives of almost everyone, at one time or another, there is either a psychological or a practical need to have an intimate relationship with the opposite sex. This might or might not fit in with other life plans, and sometimes the conflict is difficult to resolve especially when independence is at stake. It is self evident that all people desire love, and they wish to have it from early in life, but if they do not get it, they will try to find it with other people, such as friends, roommates, lovers, or spouses. Thus, a husband might say 'I love my wife', but he does not really love her, because he married her *to be loved*, not necessarily because there was the good possibility of *mutual* love. Within the ideal of love is the concept of wholeness, which we explored in terms of family life; if it could not be found there, then people search elsewhere, often to their own and another's detriment. Since people do not seem to understand what is necessary for real love, true wholeness, namely virtue, then we must investigate the other factors that make for a close relationship. In previous chapters, it became apparent that people place a high premium on the need to be understood and recognised, to be taught and comforted. When one does not operate in a sophisticated manner to attain these goals, one devolves to using simple devices to get what one wants. Since depth and cooperation are now lacking, only a superficial agreement is perceived to be necessary in companionate relationships. People therefore determine the usefulness of other people by evaluating them according to the most basic intellectual principle: cataloguing similarities and differences. One holds up the mirror to see one's own personality, and then puts it down to see how others compare. Hence, we study in this chapter the importance that both similarity and complementarity in background and temperament have in fulfilling the personal ideal of love.

A married couple's relationship contains all the same functions as an ordinary dyadic friendship, including factors that control distance, support, and advice. The fundamental principles underlying the need for similarity and emotional gratification are obtained in the same way between any two people, regardless of gender. However, the *priority* or order of these factors is not the same. One can be attracted to someone else because one sees a trait that one approves of or admires. What is admired is either a trait that one possesses, or a trait that one would like to possess but does not. Working under the assumption that the individual is as equally pleased to see a trait in himself as in other people, the list of admired traits that he desires in the perfect mate would be very similar to the one that he believes himself to possess. That being the case, we would expect that in relationship dyads, both individuals possess at least a few major traits in common. The principle can be summarised by using the oft-used but accurate expression: 'Like attracts like'.

Besides the statement by the Greek philosopher Democritus that 'Similarity of mind makes friendship', there is ample evidence from various cultures attesting to this principle as a major factor in settling on a mate. Primitive societies restrict marriage to within classes (such as in India), moderately advanced societies control various social gatherings as part of mate choosing mechanisms, and advanced societies use informal but nonetheless essential procedures that reduce choices of individuals that are likely to be too dissimilar.[143] These customs reflect a collective interest in reducing the pool of potential candidates to people with a background similar to oneself. Nevertheless, it is possible that one can be strongly attracted to another because the latter has a trait or traits that one does not have. Although it would be irrational for someone to be drawn to someone else if they evoke repugnant characteristics, it is not at all irrational to desire the companionship of someone who is fundamentally different, if a mutual *enhancement* of life can take place. Indeed, it would be irrational *not* to take advantage of this *complementarity*, which can lead to firmer, more resilient marriage, through a dovetailing and interweaving of interests and background. When someone is able to effectively draw upon the resources of another, only an improvement in the life situation can occur. The couple act as a coordinated unit, and every challenge strengthens the relationship, making it more and more difficult for them to separate. Therefore, the relationship is made whole and functional by different aspects; whilst deep mutual respect of virtue is the skeleton, similarity of temperament, traits and experiences makes up the flesh, and dissimilarity is the muscle and sinew. Indeed, the couple no longer have a mere 'relationship', but have attained a true, deep bond, an inextricable connection with each other.

The term we shall be using to refer to substantive difference is *heterology*, and to refer to the positive emotional response to such a difference as *heterophily*.

Thus, we can say that X, a trait, belief or attitude found in one partner and not the other, is a heterology, whilst the *attraction* that exists between these partners because of this incongruence is heterophilic. We can refer to a basic likeness as a *homology*, and the satisfaction that arises from the matching of ideas as *homophily*. Often the word homology refers to any similarity that is the result of common origin. In this case we are not using it explicitly as such, although frequently people who do have very similar attitudes and behaviours tend to come from the same background, social class or region.

Heterology and homology have multifaceted effects on the individual, effects that are as varied as those engendered by the virtues, but the impact is not immediately apparent. Differences between people can be quite beneficial. The recognition of dissimilarity in experience leads to the establishment of one's own unique domain of knowledge, which builds respect and thus a more open relationship, where independence can be tolerated. In contrast, one cannot really interfere in a domain one knows little about. Heterology also tends to keep a critical distance between individuals and stops them from becoming overly assertive and thus imperiling the relationship.

There are also many advantages in having two people who are substantively similar, but here we will focus only on those areas that are connected to the issue of independence, namely where homology provides a *supportive* function. Similarity in basic habits creates a mutual understanding and an *ease of doing*. There are relatively few restraints in situations where homology is present, such as in a relationship where the parties cohabitate or otherwise spend a great deal of time together. Synchronisation of habits, temperament, desires and so on become significant when the situation is one where they both want to engage in some activity at the same time and in the same depth, such as studying, shopping, going out to the movies, or going on holiday. When a mutually beneficial activity can be performed alone, such as reading, gardening, cooking, or filling out forms, then one does not necessarily have to seek out companions with similar traits.

Similarity between persons is also important for those times when an individual feels a sentimental or nostalgic need to reminisce; shared experiences and attitudes are necessary for this important social function. More frequently, similarity is desired when balancing an uncertain and chaotic period with a secure, calm predictable period. Personality and experiential resemblances bring ease of social transaction which compensates for the dissatisfaction of dealing with people who are dissimilar to oneself. Communication can also be greatly facilitated when terms, metaphors, and ideas are mutually understood. For example, an educated person cannot deal effectively with an uneducated one because the latter would not understand the former's allusions.

Just as individuals choose friends based on similarity in race, personality, background, attitudes, and behaviour, they choose an opposite-sex love interest using comparable criteria. However adequate one might find general similarity in a same-sex relationship, a deep friendship between the sexes requires extensive mutual support and compensation. Young people form associations in the attempt to find a 'mirror' for their attitudes and behaviour, without necessarily seeking to obtain something more deeply emotionally gratifying. Such a relationship is bound to be more self-centred, where people surround themselves with a fortification built of interchangeable figures. The lack of experience with complementary relationships does not usually have deleterious effects, as young people have others readily at hand, often parents and teachers, to compensate for their weaknesses. When it comes to relations with the other sex, however, they are out on their own, and then this lack of experience becomes a hindrance. Thus, what is important in a same-sex relationship might not be very important in a cross-sex friendship, and vice versa. Consequently, out of awkwardness, and in an attempt to find common ground, young men often focus on the rudimentary or biological nature of male-female relations, conceptions which are tied to perpetuation of family and race. Everyone agrees that this is, after all, what 'mating' is ultimately about in the larger world of nature. With human beings, however, there is an added psychological goal of a perpetuation of self, specifically by defining and maintaining one's own self-image. The physical charms are thus accentuated, and a man finds some safety and relief in the soft, warm, sweetly perfumed embrace of a woman, which validates his manhood without threatening it.[144]

Studies demonstrate much can be said for establishing common ground between men and women. Harmonious relations in an intimate opposite-sex relationship depend upon similitude in education and social class,[145] race,[146] and religion.[147] Homology in personality and status also produces greater equality in the performance of physical and emotional tasks, as well as a greater dependence and commitment, a lower level of conflict and a higher level of satisfaction with the relationship.[148] Differences in personality traits and social background, on the other hand, increase the risk of breakup.[149] Close friendships between young people are *not* predicated on coincidence of ideological positions and social policy questions. Religious matters are important only when such ideas are endorsed and circulated by organised social movements. Thus, 'trivial' habits and matters of taste are *highly* important.[150] We can see that there is evidence that individuals in seeking a mate focus more on similarity in personality than in building an autonomous lifestyle, such as produced by achieving higher rank or prestige.[151]

This is not to say rank and other social components have no value, but rank simply has a lesser value in these relationships than in same-sex relationships. Often cross-sex associations are based on a male trying to 'score' with a girl, in order to raise his status by getting a girlfriend, daring behaviour or rule-breaking. However, aspects of the close friendship are prioritised in the same way regardless of romantic involvement. In same-sex relationships, concordance in personality evidently comes first, then rank; in opposite-sex relationships, personality is also primary, but is followed more distantly by rank compared to same-sex relationships. Perhaps anticipating that this will bring stability and predictability, people go out of their way to choose mates who have similar traits, especially in regards to 'minor' aspects of temperament and disposition. They might use the relationship to improve their standing in the group (as young people often do), but the test of relationship viability is agreement in feelings towards music, clothes, food, school, teachers, etc. Hence, homology is extremely important in the *formation* of relationships between men and women, with heterology and thus complementarity taking a secondary role.

Considering how well the evidence shows that similarity between partners can preserve individual independence, there should be little surprise about the finding that most marriages in the present day are strongly homologous.[152] Indeed, on attributes such as age, race, region of origin, education, attitudes, political and religious affiliation, matching is very high, on the order of 50% to 100%. Matching in cognitive abilities and psychiatric disorders is only about 20% to 50%; intriguingly, those attributes relating to 'personality' are usually below 20%. There is little evidence for negative correlations, where people seek dissimilarity more than similarity. Attributes do not appear to converge during marriage, but are there largely from the beginning.[153] The strong correlations in the larger areas of background are in keeping with our postulate that people seek homology.

But why is there so little correlation between spouses in the area called 'personality'? One reason might be that people first use 'plain facts' about individuals as the basis for judging whether a relationship should proceed. This would include factors of age, race, education and so on. For the relationship to blossom, there must be some constructive differences in personality, whilst other areas of personality are allowed to be similar, thus resulting in an absence of high correlation. The mixing of similarity and complementarity in personality would largely nullify correlations, indicating that homology is important for larger factors but not many individual specific traits. Another reason might be that 'personality' is difficult to quantify and an estimation of it might not substantively contain all the traits that are relevant to a companionate relationship, such as minor habits, everyday decision-making, and ideology. Finally, research demonstrates that much, if not most, of temperament (namely, level of extroversion, work and leisure habits) is genetically derived. Thus, members of an ethnic group are going to be more similar to each other in genetic material, and so in temperament, than members belonging to different groups. Although members of the same ethnic group might have similar temperaments, which might produce similar habits and thinking patterns, it is the *interaction* of innate traits with social entities and affiliations that determines what type of personality is eventually manifested. Temperament per se is often not incorporated into personality assessments, so couples might not betray much similarity in 'personality' when it is measured.

If it were true that there was not only a major genetic difference between the sexes in temperament, but also a fundamental innate divergence in personality, encompassing intellect, emotions, and temperament, then it would become quite difficult to create a good match. If most men and women are servants to many different inalterable instincts, arranging a homologous union would indeed be frustratingly arduous. The ordinary expectation would then be of a 'romantic relationship' streaked with discord and enmity. We do not, however, have any evidence of such a difference in personality. There is reason to believe that *differences* in temperament might exist between the sexes, which are not only an essential element in the deeper attraction between the sexes, but also function to create a mutual improvement of personality, character, and lifestyle. Differences in personality no doubt can produce friction, yet to be attracted to someone unlike ourselves makes sense if one acknowledges an almost indomitable fascination with things unknown and the strong innate human propensity to learn. Nevertheless, it is more than simple curiosity that produces a truly complex and intense fascination with another person. There has to be an understanding at some level of consciousness that transformation is possible. Since such unions can and do occur, the belief that major trait differences are innate and counterproductive is largely incorrect.

Thus, similarity or homology might be what people are comfortable with, but complementarity is what they ultimately seek for true love to come alive. It cannot be overemphasised, however, that *although the founding and continuing vitality of a relationship is often expedited through homology, a deeply rewarding relationship can only be attained through the critical presence of positive heterology.* The most successful way in which homology and heterology can enhance a relationship is through joint learning as a central experience. Whether the learning occurs due to individual interest or due to external necessity, it provides the couple with critical information about each other's strengths and weaknesses, information that acts to build respect. Further, both add important shared experiences to their lives that increase the level of similarity between each another, hence increasing mutual attractiveness. Most importantly, where weaknesses are revealed, and difficulties threaten successful completion of a project, another can use their strengths to step in to 'save the day', which also increases desirability and respect. Unfortunately, this arrangement can be hindered by the independence ethos, where people often believe that they can handle a challenge in their own way, without assistance, direction or education. Independence indeed creates a storehouse of experiences upon which one can build competence and social rank, but it is not 'sociable' in the sense that a companion or spouse is prevented from gaining a whole view of one's personality. Instead of calling for this curtain, this veil, to be removed, so that openness and cooperation might be possible, society has moved to keep it in place whilst putting increasing emphasis on making similarity the cornerstone of the 'happy' marriage. Such an interference in free decision-making makes courtship difficult and marriage potentially volatile. In the next section, we will identify one major method society employs for increasing similarity between people.

EDUCATION, THE GREAT EQUALISER

Education, employment status, income, ethnic group, age, hobbies, number and sophistication of previous dating relationships, social and antisocial activity—all are attributes that men and women take into consideration when searching for a companion. Perhaps the first critical appraisal made by the dating couple is not of each other's background, but of each other's *opinions*. It is easier to ask for an opinion than a detail about one's background, because the latter might be seen as 'intrusive'. Further, since opinions do not only concern the past and present status of a person, but the future status as well, they are actually more important than most other attributes. Beliefs on what rules govern the relationship itself would be particularly apposite, since without congruence here, the relationship might easily falter. This is especially important since intimate relationships have more rules that facilitate closeness, and cover social and emotional factors, than non-intimate relationships, where rules used are primarily for maintaining distance.[154] The couple would have to agree not only on attitudes concerning abstract and practical matters, but also on the rules that would govern their own friendship. 'Truth in disclosure' not only makes for steadier and deeper relationships, it is also a critical component in the character of the virtuous person. However, it might not be possible to fully determine the facts until one is well into a relationship, and so one is exposed to some significant risk of loss.

Clearly, belief similitude is essential in the formation and maintenance of the relationship, and it would be advantageous for us to identify *which factors most strongly influence opinion and in what directions*. We have seen in previous sections that one area is common in the formation of friendships, careers, personal habits, status, and social rank, namely that of education. As education would logically be expected to exert an influence on thinking, and as education is a critical part of the modern life course, the amount of institutional instruction might be associated with the direction and strength of general opinions. Whilst we might reasonably assume that a correspondence in opinion would be parallelled by correspondence with other background attributes, education is evidently exceptional in that similar school experience does *not* necessarily mean similar opinions. It would be an intriguing finding indeed, if, contrary to what one might expect, the higher the education of either men or women, the more *diverse* their opinions become in certain areas. Although the experiences of obtaining higher education might be similar, and thus draw a couple together, that very education might have created a divergence of opinion that makes concurrence difficult on other issues. From observation, we know that the better educated often tend to be somewhere in the middle values on an opinion scale, but less educated people are less tolerant of ambiguity, of 'grey areas', and tend to cluster at the extremes. However, educational experience might also create greater similarity in opinions in other areas, thus making it difficult to offer any easy explanation for this phenomenon. We stated in the last section that if there are unchangeable innate differences between the sexes, implications arise as to how people court and choose marriage partners. If it can be proven that one major area of life can change thinking, then this theory is seriously weakened. It will be shown that at least education, of the variables people commonly experience, can affect opinions, with differing results for men and for women, thus rendering the methods to fulfilling the social preoccupation of matching 'like for like' in marriage that much more arbitrary.

Agreement on certain issues is highly important in setting the pace of interactions during courtship. Initial evaluations of another person during the pre-dating or early dating stages are limited to a general consideration of characteristics such as race, religion, appearance, and previous marital status. Because of the large number of candidates available in modern industrialised societies, the mental and physical resources made available for such an evaluation must be considerably limited if all candidates are to be dealt with equally and fairly. The belief is that if one matches both in theory and in practise opinions on these areas, there is greater likelihood that there will be congruity in other, more detailed questions. When well-educated people have a stronger convergence in these areas, they are more likely to be well-matched. Thus, being in a social environment of campus or classroom is more likely to yield quick easy 'yes' to a date enquiry. Random encounters on a college campus, in a dormitory, classroom or social function, often carry a good chance of turning into friendships because it is likely that people will have the same opinions about a number of important issues, such as their personal outlook on married life and on dating a member of another social group.

However, different phases in the relationship bring different kinds of questions and different kinds of answers. When a man and woman first meet, they attempt to discern each other's position on important issues pertaining to a potential relationship. If general opinions on an issue do not have much clustering, then there will be many encounters that end fruitlessly, bringing frustration and animosity. If a time limit is imposed, people go through a number of such encounters, then settle on the best person; there is a greater likelihood of opinion incongruity and thus greater friction in the relationship. If no time limit is imposed, then the educational groups that are more variable in opinion will take longer to find the right person compared to those who have opinion clustering. In the latter scenario, the 'goodness of fit' of a relationship originating in a low-variability (homogenous) versus a high-variability (heterogenous, diverse) group will not be very different, if random chance appertains in all cases. Hence, 'deadline' pressures can often be implicated as one reason for bad marriages in culturally diverse societies.

There must be a delineation between the first stage, where simple procedures are used to see if the couple can get along at all, and later stages, where complex and sometimes protracted methods reveal the filigree work of personality. The congruence of ideas about the 'goodness' of the relationship itself only validates its existence, allowing it to move forward, but does not actually bring the couple any *closer* together, as only true homology in temperament, attitudes, opinions, and behaviour can do that. One should not forget that major differences in culture and family background become quickly apparent in a relationship that is mixed in fundamental views, perhaps eclipsing an initial rosy assessment that was based only on an evaluation of beliefs of a general nature. Even though it is important at all stages to reassure oneself that a cognitive alliance exists in the major arenas of life, certainty is all the more critical in later stages if emotional consummation is to be achieved.

After dating over a period of time, and after the relationship has deepened to an extent, the couple invariably believe they have learned more about one another than what would be known in a casual friendship. Although not yet married, the couple do experience many parallel situations to that of a married couple; hence, possible friction might still arise over differences in opinion, for example, about the roles of men and women in married life. However, because there is already some investment of resources in the relationship, the likelihood of a breakup might be less than expected. It is only after marriage, when abstract issues and questions become quite concrete, that genuine disagreement is likely to arise. If agreement on issues is forced, and ideas not clearly and genuinely expressed during courtship, then the married life can be quite a disappointment.

Let us now examine the effects that education has on the direction and strength of opinions. Since a wider range of responses includes 'ambiguous' replies, and this creates more diversity of opinion, and more diversity often creates problems in matching people, we might first entertain possible answers to the fundamental question: Why would education produce a toleration of ambiguity? It is beyond debate that the more college education one has, the more theories and information one is offered and one assimilates. Well-educated persons have been exposed to a wealth of putatively factual knowledge and theories, which, however, often contradict one another, making it difficult to hold convincing opinions with absolute certainty. College also encourages dissent and novelty, so individuals are likely to form their own theories, in some cases not because they really find it necessary, but because they simply wish to appear 'academic'. Further, experiences with prioritising and sorting data and constructing hierarchies of information, make well-educated individuals more comfortable with spreading out responses along an attitudinal spectrum. On an opinion scale of say 1 to 7, with 1 being very much in favour of something, and 7 being very much against it, middling, equivocal, or 'weak' values (3, 4, or 5) are not uncommon. The confluence of these factors results sometimes in an alteration in beliefs. Indeed, it is not unusual that long-held and strong convictions, whilst not rejected, are significantly reduced in intensity. What might start out as a belief on one end of the scale, say at 7, might at some point settle somewhere in the middle, such as on 4. Diversity, although making debate between friends and/or colleagues spirited and interesting, can produce acrimonious arguments between husband and wife. Therefore, if education does indeed have the impact on opinions that we postulate it to have, it would be of interest to discover the specific dynamics involved.

The most important issues a couple would confront would be those relating to the relationship itself and the people involved, and we therefore studied a selection of questions relating to those issues, asked in a survey of unmarried, non-cohabitating people under the age of 35.[155] We find clear evidence of patterns in the strength and direction of opinions, and we summarise the results in the following table:

Table 5

QUESTIONS (paraphrased)	CHANGE IN DIVERSITY OF OPINIONS (as education increases) MALE	FEMALE	CHANGE IN AVERAGE OPINION
Would you like to get married? (A3-2.)	Moderately diverse to moderately strongly singular	As for males	From 'agree' to 'strongly agree'
Is it better for a person to marry than to be single? (A3-3.)	Moderately singular, little change	Moderately singular to moderately diverse	From 'agree' to 'neither'
How would life be different now if married, in terms of personal freedom? (A3-6.)	Moderately diverse to strongly singular	Moderately diverse to moderately singular	From 'same' to 'somewhat worse'

Comparison of ranges of opinions on married life.

Table 5. (Cont.) Comparison of ranges of opinions on married life

	Singular, little change	Moderately singular to strongly singular	From 'somewhat better' to 'same'
...in terms of friendship with others? (A3-8.)	Singular, little change	Moderately singular to strongly singular	From 'somewhat better' to 'same'
...in terms of relations with parents? (A3-9.)	Same as above	Same as above	Same as above
How important is saving money before marriage? (A4-1.)	Strong singularity to great diversity	As for males	From very important to centre; outlier at 'not at all important' for females
How important is it for you to have a job? (A4-2.)	As above	As above	As above
How important is it for you for your partner to have a job? (A4-3.)	As above	As above	As above
How important is it for you to finish your education? (A4-4.)	Moderately singular to moderately diverse	As above	As above
How important is it for your partner to finish his/her education? (A4-5.)	Moderately singular to great diversity	As above	As above
Would you marry someone who has been married before? (A4-8.)	Moderately diverse to moderately singular	Moderately diverse to moderately singular	Males: from about centre to moderately unwilling; Females: remaining at about centre
Would you marry someone with children? (A4-9.)	Diverse to moderately singular	Diverse to moderately singular	Females: generally not willing to not at all willing; Males: Moderately willing to moderately unwilling
Would you marry someone who earned much more than you? (A4-12.)	Moderately diverse, little change	Moderately high singularity to moderately high diversity	Females: very willing to moderately willing; Males: moderately willing

Table 5. (Cont.) Comparison of ranges of opinions on married life

| Would you marry someone of a different race? (A4-16.) | Moderately diverse to moderately singular | As for males | From moderately not willing to quite unwilling |
| Would you marry someone who was not good looking? (A4-17.) | Greatly diverse to strongly singular | As for males | Females: centre to moderately strongly centre; Males: centre to moderately not willing; |

The first two questions in this table have the following possible replies: strongly agree, agree, neither, disagree, strongly disagree, and refused/no answer.

The next three questions have the following possible responses: much worse, somewhat worse, same, somewhat better, much better, refused/no answer/don't know.

The remaining questions have responses placed on a scale of 1 to 7, with not at all willing (or important) at 1, and very willing (or important) at 7, with an additional response of no answer/refused/don't know.
Source: Chadwick & Heaton (1992, pp 22-47).

We see that *higher* education *reduces* diversity of opinion concerning questions of a general nature that are relevant largely *before* serious dating (courtship) begins: whether one oneself should marry (strongly agree); whether one's relations with friends and parents after marriage are improved (remain the same); whether one should marry someone who is physically unattractive (centre opinion); whether one should marry someone of a different race (not willing); whether one should marry someone with children (not willing). We might believe that the emphasis on marriage is unusual, given the impression that a life incorporating various activities and a career would offer a suitable alternative to marriage. The better-educated usually have higher incomes, and so are often engaged in many different activities. However, this kind of lifestyle makes one more willing, not less willing, to marry. Activities in and of themselves do not seem to offer much of a substitute, underlining the preeminence of companionship over autonomy in modern life. In any case, in the above areas, well-educated couples reach more agreement, and thus would tend to have a more harmonious dating relationship.

On the other hand, greater education brings *more* diversity in issues that are more substantive, specific and that become important to life *after* marriage: whether savings, a job, and finishing an education are important in married life; whether husbands should earn more than wives; whether someone should marry in general (for oneself and others); whether marriage increases freedom. Increased heterology in opinion arises because of a confusion between separating roles, such as wife and career woman. A woman with high education credentials, it is believed, *should* live out her potential by earning a good deal of money, but at the same time she should *not* compete with her husband. Perhaps the higher earnings engendered by advanced formal schooling makes people less concerned about economic issues, because education gives them freedom in a career. This reveals an interesting potential area of conflict between independence and marriage, where wifely dedication to home life is devalued by the belief that the freedom 'bought' by education must be exercised. There need be no conflict as long as the individual understands that the primary role of education is intellectual, not physical, emancipation.

Thus, the latter questions cited above, concerning earnings and employment, are especially important, as it appears that divergence does not bring heterophily, that is, a delight in significant differences. No constructive compensation is found in these kinds of differences, instead causing challenges to status. Evidence for this unhappiness is found in the observation that highly paid college-educated women find marital dissolution a considerably more probable occurrence than their lower paid educational cohort.[156] This is partly the result of a reification of issues such as whether a husband should earn more than his wife, whether he should be fully employed, and whether marriage significantly decreases personal freedom; significant divergence produces the feeling that mutual respect no longer exists.[157] For those wives who do not work or who have a low-paying part-time job, their divorce potential is much lower than their well-educated counterparts because attitudes about a husband's relative earning power are never treated as anything more than mere conjecture.

We should now turn to examining the dynamics that opinions exert on the courtship process. If within a particular environment there is *less* variability (i.e. more similarity) on opinions, there is usually a greater chance of a favourable union for two people if they meet by simple random chance, as the odds that they will have the same opinion on an issue are increased. For example, if two people sitting side-by-side in the campus cafeteria begin to discuss marriage, then there will be a fairly high likelihood that they will both state the preference that they themselves wish to marry, as the majority of people on that campus hold these very beliefs. Obviously, the dating process is facilitated in this case.

We should realise that not only does being in the majority help people finding others with similar thinking, but also being in the *minority*. When dissimilarity is high, the chance of a match is actually increased as well. This less than obvious factor further illustrates the dangers of forced similarity. When there is clustering of opinions around one point of the scale, then there is a clear majority group and clear minority group. The member of the minority will become disenchanted with the views of the majority and will seek others who believe what they do. At social functions of a generally idiosyncratic variety, two such 'outsiders' standing side-by-side might make conversation and possible friendship. The stronger the outsider status, the more likely they would be to actively seek others of similar beliefs, increasing the odds of making a match. Randomness is being circumvented because people are assiduously looking to connect with others of the same type of thinking. Thus, if one is indifferent to marriage, and the majority are strongly in favour of it, then one might associate with those who are similarly indifferent. 'Indifference' does not mean absolute refusal, so it is possible that an individual with weak feelings about marriage might marry anyway for material or status purposes. It might precisely be this minority association that makes it *more* likely that both spouses are indifferent to marriage, since they were more likely to fraternise with each other than with people who strongly believe in matrimony.[158] This situation is most likely to occur when the persons holding dissimilar beliefs are clearly different from most other people within a particular social context.

It is in the area of race that this effect is most socially obvious and most potentially divisive. One could initially believe that since college educated individuals generally are not willing to marry someone from another race (see the table above), that these types of couples would be more poorly educated than average. However, it would appear that both husbands and wives in mixed marriages (black male-white female, white male-black female) tend to be significantly *better* educated than black-black or white-white marriages. White men and women in college who tend to believe in the fundamental propriety of mixed-race relations and marriages would actively seek others who have the same attitudes. As racial minority groups in society are likely to believe in such mixing, usually out of necessity, these would be more likely to meet, socialise and possibly marry the whites they meet at 'idiosyncratic' or 'undergound' gatherings. The effect is similar to that experienced by people who leave home in order to find love and support. Where a person in one case might go from one household to another, in this case, a person might go from one peer group or social group to another.

Notwithstanding the similarities in certain basic beliefs, and the relative ease of courtship, the black male-white female marriage is evidently a stormy match, as it is much shorter in duration than same race marriages; marital duration is on average similar between white male-black female and same-race marriage couples.[159] The fact that there is initial agreement on issues does not guarantee marital longevity, a point we make elsewhere and that cannot be overemphasised. People might be very happy that they have met someone who shares their views, possibly after a long period of searching. The relationship might blossom into a good friendship, but might not grow into a deep affectionate bond if a full dovetailing of characteristics is not made.

However, even though they must deal with cultural clashes that are as apparently unique to their relationship as a black male-white female pair, white male-black female relationships seem to have less divorce than other mixed-race marriages. White male-black female marriages might endure longer than black male-white female marriages because in the latter case, the couple are in a minority, and so disadvantaged, in three significant respects. One, their opinions are in the minority for their educational group; two, their marriage type is of a minority type for their education group and in general; three, the head of household is a member of a minority race, resulting in an unusual type of household structure. The last factor might make the marriage untenable because it is beyond the conceptions of most people, that is, it is too deviant, beyond the fringe, by majority standards. Even if the couple agrees on major issues, these other divergences from social norms make it difficult for them to feel as if they fit into society. If the head of the household is a white married to a black woman, then the couple are deviant in only two respects, making them more acceptable, as they have only two 'strikes' against them but not a third, allowing a greater degree of social integration. Further, if there is some basic acceptance into society, the relationship might be made *more* tolerable perhaps because longer exposure to the educational system assists in the development of intellectual mechanisms and reasoned thinking can defuse potential conflict.

Thus, the over-demand for similarity might create forced matches that leave individuals poorly matched as spouses and as social outsiders. The initial attraction between two people was the fact that they had a more open and liberal (non-conventional) attitude towards friendships. Challenging the relationship is not only a fundamental lack of agreement and complementarity, but also a struggle with social exclusion, a fate that the demand for similarity was supposed to avoid. The principle we have been discussing, of minority groups distinguishing themselves from majority groups, would probably apply to other areas as well, but without the added factor of having to go outside one's own racial group. For example, the same effect applies to other areas where there is a division in belief, such as on the issue of physical appearance or marrying someone who has been married before. It is also possible that a higher than expected proportion of people who married divorced individuals with children are college graduates. Even though those with higher education evince the belief that it is wrong marrying someone who already has children, the fact that colleges offer venues for those who deviate from this norm might actually facilitate such unions.

On certain occasions, people consciously seek out others with very different opinions. We cite here one example, that of the merging of educated and uneducated people as a 'mixed' couple. Tired of what they see as the pusillanimous, 'wishy-washy' and even traitorous attitudes of educated women, intellectual men might be attracted to lesser-educated women, who possess strong and thus stable ideas about work, savings, a husband's position in the household. One seeks uniformity of opinions, and one more often than not finds them in the lower classes. Hence, those men who spend their time in education developing their intellect, and thus putting off marriage, have a tendency to form heterologous unions, such as marrying well beneath their social class. Two examples of this phenomenon can be adduced. Rousseau and Descartes, both highly intelligent men who encouraged refinement and sophistication, took ordinary and probably illiterate servant girls as 'unofficial' wives. We know that Rousseau, much-attacked in his lifetime, saw loyalty as the main virtue of his mistress, whom he would eventually wed when he was 56. In contrast to their intellectual side, the emotional side of such men is poorly controlled and developed. Managing anger and frustration become very difficult and a simple woman that possesses a 'strong' personality and open nature helps to rebuild a damaged ego. They might even seek the 'archaic' or 'dangerous' woman—earthy, naïve and uncomplicated.[160] As higher education has become quite common in the Western world, the man of intellectual bent, staggered by the emotionally restrained and uncertain opinions of educated women, is by no means difficult to find, and this type of relationship is also hardly unusual.

Agreement on basic issues is always of import in all phases of the relationship, and education evidently plays an important role in forming or affecting such opinions. We should reiterate, however, that the most contentious issues that a couple can face are actually *not* related to issues of background or ethnicity, since many minor disagreements over opinions will cause a falling-out long before these deeper issues become relevant. If there is little agreement in the early phase of dating or courtship due to divergent opinions, the relationship will end; if there is good general agreement, then the relationship will proceed, but agreement on more specific and more important issues, as we have been discussing in this section, will have to be achieved. Behaviour or a tendency to a behaviour, as embodied in personality and temperament, are never merely theoretical but are always concrete, thus appearing as 'deeper' issues. However, whether an opinion is minor or major depends on its pertinence to some aspect of life, either now or in the future. An opinion about an issue that does not presently touch the lives of the couple is considered 'abstract', but it can suddenly turn 'concrete' if the issue must actually be acted upon.

This change in relevance can be seen in particular where a wife's working full-time outside the home produces a number of potentially divisive issues: the issue of a wife making more than a husband, the issue of a wife's loss of freedom, the issue of a husband being out of work, and the issue of a wife launching a supportive role. In cases where the wife does not work, and/or a husband is comfortably employed and well-paid, controversial but theoretical points of view can lay dormant. Suddenly, this issue can become concrete, and the opinion is no longer minor.[161] We can all agree that virtue is most numinous and compelling in stories of chivalrous men who rescue chaste women in heroic combat, but the more common scenario in which virtue is confronted might be of the average man 'heroically' trying to pay the bills and support his wife and family. So ironically, a fall from grace occurs not because the knight could not bring himself to slay the dragon, but because a husband could not agree with his 'damsel' about the *mundane* aspects of life.

The greater diversity in opinions found among lesser-educated individuals about issues relating to attractiveness, marriage goals, children, race, and friends is to a large extent a part of the Industrial Age's overall sorry 'confusion' of values. As we shall discuss later on, the effects of migration, occupation and loss of traditional values have instigated such variability amongst local cultures that it is difficult to state what, for example, a 'typical American' believes. Education is a homogenising influence which makes one individual's opinions more similar to that of another, thus restoring a critical balance in dating and marital relationships. However, education also creates new differences in opinion, which somewhat reduce its benefits. Schooling is, therefore, highly useful to society in cultivating productive citizens, but its shortcomings must be redressed by complex social adjustments. With or without higher education, people must resort to other, questionable methods to assure similarity in attitudes and behaviour between partners.

Thus, the modern world's demand for material well-being and a high standard-of-living has resulted in the necessity of the educated citizen, yet this materialism has also created unbalanced societies largely due to migration and loss of direction from customary practises. Education brings homogeneity to opinions, thus restoring, to a certain extent, a balance in relationships. But it should be remembered that even though two people find each other, sometimes through difficult circumstances if they are outside the mainstream in some way, does not guarantee relationship viability as the very fact that the struggle took place, their minority status, might create problems with larger society. As we have seen, this affects people marrying others of different races and backgrounds, a problem in populations containing diverse cultures. More importantly, when similarity is the main focus, and not cooperation, then finding someone who is similar will increase their worth, but other areas that need to be discussed, including ethnicity and background, are ignored as value areas. This reticence, unfortunately, cannot last forever as the press of external challenges come upon the 'well-matched' couple. The crucial match, as we shall see, is not necessarily in opinions or traits, but in the willingness to change and accommodate.

Is Marriage Just Another Friendship?

The small village, a prototype of the past, contained few choices of marriage partner. Out of necessity, on many occasions people would choose a spouse not very similar to themselves in personality, background or temperament. Sometimes, family lore about the great-grandparent who married a girl 'outside the community' reveals differences so exaggerated as to offend our modern sensibilities. Although there was homogeneity of culture within this circle of villages, perfect similarity was lacking, and major dissimilarities were not at all unusual. Further, there was no attempt to increase similarity; for some reason, people accepted their fate. Were they simply indolent and accepted the aloof distance between husband and wife? Not likely, since people in Western societies often measure the success of any relationship by its closeness. And closeness was based on how much one would be willing to exclude from one's life for the sake of the other. Since married couples were presumed to have the closest of friendships, then all other things became secondary. The material, financial set- up, however, of the household is the next most important factor for a happy marriage. Once finances had stabilised, the couple would learn how to live with each other, as with all other things that God had created in Nature. They believed that strife occurred when money was inadequate; as long as the basic physical needs were met, the emotional side would inevitably take care of itself. This, however, presupposes that the couple have forsaken other people and other duties in order to put themselves in the right frame of mind for this mutual transformation to take place. The process was private but usually affected by the experiences and beliefs of others in the community. Culture, however, the accumulated wisdom of many generations, provides many elements of normative thinking. Thus, the customary mores of a parish, hamlet, village or some larger community, might have induced, influenced or reinforced the idea at all social levels that *entrustment* between two people was paramount for a successful marriage.

In spite of the force of circumstances reducing the range of potential marriage partners, society saw married life as not exceedingly difficult for a number of reasons that we can deduce from our knowledge of relationships and history. Firstly, people were willing to compromise in order to obtain an orderly family. They did not see this as some sort of personal defeat or admission of weakness. Secondly, in the less rigorously demanding societies of the past, people could be more pliant than today, readily altering their activities to accommodate the needs of others. Thirdly, people had belief systems that were located within a narrower spectrum, thus making it unlikely that the individual would be called upon to make extensive changes. Fourthly, as people grow more similar to each other as they get older, people could marry others who are mostly similar, but also quite different from themselves; there was basically no need to overstress homology. There was also no need for a lengthy 'preparation' for married life, as circumstances in marriage did not have to be radically different from that found in single life. One could marry someone significantly older or younger without worrying very much about compatibility.

In this scenario, a strong attitude of independence would admittedly be difficult to negotiate, and the essentially private strategy described above was altered with the burgeoning hallmark of the modern period, the Industrial Revolution. Most private strategies, of whatever kind, were delayed or obviated. With reference to the labour demands of factory automation, inflexibility and uncooperativeness were established as social norms. The economy did not tolerate much individual creativity on the job, nor did it allow much choice of occupation. In addition, in the fear of losing their identity, people became more nationalist, class-orientated, and group-orientated, making their beliefs more narrow and even less amenable to change. The tactic of seeking the protection of the group arose from a migration which caused people to inhabit new areas where ideas and patterns of behaviour were different from the ones they knew so well. Words that avow conformity to larger ideals and thus assure survival of the group have become more important than personal goals and virtuous *actions*. Before a person was ultimately respected for how he handled his personal affairs, his honesty and integrity; now, identity is bound up with what a person *believes*. Hence, virtue declined and simplistic notions became engrained in people's minds.

The ultimate goal of marriage, to achieve affection and support, has in no way changed, but the *methods* used to achieve that goal have steadily been revised in the past century. We could rephrase this to say that the *ideal* of marriage has changed, but this might be misleading if one were to only think of an ideal as an end result of a series of actions and not the actions and result together. It should be clear that one cannot exist without the other, and so when we speak of the ideal, we speak of both deeds and outcome. If one person refuses to marry because of objections about another person's attitudes or behaviour, then this is a case of individual devaluation, but if the suspicion is of married life regardless of who is the spouse, then it is part of a worldview where people in general are devalued. This is not something that can come about unless major changes in thinking have occurred. In our day, the talk of what marriage should be about has reached a crescendo pitch as people increasingly fail to attain even a modicum of success in their personal relations. It is precisely when marriages are *not* succeeding that the ideal is thought about all the more passionately and debated all the more loudly. Modern people make the error of thinking that we have discovered through some miracle unknown to our ancestors the transcendent quality of the ideal of love. In reality, from earliest times human beings have held a strong personal belief in a particular kind of exemplary relationship. Whether the individual reached it or not, the model of life seen as most appropriate persisted and endured. Simply because the people of the past did not analyse themselves and each other incessantly, and worry about attaining an *externally* derived paragon of family, does not mean that they did not possess one themselves. Throughout life they could have quietly carried a model of familial behaviour that would be fitting for them, their spouses, and their children.

Consequently, the *manner* in which the traditional past is viewed has made a difference in the ways the ideal marriage is viewed. Over the last four generations, it is perhaps the inordinate shift in the nature of marriage, and indeed in all of society, that has made people forget about their collective origins. The people of the past have become temporal foreigners to us, in relation to which one can put oneself in whatever fantasy or escapist orientation one wishes. Concepts different from the present time that challenge ideals can be discarded without much guilt. Probably the one fantasy most highly regarded is about noble modern man valorously struggling to reach a humanitarian 'ideal', outshining the depravity of his dull-witted peasant forbear who cared for nothing except satisfying the cravings of his belly and his loins.[162] This portrayal is often encountered in the popular media reinforcing the 'great' set of concepts relating to married life.

If the ideal of love has not been surrendered, and people have become less accommodative and under more external strain, what marital strategy has supplanted the old one? One vital aspect to the new strategy is that women and men from an early age can be, and indeed should be, more emotionally *dependent* (though not necessarily intellectually or materially) on one another, a move that one can immediately see is potentially not in keeping with the modern aspiration for independence. It is from this selfishness and dependence on others that a preoccupation with *similarity* has arisen. In essence it can be expressed as:

$$\begin{array}{l} + \textit{Self-centeredness} \\ + \textit{Emotional Over-dependance} \\ \underline{- \textit{Constructive Material Dependence}} \\ = \textit{Excessive Demand for Similarity} \end{array}$$

We can elaborate on the factors contributing to the existence of the three independent variables in the equation above. Firstly, people need more of an emotional return from marriage in compensation from losing it elsewhere. Increasing stress in the workplace, and increased dissonance with and distance from other family members, have produced a serious isolation of the individual. Secondly, in the past men and women would work harder to please the other; whatever differences existed would have been reduced or would have disappeared over time. Thus, it was not as important that they should be greatly compatible from the beginning. Thirdly, the great improvement in economic conditions has been responsible for the decline of constructive material dependence on others. Material aspects can now be adjusted and modified, making them more amenable to the individual's control. For example, sewing and knitting (traditionally in the wife's domain) are now done by professional firms and repairs, and maintenance (traditionally the husband's area) is now also performed by outside workers. Education and economic changes have spurred an increase in the study of detailed specialised materials and publications, which has expanded the exposure of both sexes to areas until recently under the authority of the other, such as mechanical repairs, food preparation, and business dealings. Individuals are now much more free to marry someone without regard as to whether they will be a supplement to the household, that is, whether they will help to form a materially integrated and whole family unit. The individual assumes that wherever he or she lives before marriage, the household is 'complete', in that all domestic functions are adequate; food, clothing, cleaning and so on are already up to par because outside workers provide the services. The only concern presently is that a spouse contribute extra income, which can be used in the ways described. Finally, the youth culture is a separate force that encompasses, in effect, the first two independent variables, and contributes to the increase in similarity. Many aspects of this preoccupation with staying young have gained a certain seductiveness in America, and possibly partly due to this, a desire for equality between the sexes has arisen.[163] Young people are emblematic of the free, independent spirit, and 'complete' autonomy for adults involves having the same cross-sex relations as adolescents. There is in this case little need for differentiation between the sexes, i.e. they generally have the same responsibilities and rights, and if the 'eternal youth' paradigm is to flourish, there must be little to differentiate the sexes even in adulthood. To assign different complex roles to each sex would be to destroy the illusion of 'staying young' mentally and physically. By virtue of cultural diffusion, other nations, neither as industrially advanced nor as modernist, have obtained and even amplified the concepts described above.

How has society brought these issues encompassed in the formula above into the forum of public discussion? In spite of knowledge of the issues, society has chosen to remain silent. Over an extended period of time—from great- grandparent, to grandparent, to parent, to the present—anxieties have steadily grown about the ability to perform complex roles in home life. Perhaps the operative word in this case should be 'willingness' and not 'ability', because it is not that people lack the mental and physical resources, but rather that they are not prepared to make the sacrifices in fully assuming their responsibilities. This anxiety, or rather this guilt, has been lessened if not expiated because of explanations offered by one branch of the same Revolution that initially gave rise to this guilt. 'Science' maintained that the traditional solution for every marital problem, that of working hard for respect within the context of household life, was an untenable idea in the face of the enlightened conclusion that human beings were destined to act and think only within the *narrow* guidelines set down by Nature. The completely happy married couple, of course, were in reality a coincidence, an accident, never the result of diligent dedication. It is no coincidence, however, that the rise of the modernist independent lifestyle was accompanied by the florescence of institutional science, from which people could easily procure this deterministic explanation of human relations as a way of excusing their own tardiness in changing for the better. As evidence mounted that genetics played a role in animal behaviour, many were tempted to see the same role in human actions. These observations were built on age-old beliefs, many correct, that inheritance in humans had a strong influence on certain basic elements of behaviour, such as shyness. However, these ideas were taken one step further in that the 'influences' became 'causes'; people were hidebound in acting out the programme that nature had assigned to them, a sensational but ultimately counterfeit idea. Indeed, scientists became convinced that ideal marriages were no longer made in heaven, but in the genetic code.

Public discussions about the 'natural' impulses of human beings could not be contained to only one area. The same need for 'separation' between different social and ethnic groups that spawned the Eugenics movement and the racialism of the 20th century, also lies behind the ethos that 'incompatible' marriages must be ended.[164] It was thought that if at all possible, such unions should never be established in the first place. Thus, like and like must be brought together because it is the way of Nature, an argument not easily refuted. The same thinking is responsible for the great social interest in matching attributes, such as background, education, and age.

It is in the last attribute, because of its fundamental nature, that we can see at work a critical part of the modern marital strategy that we have yet to discuss in detail, that of *simplification*. In the struggle to find similarity in a potential spouse, people have attempted to simplify the process by routinely matching overt traits such as age, whilst neglecting a deeper examination of temperament and personality. These ideas are grounded on the belief in distinct phases of life bringing different attitudes, challenges, behaviours and responsibilities. It would thus make sense that a person from an 'early' phase of life should not marry someone from the 'late' phase. Obtaining someone's age is probably the attribute most easily obtained; it requires only a simple question or observation. And by the same token, when this attribute is matched between husband and wife, it is the most easily determined of any homology. Therefore, reducing a persona's complexity to just a simply marker, such as age, although highly attractive, threatens the courtship and marriage processes.

Universal classifications of marriage age are used by all societies to assist people in demarcating the different attitude areas that underlie marriage. In the Western world, about one in four of any population can marry 'late', that is, well past the average age; about one in four in any population can marry early, with women being more likely to do so. Many believe the terms 'early' and 'late' signify deviations from the *customary norm,* and not mere departures from an actual mathematical average or typical age. From this outlook, we can say that in most Western nations, marrying under the age of 20 is definitely 'early', and marrying over the age of 35 is definitely 'late'. Late marriage, as a traditional concept, can be defined as a first marriage where husbands are over age 26 and wives are over age 23.[165] Although this applies to the period from the 16th to the 19th centuries, it might not really hold for earlier periods, such as the Middle Ages, or later periods, such as the 20th century. Hence, 'traditional' is a term in this case derived from an early modern period, and the practise should not be construed as going back to time immemorial. Furthermore, this definition becomes relativistic when it is grounded on actual averages, not expectations. A nation with an average age of 19 could see 'late' marriage as 23, or if the average were 25, then 'late' marriage could be considered 30. In more recent times, with the average age for men and women around 25, early marriage can occur before age 22, late marriage can realistically be characterised as occurring after age 30. Such opinions are always to a certain extent impressionistic, relating more to concepts of propriety rather than strict mathematical principles.

Historically, age was only a *starting* point in the evaluation process, not as an absolutely reliable indicator of traits, although a different attitude finds resounding endorsement today. If age of marriage does have a major effect on marital stability, then what is 'early' or 'late' has much to do with social forces that help or hinder the success of such unions. However, we notice that although matching of age is highly attractive to many people, there are still factors that override it. The proportion of marriages in North America with a large discrepancy in age between husband and wife has declined, and the proportion with nearly the same age has increased. The proportion of marriages where the wife is older than the husband has not changed much.[166] This demand for homology in ages applies to first marriages, and is somewhat less strong in subsequent marriages,[167] with the trend not being the same across all age groups. Marriages were increasingly homologous in age from 1921 until 1971, but thereafter less so. From the 1920s until the 1960s, younger men tended to select brides from their own age groups, whereas from the 1940s to the 1970s, older men had marriages that were increasingly dissimilar. Although the pattern for women is not clear, women under the age of 20 tend to select older grooms.[168] These patterns follow long trends, making it unlikely that economic forces were solely responsible.

Clearly, people have become more attracted to the belief, rightly or wrongly, that age is a significant determinant in personality development. We should emphasise that a married couple of disparate ages might still be quite similar to one another in personality and attitudes; the homophily between partners of the same age might be great, but compensating factors could intervene so that a great similitude between an older husband and young wife, for example, might also be enjoyed. People now invest fewer resources in finding a suitable mate, putting their faith in only a hazy evaluation of attributes, a 'thumbnail sketch' of a real person.

However, it is not clear why there should be an increasing tendency for *older* men to marry women not only from their own age group, but from age groups as well. The general traits older women have appeals to many older men, but other older men find that younger women offer more appealing characteristics. We can understand why young men select women close to their own age: General similarity in attributes and the availability of large pools of single females. The older man's apparent violation of the homology principle might reveal to us more about the underlying processes at work in the new marital strategy. One reason why large age disparities among married couples were unremarkable in the past might have to do with accessibility in age groups. If eligible people are not present in one's age group (one's birth cohort plus or minus five years) then one would move outside of it. If marriage within a particular age group is essential, a large surplus of females always carries the certainty that many of them, although willing, cannot marry. If such marriage is *not* essential, then people who are 'shut out' of their own age group, either because of number differences or attitudes, will, if they are able, move outside of their age group, and marry people significantly older or younger than themselves.

What happens when similarity in attributes remains a dominant factor, but men can marry freely either in their own age group or outside of it? It is reasonable to assume that if older men and younger men can both relate to younger females, it is the women who then change more over time compared to men. Obviously, these older men found something more appealing about younger women and/or less appealing about women in their own age group. If it is true that people in general desire greater *similarity* from a spouse, then it would appear that single men change less than single women as they age, thus older men would be closer in attributes to younger women than older women. What do older men and younger men have in common with younger women? To put it another way, what is the main divergence between younger and older women? Based on our previous discussions, we can divide the pertinent areas of interest into work, dependence, maturity and general personality.

Young women and young men (18 to 25 years of age) are less likely to have a full-time job than older men and women (35 to 50 years of age); however, there is little to suggest that young women are less likely to work than young men. In the second area, dependence, younger people are clearly more likely to be dependent than older people, but young women are only somewhat more likely to be dependent on parents and others than young men. Older single men and women are both likely to be self-reliant.

In the case of maturity, younger people are undeniably less mature than older people, with not much difference between the sexes. For younger women, choosing an older male has traditionally meant more stability, a more mature partner that would balance out the woman's lack of knowledge, naivete and emotionality. Many older men still favour older women due to their maturity and ability to function as full partners in the marriage. Indeed, many younger men desired older women for the same reasons. Whereas younger females and older males are fairly similar in personality and perceptions, older women and older men are similar in experiences and maturity.[169]

It is in the area of personality (habits and interests) that we find a considerable contrast between young and older women. Young women are much more likely to engage in activities that are typically *male*, with the result that young men and young men enjoy the greatest intersection of interests and activities of any combination of age groups. The easy acceptance of girls crossing over to engage in 'tomboy' activities stands in great contrast to the prohibitions boys encounter in trying to do 'girlish' things. In fact, whilst most women have engaged in activities that are typically male, the few boys who do engage in typically female activities are seen as having 'behavioural problems'. Although boys become somewhat less masculine with age, girls show a greater increase in feminine habits, so that the gap between the two sexes *grows* with age.[170] Even women who are in their late teens and early 20s probably betray more willingness to engage in male activities than older women. There are many advantages to knowing both sex roles from the inside, so to speak, as one is then less likely to feel uncomfortable or confused in a situation where the opposite sex predominates. It would appear women use the generous free time of youth to discover the world of male activities, even when occasionally thwarted by domineering boys who see this as an incursion into their domain. As adults, women must decisively take on clear feminine characteristics, which conversely means abandoning masculine ones. Younger women and men of any age are therefore relatively close to each other in regards to social activity and role responsibilities.

Similarity in general usually entails little change in personality, but it does not guarantee a smooth transition into other areas of life after marriage, if the roles of husband and wife are significantly different. Thus, we should not minimise the significance of similarity in attributes in choosing a mate, but partners of different ages, despite noticeable divergence in personality, might have to undergo *less* of a change in certain ways than similarly aged partners. Men often experience less of a change between single life and married life, as they still have the roughly the same attitudes and behaviour in both lifestyles. Women usually undergo a greater change; to name one example, they usually give up their jobs in order to raise children. As a consequence, a younger woman, who has still not grown into the habit of being a member of the labour force, will find the transition easier than for older women. For this reason, many older men in the latter half of the 20th century have found it necessary to override the advantages of marrying an older woman by marrying a younger one. If people prefer minimal shifting of responsibilities between the single life and married life, then dissimilarity is as important as similarity.

We can see that when fluency and ease of social relations are important, men and women will seek others of the same age. But when a strong, masculine response to external challenges is critical, then the older woman, despite her maturity, does not inspire the passions of an older (or younger) man. Still in both cases, *homology* between man and woman is stressed: similarity in general attributes in the age-matching scenario, but similarity in more specific attributes in the age-diverse scenario. Clearly, the focus is now on having a wife who is more masculine, and consequently less feminine, and who requires less assistance in the transition from single to married life. This kind of woman, who has become a prototypical wife in many cultures, is the product of the *simplification dynamic* of male-female relationships. As long as husband and wife have the same general interests, whatever major differences exist in personality, as in the case of an older man and a younger woman, might not be intolerable as long as each has the opportunity to express these traits. Extensive changes in the set of characteristics the average older man found desirable forced a shift in focus; now the younger, stronger, attractive, effervescent, girl-woman becomes the ideal wife, eclipsing the advantages the older woman has to offer. Hence, this change in marriage pattern results not from the appearance of a new basic paradigm, but from a broadening of long-standing ideas that in the past were widely held, albeit not often put into practise. What men once only fancied or dreamt about, they now demand.

One dynamic can actually explain two opposite tendencies. The strong desire for similarity, and thus for simplicity, explains why some people prefer to marry people in their same age group, and why others prefer to marry members of different age groups. Moreover, the tolerance, indeed the necessity, of differences between spouses, has become undone by the individual aversion to major sacrifice in personality, in addition to the exigencies of modern industrial economies. The differences between people have evidently become more irksome. It is at first glance not apparent whether there are now more differences or a greater latitude of differences than in the past, although this would be unimportant if the *level* of tolerable difference remained the same. Within this move to similarity is an all-important move *away* from complementarity, with a loss of profundity and thus fulfilment. Personal and economic reasons have changed the way people think about marriage, as was found in a study of matrimonial advertisements, wherein people described what they wanted in a suitable spouse. Over a 35-year period, the differences between what men deemed desirable in women, and what women deemed desirable in men, diminished considerably. Married life slowly became a place for mutual emotional satisfaction, more so than being a partnership where *complementarity* of material interests was of major concern.[171] What 'satisfaction' means is unclear when heterology is removed from the concept of the successful companionate relationship.

The evidence we have covered appears to point to the conclusion that people want to both reduce the number of differences between partners, and to reduce the depth or extent of each difference. The ability of married life to turn dissimilarity from a deficit into a strength has evidently been lost. Some of our grandfathers and grandmothers, no doubt, might have had little in common in temperament and interests, but they had a satisfying life because each partner conscientiously contributed his or her own unique resources to a clean, well-run household, emotional security, financial security, good child-care, and communal stability. Today, complementarity, at least without overriding homophily, is ignored if not rejected. Moreover, the trends would indicate that couples confront one or more of the following factors: Difficulty in resolving fundamental problems due to age differences; an inability to see the same advantages in dissimilarity as in past periods; certain financial and emotional difficulties in married life are now so complex as to be ungovernable.

In such an environment, men and women will often force themselves to accept each other in a relationship, where certain superficial factors match, but where deeper and more pervasive factors do not. Young couples put great emphasis on consensus and agreement, but agreement in real life is often much lower than thought.[172] Couples stress agreement in various areas, such as politics, spending habits, religion, leisure, children, and careers because like any small group they are dependent on solidarity in order to survive. However, in the wake of the millions rushing to use the 'panic door' of divorce, marriage has become much like any other group, where the uniqueness of the relationship has vanished. The idea of marriage as being unlike any other relationship has given way to the idea of an affiliation as moderately differentiated from others but increasingly similar in its various parameters to ordinary leisure and business friendships. This is not to say married life is the same as unmarried life, for the two will always remain distinct entities requiring different roles and obligations. But where before marriage was indissoluble, now it is 'partible' like any business partnership. Where intimate ideas were once passed only between husband and wife, now even co-workers are told extremely personal information. These changes have inspired an increased insistence on ideological solidarity, particularly when couples feel compelled (from media influences or otherwise) to detail activity from a much broader spectrum. The special maturity and considerations that the marital union used to demand have fallen by the wayside and now the couple have to struggle with the same pitfalls and weaknesses of any other 'dyad'.

Thus, the situations and developments discussed here are perhaps not surprising, as the modern couple arises out of a matrix that nourishes sometimes very different cultures and backgrounds, all made largely possible by migration and economic development. In the era of individual freedom and materialism, which has in many ways catalysed migration, families have taken to disassembling social traditions as they see fit. There cannot be a reversal of this depreciation of marriage except when people come to live in culturally homogeneous regions, or when people pay more attention to the characteristics of the person they intend to marry. The latter approach at the present time seems more feasible, although not necessarily likely to happen.

Notwithstanding the many advantages to homology, to press for it socially is in some cases undesirable. The ideal of similarity in attitudes when too forceful creates fewer *options* in people's lives, which in turn creates frustration, psychological impairment, and instability. Clearly, certain psychological factors have a primary role in fulfilling or denying conceptual models of household form. There is nothing in these factors that in and of itself actually is a physical obstacle to matrimony and forming a family. The modern world presents enough opportunities for forming even the most basic household, far more than in the past, where men and women in many, though by no means all, cases had to depend on inheritance for marriage. Yet the changes in ideals has produced a more complex and difficult marital situation than ever. Whilst similarity within marriage is, in general, a good thing, it should not be imposed but rather induced through natural formation, people coming together because of congruence of temperament, education, interests and occupation.

Social Disruption, Family Order

Why have people become so insistent on the ideas of a 'perfect' married life, 'fulfilment' only through marriage, and a low willingness to change, leading to an intolerance of diversity? Up until now, we have obliquely mentioned the industrial economy as a source of these ideas. In this section we shall examine in detail how the demand for freedom of movement and affiliation, as a function of business and commerce, has impacted the ability of the family to bring love and affection. Although both males and females have changed their attitudes and behaviours, causing a reduction in *connubium's* ability to fulfill, the story of the loss of affection is really one that centres on changes in the concept of home life. The activity and structure of the family were forced to undergo several revisions, and the role most affected by this would be the one which deals with most of the details of household, namely that of the wife. Thus, womanhood or the *feminine* would be the subject of transformation, with the masculine seeing less change.[173] We already alluded earlier to an aspect of this dynamic by demonstrating that older men find it important to marry younger women who are 'tough' and 'strong'. After reviewing historical developments, it will become apparent why so many consider marriage an 'institution under threat': it is because the institution has been reconstructed, with positive womanhood removed and all of the ignoble elements of the masculine sex worked into the structure, weakening it to the point where it verges on collapse.

It is difficult to know how people define roles, no more than in the past, when even the concept of 'role' was entirely connected to occupation and status. There could be no mother or father role without their being the authority inherent in these positions. As a group, the highest authority rested with the nobility, who also therefore saw themselves embodying the apotheosis of a role, be it as mothers, fathers, children, siblings, uncles, aunts, men or women. Moreover, as the nobility had the time, the education, and a definite necessity for defining their various roles, we could look to them for legitimate insight as to how Western man in general perceives the masculine and feminine. Most importantly, since they had the *opportunity* to live life, pretty much any way they wanted, freed from toiling and manual labour, freed from most material constraints except attending to official protocols, the nobility could conceive of the ideal without prejudice, as a product of the refined intellect. In short, the life of the nobleman was to be the standard by which everyone should live. Naturally, this type of life was a prototype that not everyone could achieve, no matter how wealthy. Nonetheless, ideals about family life were procured by the middle and lower classes from elite purveyors, although how much of an influence on behaviour they had is something that has to be determined. The ruling class apparently had genuine insight into these ideals, and did not merely propagate an arbitrary standard meant to preserve their power. They did peer deep into themselves and their culture to see the true nature of the masculine and feminine, of family life, the home, the ultimate 'centre of power'.

What the nobility found in their enquiries was that being a member of the elite meant not only being superior materially, but also morally and ethically. Women in particular were expected to perpetuate all the best traits of humanity. This would include compassion, discipline, intelligence and honesty; they had to show great foresight, discussing openly these matters, diligently pursuing the ideal. Most women emphasised virtue, and pursued a course that was meant to promote warmth and affection.

Conversely, they were suspicious of sexual matters and feelings, as well as all other frivolous pursuits. Regnant in the domestic but not public sphere, subordinated to men in many ways, these women nonetheless held interrelated concepts of power, wealth, virtue, moderation, all to be inextricably tied to being a member of the nobility.[174] However, it is most important to understand that *the expression of the virtues was not tied to being married, having children or any other specific social arrangement*. They were very conscious of the role that they played, more so than men and other classes in society, and so were instrumental in promoting the ideals embodied within that role. The goal of this pattern of behaviour was to safeguard affection between men and women, an ideal that was often mentioned but not very often met. In many ways, the ideal noblewoman was not very different from the model of the Christian saint, except that the former had certain temporal powers and responsibilities that the latter often did not. Perhaps it is somewhat contradictory to expect noblewomen to produce and raise heirs to keep the family name, and at the same time to promote chastity. In the same way, it is difficult to epitomise modesty and humility when being attended by courtiers and servants, whilst wearing splendid, if not opulent, garments. Nonetheless, obeying male social precepts, tightly controlling household affairs, setting the standard for morality, submission to worthy endeavours, were connected to the concept of the 'feminine'.

We cannot easily separate these factors, and few women, no matter how latitudinarian, have tried; that is, until this century. Although being called on to produce children, women in general were ideally thought to be removed from the world, taking care of the household, a place of the 'now' without past or future, a place of security and care. Social and natural circumstances would come and go, but noblewomen continued to be the protectors of the important things in life, of the things that have longevity and solidity. It did not really matter whether a woman was married or had children in order to live this ideal. The key responsibility that the ideal woman had was to skilfully arrange and organise the items and forces that were present in the household, to bring to completion the mission that God had assigned to her, after giving consideration to the needs and limitations of her personality. Where men were concerned with the transitory nature of business and politics, women cared for the things of the home, which indeed have remained unchanged far longer than anything in the 'male' world outside.

Whatever the success or urgency in implementing these ideas, the Industrial Revolution did not allow the moralisation process to continue. The public were called upon to make sacrifices not for God or home, but for industry and country. The period between the early 1800s and the 1840s was a time when the public were directing their attention on the impact of technology and machinery on society. Although many communities opposed mechanisation, it succeeded in pervading all aspects of life, and protests against mechanisation were met by stern governmental countermeasures. This new society of the machine, of migration, dislocation, confusion and violence, prompted a call by individuals and groups to bring strict order to the primary social unit, the household.[175] People were witnessing an increase of unusual or deviant behaviours, including alcoholism, illegitimacy, opium use, prostitution, membership in secret societies and occult groups, pornography, violence, riots, theft, murder, rape and fraud.

Turmoil in society grew within the context of rapid growing cities, big business and enlarging government authority, but in spite of the power of these burgeoning entities, they were unable to stop the disruption. The concept of autonomy, so crucial for commerce, had degenerated into lawlessness. To keep the economy growing, and the independence ethos strong, the family structure had to change. The last line of defence *was* the family, and measures were taken by fearful individuals to counteract the threat. Anxiety over the etiolation of the ideal of marriage made men and women stoically depend on formalism to guarantee that it would be met, even if in their hearts they did not believe it would work. Just as the labour unions forced workers to join their 'brothers' in a movement against exploitation, so too did the family 'union' wage a struggle against its own tormentors, whether they be ill-bred suitors, thieving servants, licentious neighbours or conniving relatives. Thus, we can see in the mechanical workplace and the 'mechanical' family reactions that appear companionate and virtuous, but that do not fulfill emotional needs and that also clash with a self- centred independence ethos. Although regimentation was effective in counteracting the dangers of recklessness, it left little time for the family and little spontaneous affection between family members. The model of strict adherence to the virtues was palliated by what people saw as the realities of the day; being 'soft' was quickly becoming a vice and not an asset. Respect and honour automatically paid to virtue were dwindling and women began to fear a loss of social position, indeed they felt that they were becoming only another 'ethnic' group clamouring for rights.[176] Thus, not only was emotional security being lost, but also independence; two highly important aspects of life were losing their vitality in spite of the onslaught of impassioned speeches and vigorous social action.

Although the emphasis on family life was welcome, the maternal domestic role was becoming the only viable role for women. Virtue and social separateness, although important, were being overwhelmed by the demands of achieving and maintaining a high standard of living and the careful upbringing of children. It was becoming increasingly difficult, in a materialistic competitive society, to marry a person close to the ideal, someone kind, disciplined, truthful and loyal. The changes to marriage that had taken place by the 19th century were so great as to frighten many people away from pursuing relationships outside the circle of their relatives. Homology thus became an instrument for social stability. Ideally, men and women could meet one another under the assumption that many of their ideas about marriage and family were already comparable. They could then deal more easily and thoroughly with the other problems, including employment, career, and standard of living preferences and other critical areas undergoing significant changes. This is an instance where attitudes are not determined personally, but are strongly influenced from the outside.

Society accommodated to a certain extent this xenophobia (or was it really an unrealistic fear?). For children, the households of middle and upper class Victorians were often closed to outside contact, except to relatives and close friends of the family. The few eligible individuals that a person might have met in adolescence would only have been siblings and cousins. Since the former were sexually *ultra vires*, but the latter were not, marriage between cousins fulfilled both the need for social duty and the personal need for emotional security. In the restricted climate of many families, making a cousin one's wife or husband provided an enticing solution to the dilemma of how to live an acceptable life and still avoid the awkward difficulties of discovering a suitable, respectable mate. The prevalence of marriages between cousins is not known with certainty, but in the wealthier classes it was possibly well above one in twenty.[177] The very prevalence of such marriages tends to prove the assertions made here: Why would people marry cousins unless few people apart from relatives were available, and why would availability be low unless families restricted their social circle due to a grave suspicion of the motivations of 'outsiders'? Serious distrust must have been quite palpable in English and other societies during the early part of the 'glorious' Industrial Revolution.

Marriage within the family, namely with cousins, was one convenient way for men and women to progress along the life course without undue investment in the search for partners. This was especially true of busy professional men who did not wish to take time away from their business for such romantic and basically impractical enterprises. The conveyance of family wealth into dependable hands might have been another important reason for marriage between relatives. However, the main motivation for cousin marriage was grounded in a love for the familiar and safe, as a cousin would often resemble, both physically and temperamentally, a beloved parent or sibling. Falling in love with 'outsiders' was becoming too precarious, and a cousin had an easily verifiable history and background. There was the unmistakable impression that stability and predictability in human relations were ebbing. One of the most significant books of the Victorian period, Charlotte Brontë's *Jane Eyre*, put forward a bizarre plot development that apparently did not strain the credibility of the work: the heroine's prospective husband turns out not only to be already married, but his wife is a disturbed, tragic figure living in the attic of his mansion. Evidently, this motif, and it was repeated in various forms in other works, resounded with people who had become highly alarmed at the shocking things that they themselves had uncovered.

Some historians and psychologists have seen fit to invoke the theory that cousin unions were a so-called displacement of incestuous feelings, sexual desire being shifted from a close relative to another close, but socially acceptable relative. There is little reason to suspect that this is the case; it is far from certain that the prime reason for these marriages was a *sexual* desire for close relatives. Rather, it seems that they desired a quite understandable close but *non-sexual* relationship with family members, and that they wished, if possible, to continue it in some form into adulthood. The love of a father might prompt a young girl to marry her cousin not because she wishes another father per se, but because she wishes to maintain the same type of constructive *relationship* with her husband that she had had with her father in childhood and adolescence. This is especially true if the father died young or was away on business most of the time. We have encountered this before in our discussion on how the loss of affection and guidance at home can lead to an increase in marriage tendency. Thus, close attachment to relatives has always concerned emotional security and continuity, rather than the fulfilment of secret forbidden sexual obsessions.

This marriage practise became so prevalent that it was a matter of public debate by the mid-19th century. There were critics and advocates of close relation marriage, many echoing the genetic concepts of the Eugenics movement, whose members encouraged or discouraged inbreeding because of the propagation of superior or inferior traits, as the case may be. As love was viewed as an 'irrational' aspect to life, the great Rationalists of the late 19th century, men often separated from their emotions, had little choice but to invoke a 'rational' explanation for why so many people had a fervent attraction for family members, even if they could not marry them. In time, all male-female affection became linked in some way with the 'basic' urge of sexual attraction. Carnality was seen as the unalterable basis for almost all kinds of human interactions, and was a beast especially difficult to tame when people of the opposite sex, of similar age, background and emotional status, lived in close quarters. The issue of closeness between members of a family, not surprisingly, entered into the discussions between doctors and patients, giving shape to the burgeoning sexualisation theories of human nature, the most well-known of which was Freud's Oedipal complex. Whatever problems arose in life could be traced back to the way in which people dealt with or did not deal with this underlying sexual longing. We can see in these developments the beginning of the substitution of sex for affection in relationships. According to the science of the time, real 'affection' did not exist. Deeply emotionally satisfying feeling about someone else, instigated only by the sharing of ideas, was a myth, and the basic goal of any intimate relationship was to satisfy sexuall lusts. Thus, unforseen by most, the search for homology in companionate relationship led in a twisting path to a place where a number of social and scientific programmes branched off to assault traditional wisdom and decency.

Hence, close affiliation between relatives was thought by many scientists to be nothing more than a rather pathetic attempt to live out a fantasy incestuous affair with someone that resembled a parent in physical appearance and/or in personality. It is far more likely that people cultivated deep friendships with close relations exactly as a way to *negate* or defuse the issue of carnality. In time, females could no longer take up a sisterly relationship with a male belonging outside a two-degree limit, without the apparition of sex appearing; the talk about 'keeping our women safe' was a sad reflection on a society that was quickly losing its moral restrictions. Men are now always 'on the make', and sexuality always threatens to interfere, even destroy, the emotional relationship. Alternatively, since sex between relatives such as brother and sister was unthinkable, a loving, respectful and affectionate tie between siblings was ever more popular. It *freed* the individual from having to worry about how to proceed in his emotional life; marriage, sex, child-birth, family were all removed from the equation. The spectre of the carnal was safely and quietly locked away.

It was against this background that a critical struggle was waged by the people of the Victorian period in understanding whether the affection between the sexes was always based solely on a profound emotional dynamic, or whether strong affection was always linked with sexual activity. Living the former, traditional dynamic was relatively easier than in our day, and close affectional ties between people, both related and unrelated, were common for centuries. Such ties gave people an alternative to marriage, allowing an objective assessment of one's own needs and the social environment. No one had to rush into anything that was less then secure; too many enormous changes had already occurred in everyday life to be complacent about marriage. Notwithstanding these advantages, the changes in social relations in the 19th century made friendships with people outside the family more precarious, and so many turned away from tradition and inward towards finding a new scheme. As we have already stated, the tradition of affection continued but the sphere of potential friends shrank, and at the same time, society insisted on greater personal sacrifice, on a woman's marital and maternal 'duty' to satisfy men's sexual appetites, raise children and maintain a home. The literature of the period reveals this struggle by presenting many combinations of individuals in relationships where love, concupiscence, child-rearing and marriage were all separate mental and emotional areas (see previous discussion on how modern women separate these roles). By realising the merits and disadvantages of each, hopefully a greater understanding would emerge, and people would be more in control of their destinies.

Order and control over resources in private life, which gave women the power to choose cooperative and considerate marriage partners, were dwindling however. Thus, we begin to see why we said that the changes of our era are embodied in changes in the feminine. The aversion to growing up, sex, and pregnancy were closely tied to losing the bond of intimacy, as the 'pragmatic' idea of having a marriage where sex predominated over affection was intolerable. Women reacted to this by succumbing to their first natural reaction: reject marriage and childbirth. They wished to find happiness in purely non-sexual intimacy with family members, or if necessary, no intimacy at all. There is much to indicate that such a desire for chaste love was common, but the pressure to conform to social dicta about marriage, children and domestic roles was overwhelming. Intuitively, we know that anytime large numbers of people pull away deliberately from fulfilling the ideal of companionate love, some kind of damage has occurred to the average person's psyche. What is this damage in the period we are discussing? We can see that in recent times personal antipathy is the likely cause of a delay in marriage, whereas previous generations often did not marry due to an external economic agency. However, firm, logical statements about what women found wrong with men, marriage, family and children are uncommon, and instead we see the increasing use of psychological devices that allow indirect avoidance of responsibility. Thus, there is evidence that this antipathy towards marriage was based on a reaction to an *unarticulated and undifferentiated fear*. Our role here is precisely to state the feelings and that thoughts that were concealed during this important period in Western history. As shall be seen, the damage that has occurred to the psyche is in the critical 'interface' between individual and society, arising out of an imbalance between individual need and social need. When such damage is done, both love and independence as major goals in life become unreachable.

This first step is to examine what methods were used to avoid direct responsibility for refusing marriage. One method, although radical, reveals the depths of despair into which many women had fallen. A woman could revert to a child-like status and render herself unsuitable as a wife by inducing secondary amenorrhoea. The only way such an effect could be reliably accomplished was by losing enough weight so as to cease menses, and thus to produce a 'second childhood'. Far from being a very recent disorder, self-starvation, or anorexia nervosa as it came to be called, was first noted around the year 1800, with the first professional discussion about the subject being held in 1873. This disease appeared in France by 1892, where it was tied to a fear of being overweight. Thus, the goal of attaining an hourglass, glamourous figure, the modern preoccupation with superficiality of appearance, had become established. Yet, even early on, self-starvation was connected with a definite intention to avoid entering adulthood. In the first two decades of this century, doctors in Switzerland associated it with a desire to regress mentally; by making themselves very thin, girls end not only ovulation but also their physical maturity, which in turn obviates marriage and childbirth. The inability to weigh the myriad arguments for or against marriage was symbolically rendered as psychological paralysis that was often associated with anorexia. These girls explained that in an effort to evade the onerous responsibilities they felt were present in marriage, they wished in some way to return to childhood; a more fanciful way to put it was that they simply wanted to fall sleep and wake up grown old.[178]

It is, upon examination of the attitudes of ordinary people and professionals of the time, easy to see what was feared by these women. Life had become subject to more rigid rules than ever before, where even the duties of wife and mother merited scientific and public scrutiny. By the 1890s, child-rearing needed to be standardised as well, and not surprisingly evolved into having a 'scientific' and 'professional' appearance. The individual was increasingly losing his or her personal freedom, ironically at a time when freedom was supposed to be on the ascendency. How was love supposed to flourish and be maintained in such an environment? If humorists and satirists are allowed to some extent to articulate the most disturbing thoughts of the people, then perhaps Oscar Wilde's observation on matrimony was revelatory: 'One should always be in love. That is the reason one should never marry'.[179] The implication is that the natural outcome of love, which is marriage, could never be reached; the individual found himself in limbo. Details as to how society began to seriously alter the family paradigm can be found in the 'strange history' of changes in the education and socialisation of women.[180] The changes brought on by the Industrial Age by the late 19th century created a double-stress phenomenon. On the one hand, domestic work was had become less interesting and less rewarding, but on the other hand, this work demanded greater expertise and proficiency. The accomplishments of men and women in the outside world of business and science outshone and trivialised the 'quaint' role of housewife.

However, housewives were not under any less scrutiny to fulfill their traditional duties. Indeed, now more than ever they were expected to perform flawlessly as making their own special contribution to the world. Physicists, doctors, chemists, and other professionals were careful to delineate the special demands of their occupations from that of the mere 'housewife', without forgetting the key role she still had to play in maintaining a living environment for a husband and children. Due to the fact that many women went to school or worked, they could no longer learn domestic skills by apprenticeship to their mothers. Now these skills were taught in the schools, and magazines, books and other materials were published as guides for women. One young mother from Indiana voiced the apprehension common to many in the 1920s when she said, 'Life was simple for my mother...In those days one did not realize that there was so much to be known about the care of children. I realize that I ought to be half a dozen experts, but I am afraid of making mistakes and usually do not know where to go for advice'.[181] This was at a time when the childless rate for couples was at its peak, and there was the demand on women to further education and careers. Initially, this meant using a simple model where one lived one role, but forewent marriage and the others, but it eventually became common to use a model that integrated marriage, parenthood and career.

It is in one area of married life in particular that made women lose much of their independence. During the 'maturation' phase of the modern era, the idea became firmly impressed that the actual *mission* in the life of the woman was that of *motherhood*. G. Stanley Hall wrote an influential work called *Adolescence*, published in 1904, which although it contained much erroneous information, at the very least propagated certain critical concepts that would become part of the new simplified ideal of marriage. Women, in this worldview, could never find true fulfilment without becoming wives and mothers; indeed, a woman's 'body and soul are made for maternity'. A basic, innate need to take care of children, their own or others, through birth, adoption, teaching, etc., lies at the heart of the feminine. In a society that allowed men and women to fraternise, Hall worried about women becoming too masculinised and losing sight of their true nature. It should come as no surprise that he also strongly urged against permanent celibacy and late marriage.[182] In a mixture of truth and fiction, Hall said publicly what many said privately. The ideal of 'love' was made easier by entirely excising affection, love in its most potent form. Women did actually gain some power over their lives by indisputably emphasising a unique domain: their reproductive role. However, emotional satisfaction, unless tied to a biological function, is not part of this lifestyle, and probably cannot even be achieved. Some of the more traditional females ironically saw this new 'role' as slipping several steps down, a degeneration from the time when women had true power. The new woman was acting more the 'rustic' than the peasants ever did, a prototype hardly advanced enough to meet the demands of the new age.

Complex social developments called for a major *homogenisation* and *simplification* of standards, two themes we have pursued in this chapter, themes that would restore order and defuse some of the angst surrounding married life. Although women voiced confusion over the new 'rules', their confusion was not really so much about complexity but rather about simple knowledge. The new way of life was indeed simple and direct, but the difficulty lay in finding an authentic source. There had to be a narrowing of the diverse set of household forms that existed when people had a secure traditional culture, which provided what they believed were all the answers necessary for family life. In fact, whenever couples wish to reduce instability in home life and when they wish to have more time for themselves, they reduce the number of children born into the household. For example, in the well-studied early modern parish of Colyton (Devon, England), the number of children in a completed family ranged from 0 to 10, with the period 1560-1629 showing more of a tendency to cluster around the mean of about 5, than in the period 1647-1837, when more diversity was apparent. However, this diversity pertains more for women marrying under 30 than marrying over 30. When the two groups are combined, there is less of a difference.[183] As we approach the present day, this parish, like all others in England, reduced its variance again in fertility. The variability in fertility from region to region and household to household has historically always been extensive.[184] Thus, household form, and by extension its rules of operation, is by no means etched in stone, and can be quite changeable. Women could quite contentedly have many, few or no children without an explosion of psychopathology requiring psychoanalysis, drugs or group therapy.

The equivalisation of women with maternity is not a traditional idea, but a recent one, at least amongst the middle and upper classes. Thus, it is highly significant to note that in regards to an absolutely critical aspect of life, younger married women of the past were considerably different from the ones of our day in their views on children, with the latter being far more constrained in their ideals. Older married women are similar in both earlier and modern periods in their preference of having the *least* number of children possible. Being perhaps more desirous of self-development, older women preferred having more time to themselves, and were less tolerant of disruptions brought about by numerous pregnancies and children.

By the 1880s, there is pellucid demographic evidence of a Western standardisation of marriage through the homogenisation of ideas concerning maternity, womanhood, and family life. In line with this, three cultural fertility standards were implemented in phases. In the United States, the first standard entailed reducing the number of families which had *high* fertility. Very large families (of 7 or more births) became much less common in the female cohort born in the 1860s (marrying in the 1880s). Thus, women married, stayed or worked at home, and had children, but avoided very large numbers. A second standard was implemented with the concept that anything more than *three* children was necessary. The rising trend in the incidence of one and two child families began with the cohort born in the 1860 to 1880s (marrying around 1880 to 1910) and evidently this trend has not yet slackened. The proportion of such families increased from about 20% in the 1880s to 63% in 1987,[185] an incredible transformation in fertility. In this scenario, women married, stayed home, but had fewer children than previously. Theory normally determines people's behaviour, but in this period, theory about the ideal family generally *conformed* with practise, that is, behaviour came first, then attitude. The proportion of the population who believed that having two or three children was ideal rose from 64% in 1936 to 76% in 1986. However, only about half of women past their child-bearing years were actually happy with their fertility; fully one-third said they wished they had had more children.[186] This demonstrates that people allowed the cultural ideal to be imposed on them, at the cost of their happiness and security. They accepted an abstract idea for the good of society, but were unhappy about its implementation in their own lives.

Respect for a traditional standard to a certain extent was still conspicuous when women avoided having children if they were working. This is evident in the rise in the numbers of nulliparous women parallel to the rise in the number of working married women. The proportion of women not having any children began to rise in earnest in the 1860s to 1870s birth cohort (i.e. marrying 1880 to 1900), consistent with the increasingly common phenomenon of the working married woman.[187] However, the phenomenon of married women having no children peaked in the 1920s and then abated, even though married women continued to show ever greater involvement in the workforce. Hence, the third and final modern standard was implemented, wherein women married, had only two children, and worked before and sometimes during marriage.[188] This last standard created a major change in the life of the average woman, more so than the changes engendered by the previous two cultural standards.

Today, people admit to the relevance of the third cultural standard mentioned above by saying that lower fertility is the result of wives working and the expense of raising children.[189] Interestingly, equally important but more prosocial issues now receive hardly any attention; how to raise many children in an unstable socioeconomic environment, or how to morally educate and guide children from large families, are considered either old-fashioned or eccentric questions. The present fertility model is probably one that receives wide support across social divisions, such as ethnic group, nation, class, education, region or political party. Consequently, there must be powerful fundamental reasons in support of it which makes it resilient to change. Cultural ideas about fertility are often not the result of objective examination, but social contrivances that serve the purpose of bringing a distracted society back to the critical issues in life. Having two children in marriage is the overwhelming choice of modern culture, with no differentiation between socioeconomic and demographic categories.

Changes brought about by industrialisation and migration elicited the romantic 'love conquers all' concept of marriage, along with a non-romantic 'natural' sex-related argument for marriage. A greater diversity of ideas was put forward publicly in relation to achieving a viable marriage, but less tolerance of dissimilarity and ambiguity in personal views on marriage was common, too. In some respects, standards concerning family life narrowed, as for example in ideas concerning the ideal number of children a woman should have. This homology was necessary due to a loss of virtue, especially the virtues of caution and of striving for self-perfection. In the past, people took the knowledge gained from family, community and their own observations and assiduously put it into creating a personal 'culture' for their *own* version of family, adjusting this 'culture' to the size of the household, whether it contained 2, 6, 10, or 17 people. These rules must have worked well, for how else can we explain the lack of perceptible 'family value' crises in societies with long-standing large variations in household sizes and types? Individuals in the modern age became unable to adjust and decide for themselves the proper family-level standards, and collective society put its 'heads together' in an attempt to determine standards for only one or two types of household. In this way society limited its options, and consequently, limited the rewards gotten from family life.

However, in many other respects, ideas about of 'correct' behaviour multiplied, with a parallel increase in contradictions in standards. Women in the modern age were put upon to be experts at being wives, experts at motherhood, and experts at teaching. And all this with hardly any training at all! In line with this, fertility had to be lowered. Fewer children meant more time was available for being with one's spouse, and also greater freedom for outside work due to less time needed for domestic tasks. However, the ability to work not only increased one's standard of living, but also conveniently bestowed the option of divorce. Since wives could now more easily support themselves without a husband, not least because they had fewer children to raise, they could conceivably divorce their husbands and become truly independent. The sole 'mission' of women was motherhood, yet here were the means by which she could escape such a role. It is unfortunate that the advantages that women now possessed could hardly compensate for the loss of independence they suffered in the critical life area of the family, namely, sacrificing the freedom to choose marriage, the freedom to choose one's marriage partner, and the freedom to determine how many children one desires.

A multiplicity of ideas is often good, but often it is a confusion of standards, clashes of concepts between regions, generations and classes. Science was called upon to end the commotion, to provide the light that would lead the individual out of 'darkness'. The destination brought on something of a shock, however. Naturally, at first this anxiety was not articulated but was felt, as marriage became an increasingly precarious enterprise. People were demanding that ideas and standards be similar, but at the same time a swelling diversity in standards and commitments greater than at any point in the history of Western civilisation offered enormous challenges. Since women were expected to run the household, they were the ones most affected by these changes in concepts of family, hence our statement at the beginning of this section that the changes in family were in many ways due to a change in the concept of the feminine.

Whether they like it or not, women in the latter half of the 20th century *must* marry, they *must* marry someone very similar to themselves, they *must* have children, but these children *cannot* number more than three. Of course, one can always say, quite accurately, there is no formal 'law' that forces anyone to do these things, but there are informal social rules that incorporate punitive measures that are just as effective in getting compliance as those the state uses, such as the lawsuit, jail and removal of property. The ideas that society gave to women were taken because they solved immediately pressing problems, not because they brought greater contentment than older traditional ideas. Quite simply, pragmatism is really no replacement for idealism.

What has occurred over the last six or seven generations has been a transformation of family and marriage as a result of people's unwillingness to compensate for the demographic and cultural challenges engendered by the Industrial Revolution. Let us review the transformation of the methods used to achieve the ideal of love. The first major social reaction to the disruption of the Industrial Age was to *restrict* the circle of people that could be considered for marriage. By focussing on people within one's extended family, the vagaries of marrying a person who was a stranger could be avoided. The next major reaction was a *retreat* from marriage because of certain fears: the loss of affection from a husband due to material concerns, business matters or a mistress; a large number of pregnancies; a reification of the notion of sexual attractiveness. Even marrying someone known well to the family, someone with an attachment to moral and ethical principles, could not guarantee resistance to temptation and happiness in marriage. Women used various devices to remove themselves from consideration for marriage; others used ways to delay marriage, at least until they felt mature enough to endure the problems they feared would arise. In the next social correction, the modern age began to provide a means of establishing control in the household. By finding that they could reduce *fertility* in order to increase their independence by allowing time for other tasks and to mollify their ill feelings about raising children, women became more confident about marriage. Men and women could live in a family where the option for both husband and wife to work existed, where children could be born at the time desired, the number of children could be limited to a desired number, and the option existed to end the marriage if emotional satisfaction was not achieved because women alone could now support themselves and their children if they had any. Of course, what works in theory, 'on paper' so to speak, often does not work out in reality if the theory is based on incorrect assumptions. The correct assumptions are as yet not widely known.

Love is an ideal thing, marriage a real thing; a confusion of the real with the ideal never goes unpunished.
~Johann Wolfgang von Goethe

Impulsu et caeca magnaque cupidine ducti conjugium petimus.
(We, led by the impulse of our minds and by blind passion, desire marriage.)
~Juvenal (AD 55-c 127)

Chapter 5
In the Aftermath of Pragmatism

A Balancing Act

When there is a narrowing of concerns in any area of life, people ultimately fall back on simple materialism, in other words, pragmatism, a word that can carry both positive or negative connotations. If we agree that experiencing mutual love is a greater accomplishment than experiencing independence, then we must use it in the latter sense; in our world, the focus is on methods that primarily maintain one's independence, not on methods that lead to companionship. As we have seen in this book, there are many external factors with which the individual must contend that seriously affect his or her personal desire for love and affection. Perhaps apprehensively, people learn to have their love ideal co-exist with their material aims. Then they learn to modify their relationships to make them conform to their desire for independence through simplification and homogenisation of standards. The problems arising from these two phenomena have been examined. Knowing how our ancestors dealt with materialism, dependence, cooperation and freedom, we see in the modern relationship great weakness that does not inspire confidence that the struggle between the love ideal and independence ideal is being resolved happily.

We have noted how well people fill deficiencies in their lives by establishing intimate relationships with the opposite sex; these relationships can make up for many shortfalls in home life, many lapses in sustenance and advice. It is easy to see a particular man or woman as a fountain of support, when the ideal is articulated. But that is a real man or woman on the other side, not just a projection or image. They have a unique collection of experiences, strengths, weaknesses and beliefs. Do people give much consideration to these factors? How well do people assess a relationship? How do they decide if it is right for them? How do they know what to do and say to make it work? Do they evaluate the situation with reason and forethought, or with bias and subjectivity?

In this chapter, we will examine the capacity of the average individual to develop and balance in his own mind the various issues relating to love and independence. In previous discussions, it was apparent that people are easily impressed by exogenous factors, whether it is at work, home or school. They also frequently take into account their personal needs. But it is not easy for even the most virtuous person to completely remove self-centred desires or to draw distinctions between self-interest and other-interest. Humans, because they covet self-realisation, recognition, appreciation and equal treatment, predicate their attraction to the opposite sex on, at the very least, a desire for security, material progress and success in society. Self-interest can often be veiled by thoughts and expressions of love, but in reality the desire for companionship is *only* pragmatic. The most critical factor in relation to a cross-sex relationship is how the individual develops the ideal of love, which embodies the rules that will provide companionship and affection. This ideal's development and maintenance must be examined, in its relationship to competing demands of independence and the limitations of the individual. The basic mortal drive to be praised is invariably tied to a desire for independence, since how can one be respected for one's accomplishments if they are the result of other people's actions? Thus, everyone wishes to experience independence, where the individual stands alone in his or her achievement. But this will clash with the modern version of the love ideal, which in turn is related to dependence, or more accurately, over-dependance. The modern economy has given people the opportunity to proceed through life all alone quite comfortably, and the whole of society can now offer compensation for the lack of a spouse. The independence ethos can be realised, but at the expense of the love ideal.

Because of this focus on material matters, marriage is often thought of as simply the setting up of the joint residency of two people, but that is not the case. It involves much more:

- establishing a household
- finding and keeping an occupation
- accumulating possessions, including furniture
- attaining physical security
- realising a particular standard of living
- bearing and raising children
- integrating career and business with family life
- dealing with relatives on both sides of the family
- providing for the children's future
- rearranging one's life after children leave home

At every major point in married life there is a threat to the romantic marriage concept (exclusivity and total continuing dependence) and it is up to the individual to establish which concerns are primary and which ones are secondary in maintaining love. The burden of success falls squarely on the shoulders of the individual. Hence, the complexity in juggling material concerns with emotional needs requires maturity, discipline, objectivity and good planning.

No Way to Win at Love

As we stated in the first chapter, one of the virtues is empathy. The ideal of love must develop within a context of a mature use of moral reasoning, which involves a consideration of the condition, situation or status of other people. Everyone develops this ideal sometime during childhood, probably between the ages of 7 and 10. During this period, the conflict between continuing reliance on parents and the desire for independence creates insecurity and the individual begins to think about alliances, not just mere transitory friendships. Thus, the ideal of love is cultivated against a background of childhood *insecurity*. What they need in more than just a play pal, but a real friend that they can confide in and rely upon. This theme develops, albeit slowly. As they enter puberty, they quickly understand that their closest friend can only be someone from the opposite sex, and so the beginning of the lifelong desire for affiliation with the opposite sex. One comes to the realisation of the *special* bond between masculine and feminine, to an understanding of the timelessness of it. Thus, social factors that cause uncertainty and instability in sex roles can create insecurity in life before marriage and after marriage.

The various aspects of an ideal friendship become more solidified in adolescence, but unfortunately in our day this process has for certain complex reasons been stultified. Instead of showing some haste in becoming aware of what exactly constitutes 'love', that is, the actual day to day aspects, the markers and signals, there is a tendency to add to one's knowledge but slowly. Perhaps this happens because they have come to understand that the profundity of the ideal makes its fulfilment elusive, and relationships therefore present no urgency to augment awareness. It is a simple matter for the individual then to resist the urge to add to and crystallise the ideal, since it becomes increasingly apparent it will not be reached except through great effort. Without assistance from family and adults, the ideal is left in pieces, hardly mature or integrated. There is much fumbling around by individuals, trying to understand how society and relationships work and interact.

When the children of our day are left to their *own* devices in determining the parameters of love and affection, they encounter many problems, not necessarily because they lack the potential to do it themselves, but rather stemming from surprisingly slow to develop moral reasoning mechanisms in modern life. EISENBERG ET AL. (1991) queried the attitudes of three groups of middle class children. One group of 32 children were tested a total of seven times as they progressed through the ages of 4 through 14. Two other groups of children, one eighth graders (about 13 years old) and the other tenth graders (about 15 years old), were interviewed only one time using similar questions. Although pragmatic concerns, stereotypes of good and bad persons, role taking (taking the perspective of the other person), and positive affect relating to consequences of actions all *increased* by a sizable amount, other aspects hardly changed at all. The most notable of the latter are (* denotes especially *low growth):* improving the community or society*; responsibility to uphold laws, duty, norms; generalised reciprocity (exchange not on a one to one basis, but of benefit to a larger group); sympathetic concern for others*; negative affect relating to consequences; positive or negative* affect regarding living up to internalised values; protecting individual rights preventing injustices to others*; equality of individuals*. The oldest children in the study were the most motivated by physical, material or psychological needs of the other person, stereotyped views and pragmatic concerns. Moreover, although reasoning increases with age in general, some areas actually *declined* in most children from ages 13-16; some children experienced large declines in ability at certain points.

This study presents a troubling picture of modern humanity at a stage in life when they have responsibility and power, but do not have the inclination to use these resources wisely. The authors of the study are strangely quiet about this finding, with the only substantive comment being that '[t]hese categories of reasoning were used quite infrequently...'.[190] Even though the researchers were specifically concerned with trends of moral reasoning during childhood, they could hardly have overlooked the larger social relevance of their findings.

As these moral understandings are considered essential to the formation of a proper loving relationship, it is disturbing that a 15-year-old individual, whose moral reasoning is really no better than a five-year-old's, might become entangled with high-stake physical and emotional intimacies. Processes of integrity such as sympathetic reasoning, conscience relating to violation of own norms, an ambition to see equality, justice, in a better world, are hardly developed, yet these are necessary in establishing a solid, lasting intimate friendship.

There is little question that 'other-oriented concerns and perspective-taking tendencies are intimately involved in moral reasoning'.[191] Such concerns and tendencies are fostered by parents, relatives and teachers, who must give children a wide-ranging understanding of human behaviour and clearly defined behavioural boundaries. Children aged 10 to 18 have moral judgement that is largely dependent on positive intra-family relationships and stimulation of moral reasoning, more than on family structure.[192] Teenage children of authoritative parents use the most moral or post-conventional reasoning, followed by children of permissive parents, then authoritarian parents.[193] In addition, influences that come from outside the home, such as cultural attitudes and educational experiences, might make a major impact on the development of moral reasoning, especially ones that encourage democratic processes, active decision-making and mutual responsibility.[194] Egocentrism, irresponsible social relations, and reckless sexual activity are clearly outgrowths of an indifference to moral issues, and of a thrill-seeking and ultimately autonomous mentality. For example, girls aged 14 to 17 who have had a pregnancy were less concerned about morals as restraints, less concerned about the impact of their current relationships on their own or a future husband's feelings, more likely to date more often, more likely to see soap operas and romance novels as reflecting real life, and more likely to become aroused to erotic scenes in films.[195]

Young people in our day, who often lack proper parental guidance and are exposed to ideas that encourage self-centeredness, generally have difficulty even *assigning* responsibility for inappropriate behaviour. For example, a sample of 8th graders from the Northwest US were given hypothetical scenarios. In one case, a teacher angrily reprimands a student who disrupted the class by loudly asking someone else for lunch money. The teacher was wrong for reacting irritably, and the student was wrong for speaking in class. In spite of the apparent simplicity in assigning culpability, many were confused or clearly showed a tendency towards antisociability. In fact, 26% of the males got no or only one answer right out of a total of four such questions.[196] It is easy to see how conflicts in dating and other relationships can multiply as both persons make false charge and counterchange, a situation which is exacerbated by the increasing variety and depth of deception practised by young people. Deception is facilitated if the individual believes he is doing nothing wrong. For instance, if speaking in class is morally acceptable, then lying to say it did not happen is also acceptable, as a means of protecting oneself from unreasonable exercise of authority. Where one's personal agenda is at stake, such as passing a test necessary for success in career, mendacity is most likely to occur.[197] Dating relationships are likely contexts for dishonesty to manifest itself because the importance of a match, so critical for teenage concepts of self-worth, prompts males to lie in order to obtain intimacy quickly. Such weakness takes the form of falsely claiming that one is in love, or wrongly averring that one wants to continue the relationship, or statements that aim to predicate the relationship on sex.[198]

In addition, a lack of congruence on opinions can foster conflict and suspicion. The process of age can often function in a way similar to process of education in changing opinions, as was discussed earlier. One would expect that couples who inaugurate dating at an earlier age, say by the age of 15, would be similar to the lower educated adults, as their education is the same as that of an adult but who finished school before completing secondary level requirements. Although formed at an early age, opinions go through a steady evolution throughout life, mediated by both the educational system and the intellectualisation process itself. Thus, teenagers would probably be more likely to *disagree* on whether they themselves should marry, whether marriage would affect their relationships with friends and relatives, and whether they should marry someone of a different race. Of especial importance is the divergence of views on whether good looks are a critical component in attraction, since teenagers put far more emphasis on these matters than do adults. In addition to a lack of maturity, an inability to agree on basic issues concerning life attitudes would make it quite difficult for young people to make close, intimate friendships.

The overall situation seems clear. Children are evidently conditioned to seek *dependence* on others, first through school groups, then in smaller groups, and then in the dating relationship. Perhaps even more importantly, since people lack moral understanding and feel they cannot obtain it on their own, they might press a marriage partner 'into service'. It is precisely this lack of moral thinking that unfortunately makes them unconcerned about their capabilities as a spouse. In addition, young people take on adult responsibilities too early in their mental development and engage in possessiveness, manipulation and sexuality, instigating difficult male-female relationship experiences. Overall, the individual has great difficulty cultivating a standard response wherein he takes into account the necessity to strictly follow sensible rules, and wherein he is concerned with the well-being of others, especially those who are not directly affected by his behaviour. Lying becomes an easy way out of difficult situations, facilitated by his lack of concern about the negative effects. Thus, egotism, fantasy proneness, escapism, and hedonism figure prominently in the decisions that lead to how individuals deport themselves; goading themselves into habitual use of inspection, accumulation of evidence, categorisation, and careful evaluation is evidently beyond their willpower.

We should stress that often deception results in a worsening of relationship, bitterness, and general suspicion of motives. In short, a deterioration of social interchange occurs due to poor use of reasoning mechanisms. Undoubtedly, fulfilment of self-centred, materialistic wants are obtained through crude generalisations, and lying, cheating, evasion, are necessary to avoid failure and discovery of deviance. For those younger than the mid-20s, *weakness* is the characteristic response to the complexities of intimate male-female relationships.

We should also emphasise that information depends on parents assisting their children in finding important values and in correcting them when they err. A shortage of advice and support by parents, and deficient attention paid to emotional needs, was often in the past attributed to losing a parent or living with a large family. There is little doubt that these factors today figure prominently in the early search for a romantic partner. However, clearly the current widespread paucity of maturity could not be due to large families or high parent mortality. The most likely culprit would be simple abandonment of parental responsibility, though this is far more difficult to measure than death or family size. Therefore, we can at this point only refer to the high divorce rates in the Western world as the strongest evidence of the conflict between spouses and as pointing to a failure to provide proper child-rearing.

After the desire for love is established, a conflict arises with the ideal of independence, a conflict taking place within an immature and poorly developed psyche. It would make sense then that young people would have to rely on the advice of adults, who have themselves undergone similar experiences, and can disclose the advantages or disadvantages of a particular behaviour in a particular situation. However, we are not very sure that even middle-aged adults could attain a highly mature response to a complex situation. Their greater experience in the matters of the world does not guarantee that they have acted correctly themselves, or have admitted to poor judgement. Thus, young people should consult whatever sources are available on long-standing cultural practises, the 'collective acumen' borne of multifarious incidents and conflicts. We can visualise this process of discovery as an inverted pyramid, where a young person first draws on his own limited experiences and immature thinking processes; being frustrated with the results gotten thereof, he then proceeds to ask his friends, who have some more knowledge than he does; he then asks his parents, who can rely on an even wider range of personal experiences and second-hand information; and being not entirely comfortable with this, he then moves to the upper reaches of this structure, where information is at its widest and most secure, because it draws upon the experiences of literally thousands or millions of people.

The fact that young people today do not draw upon the traditional cultural well of experiences might very well leave them oblivious to the fact that the desire for material well-being and the desire for love *can* co-exist successfully. As long as people are willing to make sacrifices, then independence, love, and material security can all be achieved simultaneously, although self-determination must to a certain extent be curtailed. Critics of the present cynical age can contend that the driving ambition in life is not love, but it is to reach a high material standard, with a concomitant predilection for autonomy and separation from others. When one steadfastly waits for inheritance of property or money before marriage, it is, they argue, only to protect one's own physical welfare, and a spouse and children are added merely as part of a further effort to fulfill that end. But is it unrealistic to maintain that it is a *considerate* and kind nature that prompts a man or woman to gather the appropriate funds together before marriage? Perhaps in past times it was a great love of people that motivated the individual to wait for the time when the household would be secure and relatively free from financial worries. Although it is true that many couples might have been able to eke out a living before inheriting property, the dangers of such a situation were many. A loving relationship might have been attained but within a precarious context. A man might have thought, What sort of husband would I be if my wife and children starved, or wore rags for clothes? The concern for material security might be for oneself, or it might be for oneself *and* others. Thus, it is living the virtues of empathy and caution that make one attentive to material matters. It is a dangerous assumption that strict adherence to financial protocols is only limited to simple-minded and cold-blooded egotists.

Interestingly enough, the present cultural ethos is analogous to a childhood belief, where immature individuals expect freedom and love whenever and wherever they find it necessary. However, unlike many other situations, in this case, the childhood 'fantasy' can be reality, but only when one constructs it properly. Although love will always exist as a preeminent force in human nature, there will always be tension between love and another main force, namely, the desire for independence; these forces *cannot* be congruent, though they are *not* mutually exclusive. To want love means to be reliant on another, and this cannot easily co-exist with one's struggle for independence. When reliance turns to over-dependance, then any kind of independent behaviour becomes impossible to achieve. The need for love is necessarily one of dedication and sacrifice, since love cannot occur without it. The other force, independence, interferes with this and so the two can fight for attention, but a relationship does not have to be a constant struggle of wills. People are usually impelled by the desire for independence to seek similarity and complementarity, for it is through these factors that one is able to realise one's goals and are instrumental in finding a good life, one that incorporates security and stability as well as progressivity.

There is often a fine line between exploitation and acceptable employment of resources, between manipulation and making the best use of what one has. People therefore might be attracted to one another because they see the ideal and because they see the potential to further their own interests. There is no disgrace in wishing to reach one's goals through the assistance of another, as long as there is no dishonesty and misuse of favours. However, in a materialist society, where immediate, physical gratification takes precedence over that of emotional satisfaction, it is difficult not to abuse the friendship between two people, even where there is an affectionate, caring attitude.

Thus, tensions can only be resolved through cooperation and sacrifice, without which the long-term viability of a relationship is extremely dubious. For the sake of the relationship, every shrewd person appraises the present and future pragmatic and emotional characteristics of the other in a sincere, thoughtful, and exhaustive study; considering the consequences, anything less would be reckless. A man dating a woman who attends law school, for example, must take into account the fact that when she graduates she will, for at least a few years, work very long hours. If he finds this unacceptable, social engagements might diminish or end altogether. If a woman in college gets along well with a man who works as a mechanic, the fact that her own income might ultimately be considerably higher than his could present status difficulties, making her reluctant to continue the relationship. Any temporary or short-term problems, such as attending a school in another state, can be overcome, if the longer-term pattern of behaviour by both people has been visualised. These short term obstacles are not large compared to the rewards that await in a future transformed by support and affection.

The most satisfying relationship contains two people who both are as committed to each other as they are to living all the virtues. Nonetheless, most people have ideals which incorporate only one to three of the seven virtues. There is a cultural archetype of 'everyman's dream woman' and 'everywoman's dream man' which includes the whole set of virtues, yet a virtue is perceived as being 'cloaked' by a negative trait. For example, a woman should be chaste, but also sexually attractive to her husband; a woman should be reserved, but must still be able to deal aggressively with people she meets in carrying out domestic chores, such as servicemen, clerks, salespeople; a man should speak the truth, but often tells inaccuracies about his behaviour so as not annoy his wife; a man should be empathic to people's concerns, but also be a hard-driving businessman. The individual realises that it ultimately makes no sense to denigrate or compromise a virtue, which is the pinnacle of human achievement. Compromise virtue, though, he does, in order to compensate for the buffeting crosswinds on the way to autonomy. He might blame outsiders for denying him the ideal love, but by attaining the *other* ideal, that of independence, it is clear that he has only himself to blame for his predicament. No one can be both in toto free and unfree at the same time.

When the ideals of love and sacrifice are not taught and adequately assimilated, and are not connected to virtue, young people are left to construct it themselves with all the imperfections seen above. The goodness that we feel about someone else invariably has to do with how much the other person can understand, feel and empathise with us. For this to occur, the other person must be sensitive and concerned, and they must put aside their own perspective at times to see the other viewpoint. Being from the same background as ourselves certainly would help in this, but it is *not* essential. However, if one is not inclined to *sacrifice* one's ideological territory, then for a harmonious relationship, it might be necessary to have two people that are similar to each other in temperament, education, and experiences. Similarity and difference in a relationship can therefore yield losses in addition to rewards. When the individual has an immature personality, weak mental processes, and a love ideal that is in constant struggle with materialism and independence, then the major goal must be finding homology over that of heterology. Human beings are adaptable enough so that even individuals that are morally deficient can have marriages that are stable and harmonious, if not especially resilient to *outside* destabilising forces or conducive to personal growth.

Hence, because of what he or she might substantively bring to a relationship, there are a wide variety of ways that the individual can be made attractive to another person. Attractiveness, although always appealing to the emotions, can nevertheless be a dangerous trap. We are by nature attracted to a clearly defined entity called the opposite sex, but what about the 'opposite gender' whose attributes are not clear? Self-serving interests are often at the heart of evaluations between men and women. People often find it intolerable that anything should deviate from their personal plans, so they mentally project what they wish to see on a situation, person or object. The financial markets, for example, would behave in a distinctly unprecedented fashion if everyone based their investment decisions on carefully obtained objective truth and avoided avaricious, quick-money schemes that bias judgement. In the attraction between male and female, this type of blindness is all too common as well. Is the affable, caring, devoted woman a man sees really there, or is it just an illusion? Is the strong, decisive, protective man a woman loves a true assessment, or merely self-deception? Furthermore, since culture and genetics do much to differentiate the sexes, the individual must be careful to assess whether what they feel is simply attributable to a pre-existing concept of goodness or whether they truly feel attracted. When drawing up the list of 'attributes of the opposite sex', do we appreciate or favour these attributes because society tells us that this is what it is to be, in the gender sense, a 'man' or 'woman', disregarding the personal implications? People should ask themselves whether their attraction is genuine, or whether it exists because someone essentially handed them a 'list' that tells them what makes for a good man or woman. Society can easily link personality attributes to physical attributes, precisely because the latter are so much clearer than the former. In many cultures, physical traits frequently have corresponding personality traits, which might or might not be accurate. For example, a tall, muscular man will be 'virile' and 'decisive', a small, curvaceous women will be 'undefended' and 'adaptable'. A prominent physical trait can often mislead people into thinking that the individual has control or mastery over an intellectual or emotional factor often associated with that trait. Hence, in parts of Europe where the sexes are more dimorphic, that is, where the average man and woman are noticeably different from each other in many physical traits, evaluation is possibly more problematic. Do a 'he-man' and a 'baby-doll' fall in love because they erroneously believe each has a command over his or her own gender-specific psychological traits, basing their opinion only on a casual inference from their physical features? Being fully aware that the differences one sees might not be universal but dependent on culture or genetics, accidents of time and place, makes one think twice before becoming seriously involved. Knowledge of deviation from the norms is the best antidote for self-deception and the quickest road to maturity. Putting ourselves in other situations, where things might function equally well, or better, makes us question our assumptions about what is 'good' in a person.

Apathetic Dependence

One is often inclined to improve or upgrade one's personal situation. The attraction between the sexes is ongoing because it is a way for the individual to bring more pleasure into his life. It would then follow that open and frequent dialogue about these matters of attraction would come about, yet even informal discussions about the subject are rare, especially when the attraction is based largely on homology. Perhaps this is due in part to the fact that from a public policy perspective, which deals with short-term direct social impact, little can be said about the phenomenon of homology except that within a particular context it favourably exists, although one can say considerably more about heterology, since the points of difference can become divisive and thus immediately injurious to society. Unlike differences in opinion, one hardly ever hears that a similarity between two people has become a bone of contention between them. Further, although the similarities that people find in each other become the foundation for all other aspects of the relationship, they can be quite mundane or 'trivial'. Consequently, we must not worry about 'public policy' in the present discussions and instead concentrate on the effects of attraction in both the long-term and short-term.

In the section we will examine the effect two crucial components of love, homology and heterology, have on the most important aspect of human existence, namely, the process of attaining life fulfilment. Let us review what has been said so far in this work. Whilst the search for similarity is centred on temperament, similarities in experiences and education are also very important. It might be fair to say that the search for similarity is more a routine aspect of any male-female relationship than the search for positive dissimilarity. The latter arises, sometimes prominently and sometimes unexpectedly, to be confronted with great interest by both sides. How one deals with the issue is dependent on one's aims in life. If information and knowledge about oneself and the world are critical, then personality or background differences become a part of the relationship. If certain differences produce a justified fear, then the difference can become the basis for an end to the relationship. The most positive use of diversity is for compensation of one's own weaknesses or inexperience, in which case similarity still plays the main role in the relationship, with dissimilarity cropping up from time to time to play a supportive role.

Relationships are the building blocks of social existence, and relationships are in one way or another always affected by the congruity of ideas that pass between people. Do people use similarities and differences wisely in relation to their quest for fulfilment? We answer this question by first probing the 'health' of adolescence, which constitutes the beginning of personal independence and thus forms the foundation for later developments. We note that teenage friendships are controlled largely by one important dynamic we have been discussing: the peer relationship is seen as providing a path for happiness, but only when it stresses reinforcement of personal ideas as a means of emotional support. The multifarious challenges of modern living make adolescents crave confirmation from their peers at a level not seen in recorded history. In this regard they quickly establish a 'mutual admiration society', where one person supports and validates ideas of another. For this dynamic to be maintained, there must be fundamental similarity between the various participants. The differences that they see in each other are attractive, but the benefits are only realisable in the long-term, in circumstances where they are closely working together. Thus, what people initially desire from a relationship is mutual support, but what eventually attracts their attention is the set of positive differences. Incongruously, the allure of diversity proves strong, yet young people hardly ever understand it, much less put it to good use.

But support by definition means gaining from someone else something that one lacks. It also implies weakness, since to rely on another means losing power and autonomy. Great social stress, coupled with immaturity, yields a strong desire for emotional sustenance. Once this desire is set into motion as a strategy, however, the individual is making an unintentional symbolic admission that there is a certain weakness to his character. Consequently, modern concepts of dating and relationships are ambiguous to say the least, where they put great emphasis on *dependence*, but tempered with at least a few major reservations. The ideal of love has been modified so as to make the individual more desirous than ever to experience love (support, desirability, praise) early and frequently, with the *quality* of that love being made secondary. The same reasons why people feel the tremendous urge to marry are appropriate in explaining why girls and boys find it so necessary to establish and maintain ongoing relationships with the opposite sex at an early age. For example, a teenage girl with school and work obligations tries to juggle a boyfriend as well in her schedule, in order to adhere to a strategy. Her other activities might bring her satisfaction, but the stress arising directly and indirectly from those activities makes her feel inadequate without a boyfriend, especially if close female friends each have one.

Since one is acknowledging a sacrifice of personal choice, especially in manners and temperament, when one depends on a steady dating partner for emotional satisfaction, the relationship must offer a repayment for that sacrifice in some substantial way. This usually entails a transmutation of lifestyle, from being alone (dissipation and deficiency) to living together (concentration and synergy), either with or without marriage. To *not* proceed to the next level of cohabitation or marriage would be, in the view of those who believe in this concept, to foolishly lose one's investment, in the same way as working in a job that does not make use of one's college education, or building up a career for several years in one occupation only to begin at the bottom of the ladder in another. Each partner has made significant allowances in his or her mind and heart to accommodate the other; each has sculpted from the days a contour that cannot be filled by anyone else but that special person, a 'favourite'. This pattern clearly clashes with the independence ideal, and both dependence and independence to some extent must be experienced *simultaneously.*

Young people are burdened with the demands of maintaining independence in peer groups, education and career. They use sex as a substitute for affection and as a way to deepen the relationship, and they also make poor decisions in dealing with a dating partner because of their immaturity. Because of the simple-minded use of another person as a crutch, the character of the relationship itself is prone to denigration as a result. If we can agree that the only factor of the ones mentioned that is amenable to change is maturity in thinking, which is also the only factor that affects the others, then the primary method we have at present in preventing catastrophic relationships is to keep dating as far in the future as possible, that is, to increase the age of dating. The signs for this are not encouraging, since the age at which people begin to date has become progressively lower throughout this century. In the years following the Second World War, the age at which individuals began to date was about 16. Actually, the 'sweet-16' party or the debutante's ball was the 'coming-out' ritual where the girl became a woman, and thus began the long road of experiencing distinctly adult activities. Maturation was viewed as a gradual process, culminating by the age of about 21, after which the girl no longer 'matured' in the sense of learning about fundamentals, but rather put into practise the knowledge she had gained. Thus, marriage could decently take place only after 21. In more recent times, the age at which boys and girls begin to interact significantly has been declining. It can be as low as 12, where children participate in adult-sponsored or supervised activities, but nonetheless begin to form close affectional attachments. However, although he age of dating has declined, the age of marriage has not come down as well. As the one-quarter proportion of girls who have had sexual experiences by 15 will attest,[199] more than a few communities harbour secluded sexual rendevous between boys and girls barely into puberty, without any consideration of marriage.

One could explain this trend by saying that increasing insecurity and disruption in family life caused younger and younger children to reach out for help. Based on what we have said in earlier sections, there is no doubt that this is the case. But this factor cannot explain the trend fully. We can see that even if the desire for a companionate relationship has not decreased in age, the age of the onset of dating would have declined simply because young people needed 'insurance'. The high demand for romantic partners pushed them into forming relationships at an age when they did not actually feel a great desire for companionship. Thus, their *present* need for love was not overwhelming, but they took into account their predicted *future* needs. Let us examine this process. We posit that since the early part of this century, girls have had frequent and steady contact with members of the opposite sex; initiation of serious dating or 'courtship' began at about 18, an age close enough to the 'magical number' of 21 to be acceptable to society. Unfortunately, those boys who turned 18 found many girls to have already been taken by other boys, and thus they were *excluded* from having a dating partner their own age. Since most adolescent boys, focussing on a ready-made homology based on age, considered only girls from their own age group and two or three years below, and since younger age groups had not yet begun to date, there would logically be more potential partners if they sought girls younger then themselves. Thus, these boys, and younger siblings who had also noticed that they would have some difficulty dating at 18, began to date girls who were 17 or 16. Boys who were 17 anticipated the struggle to date at 18 and thus began to search for girlfriends age 17 and 16, lest they be shut out. When dating at a younger age became the norm for both sexes, finding unattached girls again proved difficult, and so boys moved to the next lower age group of 16 and 15, etc. Even if a boy did not really desire a girlfriend at 13 or 14, he felt he had to obtain one if he were not to be left with no choices at an older age, when he foresaw the possibility that he would *very much* desire one. The only tangible lower limit on this pattern, which we might call an 'exclusion phenomenon', would probably be the onset of puberty.

There are three factors that account for preferring to have a large pool of candidates. First, boys do not like to be turned down for dates. Dating is a test of their attractiveness at a time when they are very vulnerable as to identity and self-worth; the more failures, the greater the blow to their manhood, even if the refusals to date are because the girl is already dating someone else. Second, girls must ideally have a boyfriend at all times, but longevity is not a requirement. Hence, a girl may date someone for a few months, then break this off, and then quickly gain another boyfriend, whom she sees for another few months before breaking off with him. This type of pattern in cultures that do not tolerate more than one close male friend per girl at one time clearly makes it difficult for boys to 'cut in' and get the chance to become friendly with her. Moreover, many other girls have fairly lengthy relationships, where there are few breaks in the relationship chain, again making it difficult for boys to find unattached girls. Finally, there is no way of telling a priori, apart from using the grapevine or telepathy, whether a girl is unattached, and more often than not, boys steel themselves to go through the embarrassing ordeal of asking out girls only to discover that they were wasting their time.

Group dynamic factors which lead to the exclusion phenomenon would not have any relevance unless a single formidable issue existed: young people do not receive enough loving attention at home and seek affection elsewhere. The widespread domestic disruption in modern society leaves young people feeling unloved and alone. Forging ties with aunts, uncles, cousins, and siblings might be attempted, but find them either unwilling or preoccupied by their own domestic problems. Turning to people their own age for solace is the easiest solution to this problem, not to create a relationship built on mutual respect, but one built on rudimentary affinity. As most young people are not prepared to sacrifice themselves (probably imitating the selfishness they saw in their parents), they use contrivances to create the illusion of a true bond. There is the almost inevitable descent into sexuality in order to make the relationship 'official' and to keep each person joined to the other. In such a case, the mutually supporting relationship will have a tendency to fly apart, as the requirements made by peers, school, teachers and others have to be fulfilled.[200]

As young people lack a long-term vision of their own lives, judging by the activities and standards of our time, they themselves in reality might not be sure whether an intimate relationship is a prelude to marriage or merely a temporary contrivance. Among teenagers, who in recent times rarely look upon dating as being in any way a prelude to marriage, it is not uncommon to have many sex partners, and perhaps one or two 'true' loves. Sadly, this confusion repeats itself over the course of early adulthood. In fact, in a study of five metropolitan areas, heterosexual males had on average eight partners, and females three partners by their mid-30s.[201] In a French national survey, for those under age 35, males had on average five sex partners, and females had three.[202] Clearly, one's 'beloved' is likely to be among numerous 'heartthrobs', 'crushes', 'sweethearts', 'affairs', and 'involvements', a lonely figure popping up at the end of a long line of failures.

This conflict between emotional designs and pragmatic plans has to constitute one of the more absurd aspects of modern society. The pattern might be repeated as follows: A girl of 17 or 18 finds herself strongly attracted to a boy who is around the same age. This strong affection is often 'fulfilled' by sexual activity. Now that this association has deepened, and the pair feel they are close 'partners', they might ask: Now what happens? Can we marry? Almost all the time, the answer is a resounding 'No'. As the average age for marriage is now about 27 for both sexes, the current popular belief is that only country rubes or inner-city denizens would marry at such a young age. Can they alter their life paths for the sake of an early marriage?

This is also unlikely, as both probably expect to expend a great deal of mental and emotional resources for college and career building, leaving little for a prospective spouse and children. Can they go their separate ways and 'save' themselves for each other until the time they do marry? This is also untenable, as the thought of going sexually unsatisfied for ten years or longer is unthinkable. After all, was not a primary consideration in the beginning of the relationship the fulfilment of a sexual 'need'? In spite of a reduction of casual sex since the 1970s and a move toward 'committed partnerships', the belief in the necessity of relationship experimentation over the life course is still all too prevalent. Sexual activity as a major aspect of adulthood is a subject area in its own right, an area comprising the study, savouring and perfection of eroticism.[203] Long periods of separation, the temptations of alternative activities, the desire to experiment sexually, doubts about the existence of true affection—all imperil the youthful 'romantic' relationship. And without romance there can be no marriage in the modern age.

The question perforce which confronts people is similar to this: 'Is my boyfriend (girlfriend) only good for some conversation, having some fun, or is there something deeper here?' Unless, there is a true attraction, which as we have said must be brought about by virtue, the relationship cannot continue because whatever similarities and positive differences exist will never be utilised effectively. Virtue is indeed lacking in the life of the average teenager, and 'depth' is consequently not a word in his vocabulary, much less a part of his romantic life. So what are the couple to do in these circumstances? The only answer is to break off the relationship. On the other hand, the couple have laboured so much to create a proper relationship that it is genuinely difficult to break it off. Nonetheless, the weight of competing factors makes nearly all of these relationships ultimately bound for failure. Perplexity such as this can cause suspicion about the longevity of all male-female relationships, and suspicion can easily be conveyed to married life. A terrible message is presented, in that *all* intimate relationships people have before their mid-20s are bound for failure. What about those strong desires for fondness and affection? It is all for naught. Thus, the predominating dynamic is the pragmatic one, where 'affection' must be something one can turn on and off like a switch. Society cannot tell them to hold their sexual desires in abeyance for more than a decade of their lives, and yet it cannot approve of their promiscuity. In this scenario young people drift without direction, becoming increasingly entangled in complex and ultimately injurious relationships.

Despite the friction and disappointment in dating relationships, the youth of our day find that going steady has an important place in their social life. Perhaps unsurprisingly, they do *not* view a short term commitment, such as 'going steady', as a prelude to marriage. Those who do go steady are *not* different from those who do not in terms of their level of opposite-sex socialising.[204] This would indicate that young people see this kind of conviviality, of regular dating often accompanied by some kind of sexual activity, as a form of *pseudo*-marriage. They attempt to extract from a boyfriend or girlfriend the same kind of emotional satisfaction, advice and warmth that they could obtain from a spouse. Thus, dating can be used for many ulterior motives, and once a pattern is set and the couple feel they are in love, they might push themselves to go to the next step, which is marriage. In many cultures, after exclusive dating for an extended period of time, the pressure to marry also begins to build from friends and family, who often do not take into consideration the couple's desire for a natural course of events. Is there an objective measure of time over which this 'natural' course evolves? Although a precise number can never be gotten, when considering such an important proposition, it would clearly be prudent to wait for at least three years, a time which allows the couple to see each other in different circumstances, conditions and challenges. Paradoxically, although young people seem to feel very comfortable with the current dating arrangement which easily brushes away questions of marriage, when it comes to dating their future *marriage* partner, the dating relationship actually speeds up. For Americans the time of dating before marriage (courtship) is on the average about one year, with about one-third taking more than three years, and only 7% taking five or more years;[205] this period would include the engagement period. A man and woman who take only a year between meeting and marriage might have settled on the idea of marrying each other after only six months, although neither might feel really comfortable with the idea. At a time when it is not unusual for a person to take six months or more to decide on the kind of car or house to purchase, it seems rather absurd that people would spend less time deciding on something that is far more important to their lives, and far more difficult, if not impossible, from which to free themselves. Again, a sign of immature, poorly developed rational faculties.

As we have indicated, the vast majority of dating relationships end, not with matrimony, but with a parting, which is rarely sweet or valorous. Besides the possible conflict in the relationship itself, even the circumstances of its termination can be incongruous with the goals of love and affection. Of those who gave a reason for a breakup, in about one in ten cases the individual will give a false reason as to why the relationship had to end (with women somewhat more likely to do this). The main reason for such deception is ostensibly to protect the feelings of the other person, but the real reason is usually a lack of continuing interest or the fact that the person has found someone new.[206] Although falsehood might seem to be considerate if the real reason would cause distress, it can produce feelings of cynicism and animosity towards the opposite sex since it undermines the whole process of communication. If honesty were universal, then perhaps dating and courtship would be less of an onerous and unpredictable experience. At the cost of hurt feelings, one would not be left to wonder what went wrong or to remain helpless in self-deception.

No doubt deceit, instability, forced intimacy and the conflict between dependence and independence lead many to despondency, a sign that there was over-dependence. In fact, relationship problems can be the *main* problem facing teenagers, contributing to depression and suicidalism. The self-realisation of a profound ignorance in dealing with these difficult matters does not stop them from making the relationship central to their lives. The emotional cost of a breakup is often so profound that it can be a form of 'divorce', a situation greatly exacerbated by another common youth problem, substance abuse.[207] For escapist personalities, the feelings of failure, deprivation and rejection intensify from the delay in resolving the conflict between independence and dependence. Such heedless decision-making underlines the high premium modern society puts on early dating, in spite of high costs associated sexual activity, promiscuity, dissolution, conflict and depression.

It is clear that there is a major necessity to assist the modern individual, who is alone, confused and struggling, with the competition between emotional, material and social principles. Institutions stand to give the most efficient help, by providing instruction and answers to the most common questions through groups and mass market materials. Many churches, for example, provide marital training or counselling before marriage as a way of smoothing the transition from single life to cohabitation. A typical course might meet, for example, on five consecutive Mondays, two hours each for a total of ten hours, with two hours homework, and three books to read. These courses cover, in varying levels of detail, the gamut of issues that pertain to married life: finances, communication, sexual activity, and the rearing of children.[208]

When the individual is given the opportunity to interpret the similarities and differences that exist between himself and his prospective partner, there can only be an improvement in married life, but only as long as other no other negative factors are introduced in the process. Although one might think that the courses offered by churches and other organisations are admirable in attempting to prevent people from making rash decisions and helping them prepare for the obligations of wedlock, there are a number of difficulties. Firstly, by underscoring communications, means are made more important than substance. People might be forced to take on 'scripts' and to act in artificial ways which interfere with the individual's normal personality. Secondly, courses try to cram a large amount of information into a relatively short period of time, with the complexities of relationships, and thus their most important aspects, not getting enough attention. Thirdly, courses can cause embarrassment by eliciting personal data. Why should anyone, in a class or group designed for education have to lay out their innermost thoughts and ideas to others for approval? Finally, these courses, by offering lessons in 'conflict-management' techniques, *anticipate* problems will occur between the couple. Whilst this might be realistic, should it not be paramount for a church to urge the individual to strive for perfection, to teach that it *is* possible to have a nearly problem-free marriage? It might be entirely appropriate that churches lead the way in helping people to understand each other. However, it is a contradiction to proclaim that God can make all things 'perfect', but then to imply that God cannot make the marital relationship 'perfect'; in such ways they damage their own credibility. By making concessions to 'inevitable' human weakness, the church's role as an authoritative institution that can give key insight into human nature is made untenable.

Moreover, the use of tests, again whilst commendable in bringing logic to the decision-making process, comes too late in the relationship. How are the couple to deal with the unenviable discovery that they are not compatible? As we have stated, the pressure to marry is already probably quite intense because of their long-standing relationship. Now that they are engaged, the couple are under even more pressure to carry out the commitment they have made. Furthermore, tests give dubious ratings of normalcy; even researchers cannot agree in most cases what kind of pre-marital relationship will be converted into a successful marital one. The only exception to this, and it applies in only a minority of situations, is where the couple are openly and distinctly aberrant in their actions towards other people or each other. On the whole, where experts do not agree on major points, examinations can hardly be utilised effectively, least effectively it seems in the busy but emotionally fragile weeks and months leading up to the wedding.

Using instruments and courses to try to get people to form long and short term goals is a step in the right direction, but this makes no sense when the nuptials, only short weeks ahead, are fast approaching. By putting a couple into a position where they must 'find themselves' and make difficult decisions within this narrow time frame creates not avoids artificial and socially determined commitments. People should form their life goals and ideas about married life well before the wedding, but it is unwise to think they can form them almost on the spot. It would be better if the various institutions of society would persuade individuals to get into the habit of generally forming goals as a life-long pursuit. We would emphasise the building of sound *mechanisms*, and not the sale of standard and trite answers.

*Happy they who find the goddess come in moderate might,
sharing with self-restraint in Aphrodite's gift of marriage
and enjoying calm and rest from frenzied passions,
wherein the Love-god, golden-haired, stretches his charmed
bow with arrows twain,
and one is aimed at happiness, the other at life's confusion.*
~IPHIGENIA AT AULIS (410 BC), Euripides

*True love is like seeing ghosts: we all talk about it, but few
of us have ever seen one.*
~François La Rochefoucauld (1613-1680)

CHAPTER 6
CONCLUSIONS

We have, to a certain extent, in this work given the impression that far from being dejected about marriage one should be sanguine about this venerable institution. However, we should know that marriage presents a host of dilemmas, and that there is no truly effortless marriage. Still, with careful preparation, perspicacity, and dedication, for people who desire this lifestyle and deal with it in a traditional manner, it can be immensely satisfying. That being said, the people who have made the choice of founding their relationship within a modern context are going to face dilemmas of a different order. Problems will then centre on the dynamic that puts the concept of independence between the conflicting poles of materialism and love. Ideas about autonomy affect the placement of other ideas between the two poles, one which is totally personal, the other totally social, that is, between the demands of finance and career and the needs of affection.

In reviewing the evidence presented in this book, we find we are fortunate that certain principles about love, economics and independence can be elucidated that go beyond a particular culture, place or time. The competition between two desires is clear: the need for a commitment from a partner of the opposite sex, and the need to be free of commitment. It is not an endorsement of selfishness to say that these desires are valid, but one cannot successfully find a way out of this dilemma by both obtaining commitment from someone else and yet giving little of it in return, for such a relationship obviously must end. It is also foolish to deny or relinquish a relationship merely to demonstrate independence. *Mutual* support, assistance, affection and closeness are the only ingredients in lasting relationships, a concept that has been known in the dimmest recesses of man's existence and one that has been well-integrated into Western culture. For the basically moral individual, that is, someone whose own interests and outlook are at roughly the same level as that of traditional culture, principles can be deduced which become dependable guidelines for reaching relationship, marriage, education, standard of living and career goals. Thus, it is possible to find a resolution to any modern dilemma by summarising these principles and integrating them with individual needs and personality.

By looking at the contest between love and independence from the perspective of individual goals and development, moving increasingly outward from individual to family to community to larger society, we can perhaps obtain more insight on what we have discussed in this book. We will therefore focus on the *individuation process*, where a person, simply speaking, moves from dependence to independence. It is a series of successive events through which we attain control over life and self in order to ultimately reach fulfilment. Separating oneself from others, the actual meaning of 'individuation', is only the most noticeable aspect of the process, not the result. Thus, the degree of independence in life increases with the extent to which we move outward, breaking with family forms to establish our own habits, to associate with the right people, to have the right education and career, and to live with the possessions and activities we find agreeable. In this matrix, the 'individual' largely becomes the product of the following conceptual areas: Level of extroversion, material standard of living concerns, desire for homology, desire for complementarity, family relations, knowledge, leisure activities, desire to leave home, career goals and demands.

It should be understood that evidence of independence is not evidence of individuation. In the first chapter we said that conceptualising autonomy is a difficult task, and it appears that none of the situations we have discussed really directly clarify the issue. It is only after fully understanding the underlying strong emotional demands of love, which we have been repeatedly stressing, that we can understand what freedom really means to us. We can first deduce that a person can be 'free' but still unhappy. A relative lack of dependence on other entities, an alternative to restrictions, in a larger sense is what we really mean by 'freedom'. Local or temporary examples of an escape from requirements are not proof of independence, since the individual might very well still be greatly dependent on other people. How many times do we see bohemian 'radicals' still depend on parents for money, friends for advice, government contacts for protection, women for excitement, and drugs for enhancing or stabilising moods? Simply demonstrating to others that one can do things that the average 'unfree' individual cannot do is not a sign of true liberty. Conversely, a butler might have his duties laid out for him in minute detail, and thus he might appear quite dependent and without liberty, but because he is doing precisely what he wishes to do, offering important assistance to others, and is not using people as crutches, he is genuinely independent. If he is doing what he wants to do, then the time and effort he gives over to someone else is simply an *expenditure* of resources in pursuit of a goal, not a *sacrifice*. Obviously, some independence must be given up in order to attain maximum freedom; thus, it is incumbent on us to determine what we really need from life to be fulfilled, and what encroachment on our freedom would be considered acceptable. People must focus on doing whatever possible to individuate, to become truly free, which always means periods of sacrifice, change and learning. In other words, to gain liberty, and the ultimate goal of fulfilment, one must willingly be a servant of some kind.

Before all else, in the area of male-female relationships, one must set priorities as to what one finds desirable in a man or woman, and what one expects in married life. An individual's personal set of ideals, developed early on in life, balances a mix of similarity and diversity of basic ideas and opinions. In this way, power can be attained through affiliation and compensatory validation. Basic needs never leave the individual, thus always remaining part of the personality, and comprehending the underlying dynamics of social relations is a necessary step in the process of individuation. The importance of homology or similarity between partners is quickly understood as being predicated on a desire for immediate affinity, open friendliness, and an easy-going closeness. However, although congruence in traits is easily determined, heterology or dissimilarity is not, and making a good match between personalities is difficult. Despite this, the individual must ascertain what level of similarity and difference he prefers in the opposite sex, even if external forces attempt to make the decision for him. Similarity is praised and dissimilarity is downgraded because modern life demands more flexibility to take on the tasks of a changing material economy, with the result being less commitment and less willingness to change.

The need for positive differences between people (complementarity) is often a product of family disagreement and distancing, when parents do not provide their children with enough constructive, relevant knowledge about the different areas of life so that real autonomy can be achieved. Family disruption is especially a critical influence when the individual is temperamentally disposed to insecurity. Therefore, a person growing up in a home with inadequate support and instruction has a tendency to behave unwisely, being more likely to leave home early, less likely to finish high school, less likely to attend college, less likely to deal competently with peers. Evaluating this individual in the context we are discussing, there is a failure to become an attractive candidate for marriage. He or she requires assistance in the maturation process, but is stifled in the search for a provider of this assistance because of this immaturity. The resolution of the issue of how complementarity will fit into one's life is an important sign of maturity, of reaching true individual status. Questions must be asked: Do I need support or can I go it alone? Can efficiency, orderliness, and security be obtained with the help of neutral third parties or can these aspects only be realised through the cooperation of a spouse? There are no absolute correct answers, except to say that it is self-evidently wrong to disregard the fulfilment of one's basic emotional needs. To require a spouse in order to have a fulfilled life is no weakness, but *not* to seek one when one is very much desired is a sign of pusillanimity.

Thus, family relations will often determine the ease of forming and maintaining relationships, as the household of childhood acts as a training ground for larger social relations. However, the *initial* desire for contact with other people is largely the result of a genetically determined attribute of extroversion. Innate shyness might be overridden due to the persistent prodding of siblings and parents. As conducive this is to meeting parental expectations, it has a negative impact on individuation processes, because one cannot believe one is totally independent unless one obeys a fundamental internal principle governing the need for mental and emotional intimacy. How the individual and other people deal with extroversion affects perceptions of future life. The relationships family members have with one another and the material dynamics of the household can determine an individual's attractiveness as marriage material. What happens in childhood might therefore ultimately have an impact on matrimonial prospects. When desired patterns of association are frustrated, self-image is damaged, which in turn increases the need to prove one's independence.

Other relations within the household of origin also have indirect and direct effects on one's overall psychological well-being. For example, coming from a large family can make the individual feel only like 'one of the kids', not a separate personality; one needs to leave to establish his own identity if one is to avoid loneliness and depression. But, there are also rewards. A large family gives the individual the opportunity to develop skills in dealing with people, increasing his confidence. Appreciation for the lessons learned in social behaviour might not be forthcoming if crowding, arguing and other 'people' problems are not resolved. Growing up in a home without moral guidance does not dissuade people from marrying, and indeed seems to encourage them to do so, probably because they want a family that will satisfy their unrequited requests for affection, comfort and security. The inability to have close relations with a parent or sibling might prompt a desire for true companionship in marriage that was denied at home.

The domestic situation in which the individual is raised is the closest to one which he or she will experience in his or her own marriage. Family of childhood can act as a model of married life, with the individual eager to form such an entity himself, or it might act as an anti-model, which the individual might find thoroughly disagreeable. In large families and others where parents demand a militaristic-type adherence to chores and assignments, there is a tendency to produce individuals that are inflexible and selfish, individuals whose lone desire in life is to serve only 'me'. 'Family' then becomes a family of one. Acrimonious relations within the family can impel people to leave home early in search of peace and a better 'family', although without the support of older authority figures, poor career choices and inappropriate relations with the opposite sex are likely to occur.

Consequently, we should not lose sight of one-on-one relations between family members, which, even in a crowded communal type setting, are more important that group-to-one relations in establishing a pattern of individuation. Relatives can act as friends and/or mentors, and closeness between family members is significantly affected by a variety of events, such as divorce, death and emigration. Each person in a child's life takes on one or more roles, and the departure of such a person can also entail the loss of a role that he or she was elucidating, with the result that the child is impaired in development. Men and women react more favourably to specific input from family members who are within a particular age group. Some will delay marriage partially in reference to the loss of one or more role models or mentors because the removal of such a person has created social and personality impairment. However, it is more likely that the desire for continued assistance in psychological development will motivate men and women to *hasten* marriage in relation to such a departure, especially if there is more than one. Despite this desire to marry early, the individual might not be mentally prepared for marriage because the loss of a parent is genuinely responsible for slowing down mental development. Indeed, such a decision demonstrates a victory of emotion over reason, not desirable under any circumstances. Furthermore, there is a tendency to marry earlier or to marry very late in reaction to the anticipation of a father's or relative's limited participation in family life (as indicated by a lower life-expectancy). Companionship in adulthood is assigned a higher value, although so high in some cases that the individual takes great time to decide on a marriage partner. In other words, the illness and/or death of a parent bestows upon marriage a noble compensatory function, and this will cause some to marry quickly so as to partake of something truly 'special'. Others, more meticulous in temperament, are prepared to wait to find just the right person precisely in order not to disturb the ideal 'specialness' of this relationship. On the other hand, less care is shown when a longer life-expectancy makes marriage *less* valuable; people tend to marry late but not very late, taking extended advantage of parental support into the 20s and then using this knowledge to 'buy' their own separate household. The individuation process is in either case given great attention, but in the former it is endangered by an injudicious choice of marriage partner for the sake of continuity. It is clear that the death of a role model can hinder the individuation process, because personality development is not completed and dependence on others might be necessary.

It is evident from the preceding that complex forces affect everyone. However, Western religious and customary traditions have guaranteed that personal ideals should be discovered and implemented without undue pressure from outside factors, individual or institutional. Nonetheless, it appears that incorporated within these personal desires there are larger social concerns, namely that of the average individual gaining clear independence from an early age. The appetite for autonomy is influenced by home life, friends, peers, teachers and other persons within an individual's local social sphere. But the *innate* desire for independence is determined for the most part by the level of extroversion, as we have mentioned a genetic and, for the most part, an unalterable trait. This in turn will accelerate or decelerate the process of individuation and in turn the learning that takes place through the informed support gained by being close to others. Enjoying greater intimacy with others, such as with friends, acquaintances or a spouse, means there is less need for family, although one is still not a 'free man'. Society, however, can condition people to accept various ideas of the goodness of particular forms of household.

One area whose evaluations are affected not just by family, but by larger social dynamics, is that of privacy. Private space requirements, another critical factor in home life, are an essential issue for everyone's marriage plans, because less privacy can also produce poor personality development. A person from a large family can simultaneously be less desirable as a marriage partner and also be more desiring of companionship. But the manner in which this issue is perceived is dominated by dynamics that have to do with the propagation of the independence ethos through institutions of education and mass media communication. In better educated societies, the emphasis is on the present living situation: if space is small at home, seek egress; if large then remain at home, making one possibly more arrogant towards others who are less fortunate. In less-educated societies, the tendency is to focus on the future if the limited space at home reflects the general situation, which prompts a wait for opportunity and so delays marriage; if space is large in the personal context, this indicates a better social situation and so marriage is hastened. The former educational situation is self-centred, the latter is more society-orientated. These factors can be modified by divorce, conflict and disruption in the household, especially in the better-educated variety because attention is more intensely focussed on one's personal situation. In relation to satisfaction with home life, what the individual believes in many cases to be a personal valuation is really social; it is not content but form of information that influences his decisions, because the message is the same across themes. One wonders, considering the fact that independence is a universal issue which can prompt dissatisfaction with housing and home life, whether the information obtained from the media is enlightenment or reckless propaganda.

The departure from the household of childhood, of parental guardianship, announces one's independence, but now it is evidently based more on cultural and economic considerations than personal ones. A lower age of leaving home is expected in order to achieve an earlier start to a productive life, a good, bright beginning for the responsible citizen. This event involves going from a situation of long-standing stability to another much more unfamiliar and thus uncertain. How one perceives the issue of leaving home is critical to self-esteem. Only in the case of the military draft does society have a structure ready for the individual after departure. In all other situations, society encourages egress but provides no other assistance. Thus, the individual must be prepared to make plans for himself after leaving, and to take the risks as well. When one is not prepared, either intellectually/organisationally or financially, to leave home, then one will undoubtedly feel a distinct lack of confidence about the future. This situation does not aid the individuation process because it forces compromises in key areas. If the decision to leave was not his own, the individual will eventually learn his liberation was hollow, and his independence is not complete. If the decision to leave was self-initiated, and the basis was a lack of love at home, then he will be more likely to rush to another relationship, giving the impression of being responsible whilst still being unprepared. Therefore, a person can either be 'fired' or he might 'resign', but if in either case one's plans are thwarted, and one is never truly autonomous. As one could claim that there was 'strong' recurrent pressure from parents and others to exit, the blame for failure is quite difficult to place; then again, with few exceptions, no one actually threatens bodily removal, making it more likely that the individual himself is chiefly responsible for his own plight. Accountability remains amorphous, and a critical transitional stage in the individuation process is left unresolved.

It is therefore no surprise that the 'correct' age of leaving home is based on the legal definitions of adulthood, thus dropping the blame for any problems that develop on the whole of society, and so ultimately the responsibility is 'no one's'. Some people live at home because of societal influences, some do simply because it is cheaper to do so, and others have complex reasons drawn from personal and economic areas. There is the tendency, however, to overemphasise the influence of social forces. Whereas in the past culture affected the desire to stay at home until well into adulthood, now it affects the desire to *leave* home. In reality, there is still a mix of endogenous and exogenous factors that determines the age of departing the family abode: An innate desire for independence; the wish for a better family life (a surrogate family) because of parental failures in parent-child relations; economic/work-related requirements; educational demands (including living a more independent life in a dormitory); cultural demands about explicit evidence of liberty and self-reliance. Any reason to remain at home or to leave is valid so long as it improves the individual's well-being at a reasonable emotional and financial cost. Evidence of appropriate decisions alone, however, does not indicate a fully formed personality. It is clear that the individual's level of maturity is directly proportionate to the extent to which he takes responsibility for his actions and avoids faulting others for decisions that are his alone.

Part of the range of external forces that affect one's desire for companionship, although in a weaker way, involves recreation or divertissements, which can act as a substitute for marriage or a prelude to it. When the demand is high for a mate, and there are no other acceptable 'dedicated' venues for meeting potential mates, any leisure activity that involves the opposite sex is instrumental. Thus, socialising with friends is no longer a leisurely activity, but a 'labour' that often requires effort and counteracts the idea that the event is pleasurable. Further, the level of socialising is often taken out of one's hands. Whether one is on the 'people' track or the 'academic/career' track is not really so much a matter of choice but rather the result of a combination of innate and external influences. This realisation is highly significant, because it does not merely question one minor aspect of personality but reduces one's overall sense of autonomy. Further, since the life track conforms generally to innate strengths, there are no challenges, and there is no learning if one does not confront situations that are unusual and intriguing; advancement psychologically clearly demands new understandings about oneself. It is in modern man's interest, however, to create the myth of choice and control by erecting barriers between activities and reducing their cross-influencing effect. By society creating separate ritual acts for each, recreation, entertainment, friendship meetings, and dating are now distinct entities, each with its own rules. Individuation is hampered because ritualism discourages personal initiative and solutions. As a result, casual socialising, potentially an excellent source of insight into human behaviour, is encumbered with awkward rules that limit opportunities to interact with and observe others without intimidation or commitment.

Society imposes certain obligations in relation to the economy that affect personal views of both independence and companionship. Restrictions on life choices are common, and the individual does not have a free hand in many areas. Certain ancient demands, peculiar to Western cultures, are well-known to most people, who are expected to attain a higher standard of living than the previous generation, with future income being added to an inheritance (if any) and personal savings. Intellectual and physical capital in turn is to be passed on to the next generation, who will have the same demands made of them. Consequently, one's decision about education, career, and family structure are significantly influenced by the community. Unique conflicts arise from this practise, which does not necessarily affect the individuation process, but which might be exacerbated by stress carried over from work into the home and personal life. Decisions about marriage are also influenced by economic variables, such as the cost of food, clothing, durables, and housing, since conjointly running a household might mitigate financial burdens and help one reach cultural expectations about standard of living. Hence, when expenses for food, durables and clothing are high, marriage is early.

A career does not run parallel to family but interrelates with it. Family and peer relations provide the foundation for one's work life, but the latter can also interfere with fundamental emotional dynamics in relationships. Furthermore, the interaction between members of the family affects one's sociability; some traits, however, might be less useful in marriage than in economic matters, especially in dealing with the requirements of an occupation. This interferes with individuation, causing an inability to adjust and progress. Rigidity in personality due to the demands of a career can lead to poorly structured friendships and thus a delay in marriage. In the pursuit of money, one has to be a success in one's career, and often if one is not willing to be 'tough' and inflexible, one cannot achieve a high standard of living. Simply speaking, either one is uncompromising, with a high standard of living and no spouse, or flexible, with a low standard of living and earlier marriage. If personality were the only factor affecting marriage prospects, then this principle could be accepted. However, that is not the case. When the individual is successful in a career, he finds he can then marry earlier because he has the financial wherewithal, but it is precisely the lifestyle that has bestowed this opportunity on him that denies him ease in finding a marriage partner and denies him the time to savour this relationship.

Hence, external factors over which the individual does not have as much control as over the family, such as economics, education and peers, are also crucial to an individual's life. 'Economics' in a larger sense, that is, the functioning of various markets, has always played a role in the decision to marry, with inheritance, occupation, male-female ratios, and mortality rates being of significance. Things in nature, however, do not always operate according to well-understood principles, and unpredictability in status and accidents of birth create tension. As a way of reducing this tension, the cultures of the Western world have established a common path linking education, career, marriage, and parenthood. The individual has traditionally followed a course where he would grow up as a member of a household; obtain some education; establish himself in a occupation; save money; search for an available partner; marry; raise children; inherit his parents' holdings; pass on his resources to the next generation. We would expect each step to increase responsibility and gratification, but general cultural principles usually do not jibe with an individual's personal situation. Adjustments and modifications to this plan were therefore necessary, such as foregoing marriage, or not inheriting any wealth, or giving one's assets to the Church. Whatever the personal timeline of events, individuals in the past stood a good chance of reaching their life goals.

We now know that each of these steps is not independent of the others. Education is usually a product of family relations, mediated by social activities, and good grades and participation in organisations lead to higher education. Success in college, however, seems to be affected much more by success in secondary school organised activities rather than competence in informal and routine social actions. This clashes with the often heard claim that college-educated students are better prepared for the myriad social interactions of the real world than those without this education. Further, aptitude in social relations or in education does not appear to be purely the product of choice; natural inclinations and abilities have a major role to play. It appears clear that many milestones in education, family, children, work can all be made without serious problems, demonstrating that great individual control over life is feasible. Today, the traditional timeline is no longer followed, which is not in and of itself cause for worry, but it is troubling that people lay out their life courses thinking that any combination of factors is as difficult as any other. 'Hey, life's tough' is a typical comment, implying the same total burden for whatever set of choices you make, but this is simply not the truth. The life path was never rigid and alterations could be made without opprobrium, but it was absolutely essential that the individual understood the limitations of society and nature, and this is where the modern citizen fails. Fulfilment is not necessarily possible as forces foreign and possibly antithetical to the individuation process are ignored. For example, unemployment, disputes with parents, burdensome work rules, and expensive tastes, might seem to be issues unrelated to finding a marriage partner, but they do in fact have a consequence on relationships through their ability to alter the intention to cooperate, sacrifice and tolerate. It should be self-evident that people can with effort modify their life pathways but not certain interactions and connections that are basically unalterable.

An especially complex issue is the effect that education has on personality and relationships. Obtaining a high education is the major focus today in the individuation process, as it gives the greatest opportunity to develop intellectual freedom and distinction, which many now believe to be ranked greater than virtuous action. However, family life, still not to be discounted, might have an effect on one's educational plans, which in turn influences personality, since higher education often creates a shift in emphasis on relationship issues. The desire of people from large families to seek companionship might force them to abandon education plans and might result in a lower family income and lower standard of living. Since formal education changes attitudes, if people from large families are less educated, as is widely observed, they will then have more in common, thus increasing intimacy. These steps do not appear to alter the pace of individuation, although ways could still be found to increase knowledge without formal schooling. In contrast to this, families with greater integration produce competent individuals capable of achieving notable career success, but at the cost of spousal harmony. The higher the level of schooling, the more likely opinions about matters after marriage will be varied, although pre-marital, courtship concerns, such as general background, will be more congruous. Courtship and the beginning of the relationship will be stable if opinions are parallel, which often helps to create later harmony. Balancing out this harmony for a well-educated couple is the tension that arises when rates of maturity are different from what was expected, that is, when the roles of 'leader' and 'follower' are confused, such as in the case where one spouse is earning wages higher than the other spouse. Standard of living goals, always important, might be reached but at a cost to the relationship.

On the whole, society's suggested timeline has never been overly friendly, but with deft handling these intimidating interconnections can be successfully managed. Modern cultures, although concerned about individuation, concentrate more narrowly on the economic sphere. To a large extent, a community's standard of living is now also international, and it would appear that the general dynamic across the Western world is to marry but only if there is the following set of factors:

- low male unemployment
- relatively high income
- relatively low to moderate concentration of wealth

These factors significantly impede individuation because they displace other factors such as savings and type of employment. Because of their interrelationship, their repeated appearance in analyses, and the emphasis that society places on them, three principles — employment, income and wealth — can be considered the material 'golden rules' governing marriage. Even though a person risks permanent crippling of the individuation process by not marrying because of a violation of one or more of these rules, the force of society's 'ideal happy family' is so powerful that it appears to overshadow emotional and psychological needs. Thus, social factors exist that are greater than individuation. People continue to remain unmarried and living at home for interrelated reasons: unemployment, low educational attainment, poor personality, divorce or mental illness. In the past, it was possible for people to live alone or with a spouse in spite of these problems, and conversely, people could live with parents without necessarily having any of them. The implication of these observations is that persons who return to or remain with their family of origin do not only suffer from inadequate individual development, but are victims to a certain extent of a society that no longer has compensatory mechanisms.

The way in which outside influences are generally treated today invites the idea that the individuation process was better in the past, because external influences were minimised. When the prospects for a good economy are not there, especially in relation to the three golden rules, men and especially women are not likely to marry. Hence, economic matters are still very important, but society does not discuss this issue with the thoughtfulness it deserves. Further, basic issues common to all people such as leaving home, the use of space, loss of parental contact, and higher education, were simply not as important socially and personally in marriage decisions previously as today, either because their relevance was not highlighted culturally or there were legitimate substitutes. Thus, the individual could minimise the significance of these issues and focus more on those matters over which he had greater control, bolstering his self-esteem.

Naturally, moral issues, the set of rules that creates a balance between individual and community interests, override general material and pragmatic principles, and we discover that there has been a shift in the balance between individual needs and communal needs. When reviewing all the evidence that involves material concerns, emotions, intellect, independence, in relation to dating and marriage, one finds the undeniable fact whereas in the past the tendency was for men and women to be concerned about physical issues relating to marriage as a result of concern for themselves *and* their partners, in our day, this concern is only *self*-centred. Material matters are no less important than in the past, but are done with *only* one's own interests in mind; this relates to the situations before, during and after courtship. Money in the past could not make love, but too much or too little money could destroy it or at least seriously damage the showing of affection. The customs of our ancestors could not be clearer: Marry before rigid habits set in, but not so early as to prevent reaching a minimal level of emotional self-sufficiency. In addition, the more discipline and hard work one puts into finding a spouse, the less effort must be expended within marriage. Love is still important in our generation, but the ideal about love, about what one can expect in a companionate relationship, has changed dramatically, looming so large in importance as to displace traditional principles. The individual depends on the opposite sex more than ever for emotional fulfilment, perhaps obtaining in this way life's only deep psychological satisfaction, but not so much as to forego key elements of autonomy. If, as is often the case, the relationship is poorly constructed, most available time is spent trying to repair breeches and individuation is cast to the wind. Frequently this search for gratification is pursued in pathological ways, seeking reinforcement, submission and sexual intimacy from early in adolescence. Similarity of background and personality is sought to smooth over rough spots, and the couple look for homogenisation of marital standards and personalities, so that there is no struggle to change onself. In addition, sexual contact is substituted for affection, creating a false sense of closeness, as well as engendering possessiveness.

Morality and objectivity, it seems, have fallen into disuse. Man constantly undermines his relationships, because behind him is always the shadow of Autonomy, calling out reminders that 'social identity is all'. Nowhere is the supremacy of the autonomy concept, embedded in the struggle between independence and love, more obvious than in breakdown of marriages. If we assume that young people are most affected by the independence ethos, and divorce is the result of marital conflict, then the divorce rate among the youngest couples can be an important objective indicator of the strength of the independence ethos. The higher the rate, the more important the concept of independence, and the less important the concept of affection. Judging by the high divorce rate for such marriages, there is little doubt as to which concept wins. In fact, from 18 up to the mid-20s there is a steady decline in divorce tendency,[209] with a weaker trend continuing thereafter. To demonstrate independence, a 'duty' must first be discharged and certain important things in education, workplace and peer group 'must be done', which evidently are a hindrance to marital happiness. However, the still unacceptably high dissolution rate of couples who marry 'normally' at around 25 bears witness to the fact that the individual even then is not able to form a completely devoted relationship. Whatever the specific causes, the woes of married people must be in some way an outgrowth of the modern concept of independence, with its tremendous urge for escape and solitariness carrying forward in residual form into adulthood.

We see that individuation is considerably negatively affected by a host of factors. People tend to overemphasise obvious social restrictions and neglect more subtle but vital factors. It is easy to observe when summarising the influences on the decision to marry, such as in the above paragraphs, the pitfalls inherent in modern industrialised society, where the demands of ideology, temperament, emotion, education, career, family, and friends, 'come at' the individual threateningly from all sides. Choices relating to independence are critical, because poor decisions lead to problems that make one unable to reach the twin goals of material and emotional satisfaction. Independence concepts then mediate between the two; people get wrapped up in areas that take away valuable resources, as in the case where one chooses to take a high paying career, thus gaining independence, but also reducing marriage choices because of long hours and inflexible behaviour. On the other hand, by not paying much attention to independence, one could decide to seek love and marry early, yet this restricts educational and job opportunities and income. The level of independence in one's life regulates the flow of energy between material and emotional satisfaction: open it up too much, and energy flows too much to one side; close it down too much, and energy flows too much to the other. Decisions about autonomy must be made first or in conjunction with decisions about materialism and love.

Our ancestors understood that to achieve fulfilment, it was foolish for society to limit the individual to only one course. Many known roads — some longer, some shorter — led home to life's spiritual contentment, but many other paths, equally if not more useful, could be discovered. From the well-signposted trails of traditions, rules, customs and rites, modern man emerges in the wilderness of supposed self-realisation. He proudly hikes alone, happily follows his own course, yet realises his vulnerability. Among the few important items he carries in his rucksack is the secret 'treasure map' of fulfilment. For these riches his desire never weakens, but successfully finding them requires immense sacrifices. In spite of our traveller's determination, his belief in strong ideals and a good map, it would be wrong to think all other dreams, hopes and goals will be extinguished in order to achieve it. There are many grottoes, clearings, woods, trees, flowers, and other attractions in the forest that he seeks and that draw his attention. Many people thus firmly believe in the *existence* of a considerate, honest and mutually fulfilling kind relationship with the opposite sex, but spend their whole lives buried in other business. They complain long and loud about their inability to find 'a good man' or a 'good woman', but habitually underinvest their resources to improve themselves and wastefully pursue activities that only bring temporary pleasure.

General attitudes must be modified in relation to love and affection if people are to be fulfilled emotionally. More than ever the inhabitants of the modern world are seeking emotional satisfaction from their relationship, whilst emphatically refusing to deny the material importance of the household. Yet, they have drifted further apart in really understanding each other's elemental needs. Social intercourse is as important in married life as it is in any other dyadic relationship and success in this regard makes articulate, plain, forthright, and thoughtful speech integral. But that is only the beginning of the process in development of relationships, and this is especially true in light of changes in the relations between men and women in the Age of Industry. If marriage simply promised a 'better' life than as a single person, it would have very little power to persuade us to make a major sacrifice of personal resources. The great emotional repose that beckons people to live with one another au mieux is predicated on a certain effortlessness in experience. This effortlessness is in turn based on achieving a singularity of mind. Encountering obstacles in simply getting ideas across, one has little hope of making real progress in reaching an intimate level of discourse. Hence, obstacles must be removed through simplification and homogenisation of standards. This strategy, with its tampering of critical conceptual domains, is dangerous to say the least. Without being esoteric, we can say our ancestor's concept of 'singularity' simply means a relationship where conversation is unhindered, and where ideas usually find agreement and support. It does *not* necessarily mean having the same temperament, personality or background. Two people might ostensibly be quite dissimilar, but still get along superbly because they agree on the *fundamental moral issues* in life. Actually, the closeness can be so great that another person becomes in essence a part of one's own mind, which still retains its independent thought processes and knowledge but can relate to a companion's thoughts and actions. In such a case, ideas are often anticipated, and husbands and wives often know what the other will say and do. The existence within *connubium* should be as easy as living alone, but with all the advantages of external support, love and affection.

Modern people have made it clear that they have an agenda which primarily seeks to make up for the deficiencies brought on by upbringing, education, and career; devotion and sacrifice are secondary matters. It is thought that love can be 'forced' so that no great sacrifice or forethought is necessary. Love indeed can develop in a relationship, but it must be through sacrifice. With so much thoughtlessness, coarseness and selfishness in abundance, no one should marvel at the disturbing prevalence of marital conflict and animosity between men and women. In spite of this, though, we can find solace in the very old saying that true love will always prevail over all tests. Although a couple might have major financial problems, health problems and so on, the relationship will not only last but function well because neither can think of having any other life except with each other as central components. Thus, love is not measured in the money spent on or in time spent with someone, but it is in the enduring quality of the relationship. The deepest love can occur only between people who are of the highest moral calibre. Since this love comes through relying on one another, giving and accepting trust, it cannot be accomplished if people are duplicitous. And here we hear people say, with a tinge of desperation in the voice, 'Well then, teach me to be good, make me lovable'.

In our madly physical world, people start with the idea that both true love and material pleasure can be had simultaneously, but then abandon this idea to focus more on satisfying the body and not the spirit. They build careful illusions about their 'lovers'. Eventually the illusion is shattered, sometimes as they approach middle age, and the dream has to be reconstructed. There are many recriminations, but hardly any self-examination. 'Expert' help is sought, and after some reassurances people go on thinking that true love can finally be achieved at some cost. Popular external sources of information about the modern dilemma are also for the most part useless. Media representations focus more on 'plots' and ignore characters, thus the attention seeks to justify the end result, not the means to attain it. Further, the end result, the 'true love' we are supposedly seeing before our eyes, is almost without exception only an echo of the ideal. After these disappointments, people might have to alter their time frame but not their ideals, because they are too precious to discard. Maybe career, friends, fame, money, possessions are not as important as once thought but one will eventually 'have it all'. These delusions last a lifetime for many couples, with a sort of accordion effect governing their actions: they run to each other, full of promises and hopes, and then when business calls they run away from each other, vowing not to be away for too long.

In the past, the process of individuation was understood as internal discovery, and external factors were only for instrumental use in this great effort. Men and women had what could be called an *afferent* attitude to life, that is to move inward, as opposed an *efferent* attitude, to move outward. The individual lived with a drive, one could say an enthusiasm, for moving towards a centre, a place where all forces coalesce. The home where spouse, children, relatives, possessions, accomplishments were all together, defended, secure, presented a very powerful image. In this regard, one thinks of the changes that occurred in a Christian symbol seen in many Cathedrals and churches, that of the maze. The individual's path was usually an unbroken progression inward towards the *centre*, where God or Godliness was located. The length of the paths might differ, some might be more tortuous than others, but all eventually led to Heaven. After the Reformation, the conception was radically altered, with the individual moving *outwards* from the centre, guided by a thin line or tether to God, who was located *outside* the system.[210] From the security of knowing that one inexorably was proceeding towards a single goal, a oneness at the centre of the maze (as within the structured life the Roman Catholic Church offered), modern man, intoxicated by the possibilities science had to offer, committed himself to move outwards from a secure centre towards an unknown region, guided rather precariously by the divine hand. The dull, albeit certain, journey that took men to God and salvation was transformed into an exciting and dangerous exploration into what lay outside of their 'system'; intriguingly, the Divinity was no longer in the maze or necessarily even the ultimate goal. The sum total, the 'fulfilment', of one's existence was to be found in some new and better community, family, career, or government, but yet far away from one's place of birth, or family of origin, in the far reaches of the nation, perhaps beyond the edge of the world. Thus, in this neat iconography we see mankind's great struggle to 'come home' to security and love become a restlessness to 'leave home' for a chance to become 'King of the World'. Strength no longer lay in the safety of the household and family, but in breaking out from a home that for some reason was now a trap. As men moved outwards to explore, the home, whilst never losing its ideal form, gradually faded into one of many places where one could merely hang one's hat.

Again, it is fair to say that the ideal of love will never die, either in personal life, or in some collective sphere. Although people will do the most selfish and inane things, they go on hoping that their vision, forged in childhood, will one day come true. It might be three marriages, several children, and innumerable heartaches later, but the dream, they desperately believe, will be realised. It is always possible that most young individuals will realise the foolishness in such a course, but the ever growing evidence of deviance, disruption and animosity in relationships makes this seem an unlikely reality, at least in the near future. War, famine, and plague are all horrors, but horrors that in the final analysis can be endured, for they come from the outside, leaving the individual dignity intact. Betrayal and loss in love come all too often from one's own weakness, and as such affect both the inside and the outside, the personal and cultural; one cannot easily run away. All told, it would appear that the greatest misery that men and women can create are what they make for each other. In spite of this, we can rest assured that true, pure love can always in some remote sector of mankind's existence remain viable, available and ready to deliver the greatest joy to the few who can understand what it takes to achieve it.

Never has man wanted love so desperately as today, but never has he sabotaged so many of his efforts to achieve it. Sincere effort to consummate the old ideal of love seems gone, but one hopes not forever.

APPENDIX A

STATISTICAL ANALYSES AND REPORTS, INTRODUCTION

Unless otherwise noted, all of the analyses in this section use data taken from European nations, North America and Australia. In the text, we refer to 'European data', meaning a database of information taken from various sources and analysed using various statistical tools. Note, however, that this data is not only from Europe, but is derived from the European and the descendent cultures in Western Europe, North America, and Oceania. The countries in this database are: United Kingdom, Ireland, Norway, Sweden, Norway, Denmark, Finland, France, West Germany, Austria, Netherlands, Belgium, Spain, Portugal, Italy, United States, Canada, Australia. Not all these countries ('observations' in statistical parlance) are used in every analysis, as data are not available in all categories in every nation. The names of variables and sources of their data are listed in Appendix B.

Readers might be somewhat mystified by these numbers and concepts, since statistics is not taught as an important branch of mathematics at any level of schooling. This is unfortunate, as statistical analysis can greatly reward by providing deep insight into the dynamics of a situation, often unattainable through other means. It allows one to evaluate data in a most objective manner, stripped of arbitrary attitudes, personal prejudices and biases. Such an increase in comprehension and the ability to interpret scholarly papers and books can occur if formal methods of analysis and inference were improved. We can easily say that anyone with a desire for deeper understanding of the world would stand to benefit by reading a good book on statistics. Following is a recommended list of texts, some of which are basic and some advanced:

P.S. Mann, 1992, *Introductory Statistics*, John Wiley and Sons, New York.

A.G. Bluman, 1992, *Elementary Statistics, A step by step guide*, Wm. C Brown, Dubuque, Iowa.

M.B. Harris, 1995, *Basic Statistics, for behavioral science research*, Allyn and Bacon, Boston.

J.E. Freund, 1971, *Mathematical Statistics*, Prentice-Hall, Inc, Englewood Cliffs, NJ.

N.R. Draper, N. Smith, 1966, *Applied Regression Analysis*, John Wiley & Sons, Inc, New York.

In the tables summarising analytical results, the independent and dependent variables are identified. Unless noted as 'Multiple Regression', the independent variables in a table are each correlated separately with the dependent variable; they are *not* part of the same equation. We usually report one of two types of regression coefficients, the normal (standard) coefficient, or the robust coefficient. Both reveal how much the independent variable affects the dependent variable. The number can be between zero and one, and the higher the number, the greater the influence. Robust regression can be used effectively to reduce the influence of outliers (observations that are well-outside the average) on the equation. However, because it removes observations from the analysis, it should be used with caution. The type of robust regression used is known as Andrew's Sine, with a truncation constant of 2.1. For an explanation of robust correlation, see Hamilton, L., 1991, *Regression with Graphics: A second course in applied statistics*, Brooks/Cole Publishing Co, Pacific Grove, CA. Where robust regression was used, the coefficient is marked with (#). The results of both types of regression are adjusted for sample size, thus yielding an 'Adjusted $R^{2'}$'. The other statistical results given are p, or the probability that the correlation is spurious, where the smaller the number, the better; we also cite the F statistic, where the higher the number, the better, along with degrees of freedom and total error.

Two-dimensional graphs are instrumental in analysing in more detail the relationships among the variables. Non-linear relationships are found quite often in variables concerning human behaviour, but because they are not amenable to the standard statistical techniques, they are generally ignored. It is essential to study these correlations for they reveal complex and other difficult to discern affinities.

Variables marked with an asterisk (*) were included in an analysis, even though a statistically significant regression equation could not be found, because they were either near significance, and/or a visual inspection of the graph revealed possible associations. In these cases, only r, the standard Pearson correlation coefficient, is given, not R^2.

FRIENDSHIP AND LATE MARRIAGE

Independent Variable: FRIEN.SS

	Intercept	Parameter Estimate	P Level	F-Ratio	R^2
MARR30F	-41.8249	0.8225	0.009	F(1,5)=17.04	0.7278
MARR30M	-43.4315	1.0064	0.0198	F(1,5)=11.39	0.6338

EXTROVERSION AND OPPOSITE SEX FRIENDSHIPS

Dependent Variable: FRIEN.SS

	Intercept	Parameter Estimate	P Level	F-Ratio	R^2
EXTRO.SC[1]	70.3065	12.082	0.003	F(1,4)=41.25	0.8895

1. United States is removed as an outlier.

Independent Variable: EXTRO.SC

	Intercept	Parameter Estimate	P Level	F-Ratio	R^2
MARR19M	2.425	0.7276	0.0446	F(1,14)=4.87	0.2051
MARR19F	11.0993	1.5415	0.0236	F(1,15)=6.35	0.2506

Domestic Variables and Early Marriage

Other variables that describe household spending, HEALTHC, ENER, EDUC, TRANCOM, PERSONAL, are not significant.

Dependent Variable: MARR19F

	Intercept	Parameter Estimate	P Level	F-Ratio	R^2
FOOD	-3.77	0.7179	0.0117	$F(1,18)=7.87$	0.2655
HOUS#	25.4931	-0.7127	0.01	$F(1,18)=8.34$	0.2786
RECREAT	25.431	-1.5074	0.009	$F(1,18)=8.73$	0.3006
CLOTH	-5.903	2.5193	0.0374	$F(1,18)=5.05$	0.1758
HOUSDUR#	-12.4014	3.3303	0.0407	$F(1,18)=4.86$	0.1691

Employment, Income Per Capita, and Income Distribution in the Decision to Marry

A positive correlation between such celibacy and percent of household expenditures spent on recreation is also present, though not included as it cannot be fit into any equation. The same can be said for a negative correlation with space (square metres per person).

MULTIPLE CORRELATION
Dependent Variable: NOTMAR%
Intercept: 15.9091

	Parameter Estimate	P Level	Seq R^2	Simple R^2
MAL.ECOA	-0.6695	0.001	0.3292	0.3292
INC.H10	1.2078	0	0.8414	0.4576
$F(2,9)=23.87$, p=0.0000				
Coefficient of Variation	0.1446			
Adjusted $R^2\#$ = .8062				

MULTIPLE CORRELATION
Dependent Variable: NOTMAR%
Intercept: 0.3174

	Parameter Estimate	P Level	Seq R^2	Simple R^2
INC.H10#	0.5865	0.0489	0.2907	0.2907
GNP.CAP#	-0.0007	0.004	0.7348	0.5822
$F(2,9)=12.47$, p=0.0030				
Coefficient of Variation	0.1953			
Adjusted $R^2\#$ = .6759				

EFFECT OF SERVICE INDUSTRY WORK ON INCOME DISTRIBUTION AND MARRIAGE PROPENSITY

Independent Variable: EMP.SER

	Intercept	Parameter Estimate	P Level	F-Ratio	R^2
INC.H10#	31.6146	-0.1984	0.0309	$F(1,16)=5.60$	0.2129
NOTMAR%#	19.481	-0.4577	0.0189	$F(1,10)=7.83$	0.3829

LIVING ARRANGEMENTS AND THE PROPENSITY TO MARRY

(a)
Questions were asked of those who at time of survey were not married. We are therefore removing those people who had a tendency to marry early, since the average age of the sample is 21. Only relationships where curve reached significance, or had clear direction from visual inspection, are cited. Since the average age of persons in the independent variable were over 19, MARR19M and MARR19F show social tendency, and not actual effects on individuals.

Independent Variable: PC.ALON

	Intercept	Parameter Estimate	P Level	F-Ratio	R^2
NOTMAR%*					0.7065
MARR19F#	22.4339	-0.7031	0.0324	$F(1,5)=8.63$	0.5597
MARR30F#	17.4428	0.5903	0.0421	$F(1,5)=7.37$	0.5151
MARR30M#	25.1394	0.9688	0.01	$F(1,6)=16.48$	0.7207

(b)
Independent Variable: PC.NMPAR

	Intercept	Parameter Estimate	P Level	F-Ratio	R^2
NOTMAR%*					-0.5127
MARR19F#	-21.1787	0.6606	0.0655	$F(1,5)=5.53$	0.4301
MARR30F*					-0.4985
MARR30M#	59.8504	-0.5001	0.0571	$F(1,4)=7.01$	0.5459

(c)
Independent Variable: PC.FRE

	Intercept	Parameter Estimate	P Level	F-Ratio	R^2
NOTMAR%*					-0.8532
MARR19F#	1.3994	0.2592	0	$F(1,5)=20.54$	0.7651
MARR19M#	3.1619	0.5604	0.0148	$F(1,5)=13.31$	0.6724

(d)
Since the sample contains singles, if the effect is direct, then PC.PAR must be the independent variable.

Independent Variable: PC.PAR

	Intercept	Parameter Estimate	P Level	F-Ratio	R^2
NOTMAR%*					-0.5333
MARR19F#	-19.7421	0.486	0.0421	$F(1,5)=7.38$	0.5153
MARR30M#	55.6657	-0.3065	0.0381	$F(1,4)=9.30$	0.6239

Independent Variable: PC.FAM

	Intercept	Parameter Estimate	P Level	F-Ratio	R^2
NOTMAR%*					-0.4851
MARR30F*					-0.6261
MARR30M*					-0.5544

HOUSING COSTS AND PROPENSITY TO MARRY

The results for MARR19M and MARR30M are very similar to those presented below.

Independent Variable: HOUS

	Intercept	Parameter Estimate	P Level	F-Ratio	R^2
MARR19F	25.4931	-0.7127	0.01	$F(1,18)=8.34$	0.2786
MARR30F	7.6632	0.7205	0.01	$F(1,18)=8.36$	0.2792

HIGHER EDUCATION AND ITS EFFECT ON INFORMATION ACQUISITION

Independent Variable: OV25&COL

	Intercept	Parameter Estimate	P Level	F-Ratio	R^2
LIB.LOAN	2485.062	90.4454	0.0588	$F(1,7)=5.08$	0.3379
PERS.TV	4.2647	-0.0785	0.0223	$F(1,11)=7.07$	0.3358
NEWSCIRC	410.8502	-4.889	0.0137	$F(1,6)=11.86$	0.6081

EFFECT OF SPACE ON THE PROPENSITY TO MARRY

The filter NEWSCIRC LT 250 includes countries for which there is no figure for newspaper circulation; because of other characteristics, these countries are assumed to have circulation under 250 per 1000 population.

Independent Variable: SQM.PERS

	Intercept	Parameter Estimate	P Level	F-Ratio	R^2
MARR19M#	3.709	-0.0549	0.0346	$F(1,10)=5.97$	0.3113
MARR19M*[1]					-0.1402
MARR19M*[2]					-0.5479

Filters:

1. NEWSCIRC GT 250
2. NEWSCIRC LT 250

Independent Variable: SQM.PERS

	Intercept	Parameter Estimate	P Level	F-Ratio	R^2
MARR30M	7.142	0.7123	0.002	$F(1,11)=16.7$	0.5679
MARR30M[1]	17.9801	0.5117	0.0925	$F(1,4)=4.85$	0.4349
MARR30M#[2]	4.2505	0.7388	0.007	$F(1,4)=26.59$	0.8367

Filters:

1. NEWSCIRC GT 250
2. NEWSCIRC LT 250

Independent Variable: SQM.PERS

	Intercept	Parameter Estimate	P Level	F-Ratio	R^2
MARR19F#	26.687	-0.3909	0.0407	F(1,11)=5.37	0.2671
MARR19F[1]	0.4179	0.6201	0.0848	F(1,5)=4.60	0.3751
MARR19F*[2]					-0.6481

Filters:

1. STU.TEA2 GT 13
2. STU.TEA2 LT 13

Independent Variable: SQM.PERS

	Intercept	Parameter Estimate	P Level	F-Ratio	R^2
MARR30F	-0.0246	0.5647	0.002	F(1,11)=16.13	0.5577
MARR30F[1]					n.s.
MARR30F[2]	2.3104	0.5526	0.0127	F(1,4)=18.47	0.7775
MARR30F#[3]	11.972	0.3524	0.0207	F(1,4)=13.74	0.7182
MARR30F*[4]					0.1761

Filters:

1. STU.TEA2 GT 13
2. STU.TEA2 LT 13
3. NEWSCIRC GT 250
4. NEWSCIRC LT 250

Independent Variable: SQM.PERS

	Intercept	Parameter Estimate	P Level	F-Ratio	R^2
NOTMAR%	12.6555	-0.1518	0.0155	F(1,6)=11.2	0.5941

Independent Variable: LIB.LOAN

	Intercept	Parameter Estimate	P Level	F-Ratio	R^2
SQM.PERS[1]	25.4219	0.0019	0	$F(1,8)=32.10$	0.7756

1. Without outlier Finland.

EFFECT OF FERTILITY ON THE PROPENSITY TO MARRY

(a)
In our analysis we use the fertility rates for around the year 1985. Of course, these are not necessarily the fertility rates that people marrying in 1985 were accustomed to, but usually these rates are fairly stable over time. The statistics for MARR30F and MARR30M are not for a person's first marriage, and could relate to a person's second, third or later marriage.

Independent Variable: FERTRTE

	Intercept	Parameter Estimate	P Level	F-Ratio	R^2
MARR30M#	45.8246	-8.416	0.006	$F(1,18)=9.52$	0.3096
MARR30F#	31.329	-6.957	0.008	$F(1,18)=9.04$	0.2974
MARR19M#	-1.634	2.125	0.014	$F(1,18)=7.4$	0.252
MARR19F[1]	-17.1101	17.7004	0.0143	$F(1,17)=7.45$	0.2639

1. Without outlier Ireland. MARR19F with no controls was not significant, but was positively correlated with FERTRTE.

(b)

It would appear that fertility drives men to marry young, and men and women to not marry later. Early marriage prompts higher fertility among women. The following table determines causal direction using robust regression:

Y	X	P Level	Direction	Model Type
MARR19M	FERTRTE	0.014	Positive	Pro-familial
MARR19F	FERTRTE	0.2066		
FERTRTE	MARR19M	0.2698		
FERTRTE	MARR19F	0.0011	Positive	Fertility
MARR30M	FERTRTE	0.0064	Negative	Pro-familial
MARR30F	FERTRTE	0.0076	Negative	Pro-familial
FERTRTE	MARR30M	0.9937		
FERTRTE	MARR30F	0.9031		

THE EFFECT OF PARENTAL LOSS ON THE PROPENSITY TO MARRY

(a)
Independent Variable: DEATHRTE

	Intercept	Parameter Estimate	P Level	F-Ratio	R^2
MARR.CBP					n.s.
MARR19M					n.s.
MARR19F					n.s.
MR20.29F#					0.1181
MARR30M*[1]					0.3776
MARR30F*					0.3583
NOTMAR%#	18.5634	-1.0704	0.0302	$F(1,10)=6.37$	0.3281

Filter:
1. MARR30M GT 30

(b) Correlation coefficients between death rates and rates for marriage, 30 and over, by age group death rate:

Age group	Marriage, age 30 and over, males	Marriage, age 30 and over, females
45-49	-0.3915	-0.2404
50-54	-0.4031	-0.2508
55-59	-0.4534	-0.2678
60-64	-0.2738	-0.1185
65-69	-0.3809	-0.1857
70-74	-0.4451	-0.2691

(c) The best robust regression occurs when DEA45.49 and DEA55.59, of all age-specific death rates, are used.

Independent Variable: DEA45.49

	Intercept	Parameter Estimate	P Level	F-Ratio	R^2
MARR30M#[1]	39.7174	-1.597	0.0492	F(1,10)=5.00	0.2669

Filter:

1. MARR30M GT 25

Independent Variable: DEA55.59

	Intercept	Parameter Estimate	P Level	F-Ratio	R^2
NOTMAR%#	-3.4485	0.8522	0.0291	F(1,9)=6.72	0.3638

(d)

Correlation coefficients between death rates and rates for marriage, 19 and under, by age group death rate:

Age group	Marriage, age 19 and under, males	Marriage, age 19 and under, females[1]
45-49	0.3928	0.4137
50-54	0.3821	0.4689
55-59	0.4285	0.4162
60-64	0.3243	0.2729
65-69	0.4483	0.3949
70-74	0.3761	0.3629

1. Greece is removed as an outlier.

(e)
Independent Variable: LIFEEXMA

	Intercept	Parameter Estimate	P Level	F-Ratio	R^2
MARR.CBP*					-0.2661
MARR30M	-246.3317	3.8728	0.0195	$F(1,18)=6.57$	0.2268
MARR30F#	-113.5213	1.8416	0.045	$F(1,18)=4.64$	0.1609
NOTMAR%	101.4081	-1.302	0.0982	$F(1,10)=3.33$	0.1745

COMBINED EFFECT OF FAMILY SIZE AND LOSS OF PARENT ON PROPENSITY TO MARRY

(a) MULTIPLE REGRESSION

Dependent Variable: MARR19M

Intercept: -7.460231

	Parameter Estimate	P Level	Seq R^2	Simple R^2
FERTRTE	2.3051	0.002	0.2988	0.2988
DEA45.49	1.2367	0.002	0.6467	0.2916

$F(2,15)=13.73$, $p=0.0000$

Coefficient of Variation: 0.4080

Adjusted R^2: 0.5996

(b) MULTIPLE REGRESSION

Dependent Variable: MARR19F

Intercept: 5.042519

	Parameter Estimate	P Level	Seq R^2	Simple R^2
FERTRTE	14.1806	0.009	0.4945	0.4945
RECREAT	-1.2748	0.007	0.7748	0.5355
SQM.PERS	-0.1679	0.1802	0.8176	0.1276

$F(3,9)=13.45$, $p=0.0010$

Coefficient of Variation: 0.2497

Adjusted R^2: 0.7568

(c) MULTIPLE REGRESSION

Dependent Variable: MARR30M

Intercept: -11.96012

	Parameter Estimate	P Level	Seq R^2	Simple R^2
DEA45.49	4.5681	0.001	0.1551	0.1551
FERTRTE	-6.4948	0.005	0.3891	0.3106
SQM.PERS	0.4196	0	0.5137	0.3189
RECREAT	2.0215	0	0.9899	0.8016

$F(4,5)=122.40$, p=0.0000

Coefficient of Variation: 0.0354

Adjusted R^2: 0.9818

MULTIPLE REGRESSION

Dependent Variable: MARR30F

Intercept: -16.43372

	Parameter Estimate	P Level	Seq R^2	Simple R^2
SQM.PERS	0.5115	0.005	0.3248	0.3248
DEA45.49	3.1978	0.0216	0.4585	0.0018
RECREAT	0.9544	0.005	0.8656	0.5486
FERTRTE	-2.9836	0.3084	0.8853	0.2657

$F(4,7)=13.51$, p=0.0002

Coefficient of Variation: 0.1276

Adjusted R^2: 0.8198

THE EFFECT OF MARRIAGE PATTERNS ON THE PROPENSITY TO MARRY

(a)

We assume that percent of women not married in the 45 to 49 age group can effectively be termed a 'never-marrying' group, although a small proportion will.

Dependent Variable: NOTMAR%

	Intercept	Parameter Estimate	P Level	F-Ratio	R^2
MARR19F#	4.8401	0.2855	0.008	$F(1,10)=10.97$	0.4754

(b)

Dependent Variable: NOTMAR%

	Intercept	Parameter Estimate	P Level	F-Ratio	R^2
MARR30M	13.9291	-0.1731	0.0207	$F(1,10)=7.53$	0.3726
MARR30F	13.0079	-0.2285	0.0195	$F(1,10)=7.72$	0.3794

THE EFFECT OF CELIBACY ON THE PROPENSITY TO DIVORCE

Independent Variable: NOTMAR%

	Intercept	Parameter Estimate	P Level	F-Ratio	R^2
DIV.MAR	65.5865	-3.7631	0.004	$F(1,8)=15.45$	0.6162
DIV.MAP	8.5755	-0.5818	0	$F(1,10)=27.65$	0.7078

APPENDIX B

VARIABLES USED IN STATISTICAL ANALYSES

ABBREVIATIONS TO BE USED:

EBY 96:
aume D., ed., 1996, *Britannica Book of the Year*, Encyclopedia Britannica Increase, Chicago.

EBY 91:
aume D., ed., 1991, *Britannica Book of the Year*, Encyclopedia Britannica Increase, Chicago.

EBY 90:
aume D., ed., 1990, *Britannica Book of the Year*, Encyclopedia Britannica Increase, Chicago.

EBY 89:
aume D., ed., 1989, *Britannica Book of the Year*, Encyclopedia Britannica Increase, Chicago.

EBY 88:
aume D., ed., 1988, *Britannica Book of the Year*, Encyclopedia Britannica Increase, Chicago.

WEPFPS:
urian, G.T., 1989, *World Encyclopedia of Police Forces and Penal Systems*, Facts on File, New York.

Gallup:
Gallup G.H., 1980, *The International Gallup Polls, Public Opinion, 1978*, Scholarly Resources Increase, Wilmington, DE.

UN 1982:
United Nations, 1984, *Demographic Yearbook 1982, Special Topic: Marriage and Divorce Statistics*, United Nations, New York.

UN 1985:
United nations, 1987, *Demographic Yearbook 1985, Special Topic: Mortality Statistics*, United Nations, New York.

VARIABLE NAMES AND DEFINITIONS:

FOOD
Percent of household budget spent on food. Latest figures. Source: EBY 89, pp 848-853.

CLOTH
Percent of average household budget spent on clothing. Latest figures. Source: EBY 89, pp 848-853.

RECREAT
Percent of average household budget spent on recreation. Latest figures. Source: EBY 89, pp 848-853.

HOUSDUR
Percent of average household budget spent on household durables. Latest figures. Source: EBY 89, pp 848-853.

HOUS
Percent of average household budget spent on housing. Latest figures. Source: EBY 89, pp 848-853.

ENER
Percent of average household budget spent on energy and water. Latest figures. Source: EBY 89, pp 848-853.

EDUC
Percent of average household budget spent on education. Latest figures. Source: EBY 89, pp 848-853.

TRANCOM
Percent of average household budget spent on transportation and communication. Latest figures. Source: EBY 89, pp 848-853.

PERSONAL
Percent of average household budget spent on personal effects and other. Latest figures. Source: EBY 89, pp 848-853.

HEALTHC
Percent of average household budget spent on health care. Latest figures. Source: EBY 89, pp 848-853.

MAL.ECOA
Percent of male population economically active. Mostly 1985. Source: EBY 1989, pp 776-781.

INC.H10
Percent of total national income earned by households comprising highest decile of wage earners. Mostly early to mid-1980s, some early to mid-1970s. Source: EBY 89, pp 848-853.

GNP.CAP
Gross National Product per capita. All 1985. Source: EBY 88, 770-775.

EMP.SER
Percent of economically active who are in services industries. Mostly 1985. Source: EBY 1989, 776-781.

NOTMAR%
Percent of females age 45 to 49 who are single. Source: UN 1982, Table 40, pp 810-979.

MARR19M
Percent of grooms 19 and under. Mostly 1986. Source: EBY 89, pp 764-769

MARR30M
Percent of grooms 30 and over. Mostly 1986. Source: EBY 89, pp 764-769.

MARR19F
Percent of brides 19 and under. Mostly 1986. Source: EBY 88, pp 764-769.

MARR30F
Percent of brides 30 and over. Mostly 1986. Source: EBY 88, pp 764-769.

MR20.29F
Percent of brides aged 20 through 29. Mostly 1986. Source: EBY 89, 764-769.

EXTRO.SC
Factor score indicating level of extroversion of a nation. 1960. Lynn & Hampson, 1975.

FRIEN.SS
Percent who have close friends of both sexes. 1978. Source: Gallup, p 391.

PC.NMPAR
Percent of all 18-24 year olds living with parent(s). 1978. Source: Gallup, p 375.

PC.ALON
Percent of unmarried 18-24 year olds living alone. 1978. Source: Gallup, p 375.

PC.FRE
Percent of unmarried 18-24 year olds living with friend(s), acquaintance(s), roommate(s), etc. 1978. Source: Gallup, p 375.

PC.PAR
Percent of unmarried 18-24 year olds living with parent(s). 1978. Source: Gallup, p 375.

PC.FAM
Percent of unmarried 18-24 year olds living with parent(s), or family member(s), and/or relative(s) other than parent(s). 1978. Source: Gallup, p 375.

OV25&COL
Percent of population age 25 and over with post-secondary education. Mostly 1986. Source: EBY 89, 866-871.

LIB.LOAN
Library loans per 1,000 population. Mostly 1985. Source: EBY 90, 888-893.

NEWSCIRC
Circulation of daily newspapers per 1000 population. Mostly 1986. Source: EBY 89, pp 818-823.

STU.TEA2
Students per teacher at general second level of education (high school). Mostly 1986. Source: EBY 89, 866-871.

PERS.TV
Number of persons per television receiver. Mostly 1987. Source: EBY 89, pp 818-823.

SQM.PERS
Number of square metres of residential space per person. Population and households are from latest figures, i.e. 1985-97, space is taken from estimates generally from 1989-1991. Source: Calculated from EBY 89, 842-847, 538-739; EBY 96 864-869. We use the formula below instead of simply dividing average space per dwelling by persons per dwelling. Since not all dwellings are occupied, if we had used persons per dwelling, we would be allocating unused residential space, giving people more space than they really have. The equation that is used in calculating this statistic is as follows:

$$SQM.PERS = \frac{HSH \times AREA.DWE}{POP}$$

AREA.DWE
Average area, in square metres, per unit of housing stock. See above.

HSH
Number of households or families; figures in database are about equally divided between the two types. Mostly 1986. Source: EBY 89. The figure for Finland is possibly wrong in EBY; might be 1,963,000, not 1,163,000 as it is in the book; when one divides population by number of household, one gets household size of 4.26; however EBY data says 2.5; the figure for households is evidently wrong and should be 800,000 higher.

MARR.CBP
Marriages per 1,000 population age 15 through 44. Mostly 1986. Source: Calculated from EBY 89, 538-739, 746-751.

LIFEEXMA
Life expectancy at birth for males. Mostly 1986. Source: EBY 89, 764-769.

DEATHRTE
Deaths per 1,000 population. Mostly 1986. Source: EBY 89, 764-769.

DEA45.49
Deaths per 100,000 male population age 45 through 49. Nearly all 1983, 1984. Source: UN 1985, Table 27, pp 636-697.

DEA55.59
Deaths per 100,000 male population age 55 through 59. Nearly all 1983, 1984. Source: UN 1985, Table 27, pp 636-697.

FERTRTE
Average number of children borne per woman if all childbearing women lived to the end of their childbearing years and bore children at each age at the average rate for that age. Mostly 1986. Source: EBY 89, 764-769.

BIRTHRTE
Births per 1000 population. Mostly 1986. Source: EBY 89.

DIV.MAR
Divorce rate per 1000 population as a percent of marriage rate per 1000 population. Nearly all 1985. Source: Calculated from EBY 88 and EBY 89, 538-739.

DIV.MAP
Divorces per 1000 population age 15 through 44. Mostly 1986. Source: Calculated from EBY 89, 538-739, 746-751.

$$DIV.MAP = \frac{POP \times (\frac{MARR.RTE}{1000}) \times (\frac{DIV.MAR}{100})}{POP \times (\frac{P15\_29 + P30\_44}{100})}$$

REFERENCES

Alter G, 1991, New perspectives on European marriage in the nineteenth century, *Journal of Family History*, Jan 16(1), 1-5.

Anderson NF, 1986, Cousin marriage in Victorian England, *Journal of Family History*, 11(3), 285-301.

Archer J., 1984, Gender roles as developmental pathways, *British Journal of Social Psychology*, 23(3), 245-256.

Argyle M., Henderson M., Furnham A., 1985, The rules of social relationships, *The British Journal of Social Psychology*, Jun 24(2), 125-139.

Armstrong N., 1986, History in the house of culture: Social disorder and domestic fiction in early Victorian England, *Poetics Today*, 7(4), 641-671.

Atienza Hernández I., 1989, [Women and ideology: An emic vision of the role of the aristocratic woman in the seventeenth century], *Revista Internacional de Sociología*, 47(3), 317-337.

Bachrach C.A., 1980, Childlessness and social isolation among the elderly, *Journal of Marriage and the Family*, Aug 42(3), 627-636.

Bainbridge W.S., Stark R., 1981, Friendship, religion, and the occult: A network study, *Review of Religious Research*, Jun 22(4), 313-327.

Bar-Yam M., Kohlberg L., Naame A., 1980, Moral reasoning of students in different cultural, social, and educational settings, *American Journal of Education*, May 88(3), 345-362.

Basavarajappa K.G., Norris MJ, Halli SS, 1988, Spouse selection in Canada, 1921-78: An examination by age, sex, and religion, *Journal of Biosocial Science*, Spr 20(2), 211-223.

Bennett B.W., Grosser GS, 1981, Movement toward androgyny in college females through experiential education, *Journal of Psychology*, Jan 107, 177-183.

Bentler P.M., Newcomb M.D., 1978, Longitudinal study of marital success and failure, *Journal of Consulting and Clinical Psychology*, 46, 1053-1070.

Berk L.M., 1977, The great middle American dream machine, *Journal of Communication*, Sum 27(3), 27-31.

Bernard, Jessie Shirley, 1982, *The Future of Marriage*, Yale University Press, New Haven CT.

Bitter R.G., 1986, Late marriage and marital instability, the effects: The effects of heterogeneity and inflexibility, *Journal of Marriage and the Family*, Aug 48, 631-640.

Blossfeld H-P, Jaenichen U., 1990, [Expanding education and its effects on the family. How does women's increasing educational level affect the postponement of marriage and children?], *Soziale Welt*, 41(4), 454-476.

Blum J., 1974, The condition of the European peasantry on the eve of emancipation, *Journal of Modern History*, Sep 46, 395-424.

Bolger N., DeLongis A., Kessler R.C., Wethington E., 1989, The contagion of stress across multiple roles, *Journal of Marriage and the Family*, Feb 51, 175-183.

Boyes M.C., Allen SG, 1993, Styles of parent-child interaction and moral reasoning in adolescence, *Merrill Palmer Quarterly*, Oct 39(4), 551-570.

Brennan E.R., Dyke B, 1980, Assortative mate choice and mating opportunity on Sanday, Orkney Islands, *Social Biology*, Fal 27(3), 199-210.

Buck N., Scott J., 1993, She's leaving home: But why? An analysis of young people leaving the parental home, *Journal of Marriage and the Family*, Nov 55(4), 863-874.

Bumpass L.L., Sweet J.A., 1972, Differentials in marital instability: 1972, *American Sociological Review*, 37, 754-767.

Burguière A., 1987, The formation of the couple, *Journal of Family History*, Jan- Jul 12(1-3), 39-53.

Butcher J.N., Pancheri P., 1976, *A Handbook of Cross-National MMPI Research*, University of Minnesota Press, Minneapolis.

Buunk B, Hupka B, 1987, Cross-cultural differences in the elicitation of sexual jealousy, *Journal of Sex Research*, Feb 23(1), 12-22.

Cameron P., Cameron K., Proctor K., 1989, Effect of homosexuality upon public health and social order, *Psychological Reports*, 64, 1167-1179.

Carter H., Glick P.C., 1970, *Marriage and Divorce, A Social and Economic Study*, Harvard University Press, Cambridge, MA.

Chadwick B.A., Heaton T.B., 1992, eds, *Statistical Handbook on the American Family*, Oryx Press, Phoenix.

Chalvon-Demersay S., Libbrecht L., 1995, Scenarios of crisis: Social construction of intimacy through a thousand film projects, *RESEAUX: The French Journal of Communication*, Spr 3(1), 93-110.

Christensen H. T., Barber K.E., 1967, Interfaith versus intrafaith marriage in Indiana, *Journal of Marriage and the Family*, 29, 461-149.

Christopher F.S., 1988, An initial investigation into a continuum of premarital sexual pressure, *Journal of Sex Research*, May 25(2), 255-266.

Coleman M., Ganong L.H., Ellis P., 1985, Family structure and dating behavior of adolescents, *Adolescence*, Fal 20(79), 537-543.

Corset P., 1995, Television viewing practices among youth: A way toward autonomy and education, *Recherches Sociologiques*, 26(1), 73-88.

Daume D., ed., 1989, *Britannica Book of the Year*, Encyclopedia Britannica Inc, Chicago.

De Sanctis P., 1982, [Spells, love potions and other tricks: Notes on the peasant woman and her marital destiny], *Rassegna Italiana di Sociologia*, Apr-Jun 23(2), 271-289.

Diehl, H., 1986, Into the maze of the self: The Protestant transformation of the image of the labyrinth, *The Journal of Medieval and Renaissance Studies*, Fall 16(2), 281-301.

Downey A.M., 1990-1991, The impact of drug abuse upon adolescent suicide, *Omega*, 22(4), 261-275.

Edwards G.M., ed., 1996, *Britannica Book of the Year*, Encyclopedia Britannica Inc, Chicago.

Eisenberg N., Miller P.A., Shell R., McNalley S., Shea C., 1991, Prosocial development in adolescence: A longitudinal study, *Developmental Psychology*, 27(5), 849-857.

Elder G.H., Rockwell R.C., 1976, Marital timing in women's life patterns, *Journal of Family History*, Fal, 1(1), 34-53.

Farquhar J., 1992, An American horror myth: Night of the Living Dead, *Semiotica*, 38(1-2), 1-15.

Feld S.L., 1991, Why your friends have more friends than you do, *American Journal of Sociology*, May 96(6), 1464-1477.

Flinn, M.W., 1981, *The European Demographic System, 1500-1820*, Johns Hopkins University Press, Baltimore, MD.

Gallup G.H., 1980, *The International Gallup Polls, Public Opinion, 1978*, Scholarly Resources Inc, Wilmington, DE.

Giaresso R., Johnson P., Goodchilds G., Zellman G., 1979, Acquaintance rape and adolescent sexuality, Paper presented at the Midwestern Psychological Association meeting, Chicago.

Gillis, J.R., 1997, *A World of Their Own Making*, Harvard University Press, Cambridge.

Gilmartin B.G., 1985, Some family antecedents of severe shyness, *Family Relations*, 34(3), 429-438.

Glick P.C., Norton A.J., 1971, Frequency, duration and probability of marriage and divorce, *Journal of Marriage and the Family 33*, 307-317.

Goldscheider F.K., Goldscheider C., 1989, Family structure and conflict: Nest- leaving expectations of young adults and their parents, *Journal of Marriage and the Family*, Feb 51(1), 87-97.

Goldscheider F.K., LeBourdais C., 1986, The decline in age at leaving home, 1920-1979, *Sociology and Social Research*, Jan 70(2), 143-145.

Goldscheider F.K., Waite L.J., 1987, Nest leaving patterns and the transition to marriage for young men and women, *Journal of Marriage and the Family*, Aug 49(3), 507-516.

Gordon M., Miller R.L., 1984, Going steady in the 1980s: Exclusive relationships in six Connecticut high schools, *Sociology and Social Research*, Jul 68(4), 463-479.

Grigsby J., McGowan J.B., 1986, Still in the nest: Adult children living with their parents, *Sociology and Social Research*, Jan 70(2), 146-148.

Guinnane T., 1991, Re-thinking the Western European marriage pattern: The decision to marry in Ireland at the turn of the twentieth century, *Journal of Family History*, Jan 16(1), 47-64.

Gutman J., 1973, Self-concepts and television viewing among women, *Public Opinion Quarterly*, Fal 37(3), 388-397.

Hahn A., 1983, [The fiction of consensus in small groups: The example of new marriages], *Kölner Zeitschrift für Soziologie und Sozialpsychologie*, Supl 25, 210-232.

Hajnal J., 1965, European marriage patterns in persepctive, in *Population in History*, eds. D.V. Glass and D.E.C. Eversley, Edward Arnold, London, pp 101-146.

Hajnal J., 1983, Two kinds of pre-industrial household formation system, in *Family Forms in Historic Europe*, eds. R. Wall, J. Robin, P. Laslett, Cambridge University Press, Cambridge.

Hansen G.L., 1983, Marital satisfaction and jealousy among men, *Psychological Reports*, 52(2), 363-366.

Hansen S.L., Hicks M.W., 1980, Sex role attitudes and perceived dating-mating choices of youth, *Adolescence*, Spr 15(57), 83-90.

Hastings E.H., Hastings P.K., 1987, *Index to International Public Opinion, 1985-1986*, Greenwood Press, New York.

Hawes J.M., 1985, The strange history of female adolescence in the United States, *The Journal of Psychohistory*, Sum 13(1), 51-63.

Heer D.M., 1974, The prevalence of black-white marriage in the United States, 1960 and 1970, *Journal of Marriage and the Family*, 36, 246-258.

Heim N., 1981, Sexual behavior of castrated sex offenders, *Archives of Sexual Behavior*, Feb 10(1), 11-19.

Herlihy D., Klapisch-Zuber C., 1985, *Tuscans and their Families*, Yale University Press, New Haven.

Hertel B.R., 1988, Gender, religious identity and work force participation, *Journal for the Scientific Study of Religion*, Dec 27(4), 574-592.

Howard J.A., Blumstein P., Schwartz P., 1989, Homogamy in intimate relationships: why birds of a feathers flock together, paper presented at 84th annual meeting of the American Sociological Association.

Hurwich J.J., 1993, Inheritance practices in early modern Germany, *Journal of Interdisciplinary History*, Spr 23(4), 699-718.

Jencks C., Crouse J., Mueser P., 1983, The Wisconsin model of status attainment: A national replication with improved measures of ability and aspirations, *Sociology of Education*, Jan 66(1), 3-19.

Jung C.G., 1959/68, 'Psychological aspects of the mother archetype' (1939/54), in *The Archetypes and the Collective Unconscious*, Princeton University Press, Princeton, New Jersey.

Jung C.G., 1964/70, 'Woman in Europe' (1927), in *Civilization in Transition*, Princeton University Press, Princeton, New Jersey.

Jung C.G., 1968, *Analytical Psychology: Its Theory and Practice: The Tavistock Lectures*, (1935) London and New York.

Kandel DB, Raveis VH, Davies M, 1991, Suicidal ideation in adolescence: Depression, substance use, and other risk factors, *Journal of Youth and Adolescence*, Apr 20(2), 289-310.

Kermode F., Kermode, A., 1995, *The Oxford Book of Letters*, Oxford University, Oxford.

Kilmann P.R., Boland J.P., West M.D., Jonet C.J., et al., 1993, Sexual arousal of college students in relation to sex experiences, *Journal of Sex Education and Therapy*, Fal 19(3), 157-164.

Knox D., 1985, Breaking up: The cover story versus the real story, *Free Inquiry in Creative Sociology*, 13(2), 131-132.

Koller K., Gooden S., 1984, On living alone, social isolation, and psychological disorder, *The Australian and New Zealand Journal of Sociology*, Mar 20(1), 81-92.

Kuklo C., 1991, Marriage in pre-industrial Warsaw in the light of demographic studies, *Journal of Family History*, 15(3), 239-259.

Lampe P.E., 1985, Friendship and adultery, *Sociological Inquiry*, Sum 55(3), 310-324.

Landale N.S., Tolnay S.E., 1991, Group differences in economic opportunity and the timing of marriage: Blacks and whites in the rural South, 1910, *American Sociological Review*, Feb 56(1), 33-45.

Leppel K., 1987, Income effects on living arrangements: Differences between male and female householders, *Social Science Research*, Jun 16(2), 138-153.

Liehm A.J., 1975, The contemporary social film: Its content and aesthetic character, *Praxis*, Spr 1(1), 111-114.

Lipsitz G., 1990, *Time Passages: Collective Memory and American Popular Culture*, University of Minnesota Press, Minneapolis.

Lynn R., Hampson S.L., 1975, National differences in extraversion and neuroticism, *British Journal of Social Clinical Psychology*, 14(3), 223-240.

Malony H.N., 1988, Men and women in the clergy: Stresses, strains and resources, *Pastoral Psychology*, Spr 36(3) 164-168.

Marshall W.L., 1989, Intimacy, loneliness and sexual offenders, *Behaviour Research and Therapy*, 27(5), 491-503.

Mersmann H., ed, 1986, *Letters of Mozart*, Dorset Press, New York.

Mieder, W., 1986, *The Prentice Hall Encyclopedia of World Proverbs*, Prentice- Hall, Englewood Cliffs, New Jersey.

Miller K.A., 1985, *Emigrants and Exiles*, Oxford University Press, Oxford.

Miller B., Marshall J.C., 1987, Coercive sex on the university campus, *Journal of College Student Personnel*, Jan 28(1), 38-47.

Mitchell B.R., 1975, *European Historical Statistics, 1750-1970*, Columbia University Press, New York.

Mitchell G., 1981, *Human Sex Differences*, Van Nostrand Reinhold Company, New York.

Moulton R., 1977, Some effects of the New Feminism, *The American Journal of Psychiatry*, Jan 134(1), 1-6.

Muram D., Rosenthal T.L., Tolley E.A., Peeler M.M., et al., 1992, Teenage pregnancy: Dating and sexual attitudes, *Journal of Sex Education and Therapy*, Win 18(4), 264-276.

Murstein B.I., 1980, Mate selection in the 1980s, *Journal of Marriage and the Family*, Nov 42(4), 777-792.

Netting N.S., 1992, Sexuality in youth culture: Identity and change, *Adolescence*, Win 27(108), 961-976.

Orbuch T.L., Veroff J., Holmberg D., 1993, Becoming a married couple: The emergence of meaning in the first years of marriage, *Journal of Marriage and the Family*, Nov 55(4), 815-826.

Ozment S., 1983, *When Fathers Ruled: Family Life in Reformation Europe*, Harvard University Press, Cambridge.

Ozment S., 1986, *Magdalena and Balthasar*, Simon and Schuster, New York.

Palisi B.J., 1984, Household crowding and well-being: A cross-cultural analysis, *International Journal of Sociology of the Family*, Spr 14(1), 17-31.

Peres Y., Meivar H., 1986, Self-presentation during courtship: A content analysis of classified advertisements in Israel, *Journal of Comparative Family Studies*, Spr 17(1), 19-31.

Prokopec J., 1977, Determinants of interaction behavior and preference values in the choice of life partner, *Demografie*, 19(1), 11-20.

Raboch J., Barták V., 1980, Changes in the sexual life of Czechoslovak women born between 1911 and 1958, *Archives of Sexual Behavior*, Dec 9(6), 495-502.

Ramu G.N., Tavuchis N, 1986, The valuation of children and parenthood among the voluntarily childless and parental couples in Canada, *Journal of Comparative Family Studies*, Spr 17(1), 99-116.

Rankin R.P., Maneker JS, 1987, Correlates of marital duration and black-white intermarriage in California, *Journal of Divorce*, Win 11(2), 51-67.

Rao K.V., 1990, Marriage risks, cohabitation and premarital births in Canada, *European Journal of Population*, 6(1), 27-49.

Reher D.S., 1991, Marriage patterns in Spain, *Journal of Family History*, 16(1), 7-30.

Rifkin J., Timms C., 1985, *Heinrich Schütz*, pp 1-150 in *The New Grove North European Baroque Masters*, 1985, S. Sadie, ed, W.W. Norton & Company, New York.

Roman Catholic Church, 1983, *Code of Canon Law*, Latin-English Edition, Canon Law Society of America, Washington, DC.

Scanzoni J., 1968, A social system analysis of dissolved and exiting marriages, *Journal of Marriage and the Family*, 30, 451-461.

Schab F., 1991, Schooling without learning: Thirty years of cheating in high school, *Adolescence*, 26(104), 839-847.

Schoen R., Baj J., 1985, The impact of the marriage squeeze in five Western countries, *Sociology and Social Reearch*, Oct 70(1), 8-19.

Schroeder H.J., 1978, *Canons and Decrees of the Council of Trent*, English Translation, Tan Books and Publishers, Inc., Rockford, Illinois.

Segalen M., 1991, Mean age at marriage and kinship networks in a town under the influence of the metropolis: Nanterre, 1800-1850, *Journal of Family History*, 16(1), 65-78.

Sharma A., Rajlakshmi S., 1979, Opinions of married couples regarding the selection of the marriage partner: A study of couples residing in Baroda, *Sociological Bulletin*, Mar-Sep 28(1-2), 71-82.

Shively J., 1991, Cultural compensation? The popularity of Westerns among American Indians, Association Paper.

Shorter E., Schmalfuss A., 1972, 'La Vie Intime'- Contributions to its history on the example of cultural change in the Bavarian lower classes in the 19th century, *Kolner Zeitschrift für Soziologie und Sozialpsychologie*, 16, Suppl, 530-549.

Shorter E, 1980, Illegitimacy, sexual revolution, and social change in modern Europe, in Rotberg & Rabb (1980), p 85-120.

Shorter E., 1987, The first great increase in anorexia nervosa, *Journal of Social History*, Fall, 69-96.

Shotland R.L., Goodstein L., 1992, Sexual precedence reduces the perceived legitimacy of sexual refusal: An examination of attributions concerning date rape and consensual sex, *Personality and Social Psychology Bulletin*, Dec 18(6), 755-764.

Siddiqi M.U., Reeves E.Y., 1986, A comparative study of mate selection criteria among Indians in India and the United States, *International Journal of Comparative Sociology*, Sep-Dec 27(3-4), 226-233.

Smith G.W., Debenham J.D., 1979, Computer automated marriage analysis, *The American Journal of Family Therapy*, Spr 7(1), 16-31.

Spagnoli P.G., 1983, Industrialization, proletarianization and marriage: A reconsideration, *Journal of Family History*, Fall 8(3), 230-247.

Speicher B., 1992, Adolescent moral judgment and perceptions of family interaction, *Journal of Family Psychology*, Dec 6(2), 128-138.

Sprecher S., McKinney K., 1987, Barriers in the initiation of intimate heterosexual relationships and strategies of intervention, *Journal of Social Work and Human Sexuality*, Spr Sum 5(2), 97-110.

Stycos J.M., 1983, The timing of Spanish marriages: A socio-statistical study, *Population Studies*, Jul 37(2), 227-238.

Sugarman L., 1980, Choice and values among students, *Educational Research*, Feb 22(2), 143-146.

Tambs K., Moum T., 1992, No large convergence during marriage for health, lifestyle, and personality in a large sample of Norwegian spouses, *Journal of Marriage and the Family*, 54(4), 957-971.

Temple M., Polk K., 1986, A dynamic analysis of educational attainment, *Sociology of Education*, Apr 59(2), 79-84.

Teti D.M., Lamb M.E., Lester A.B., 1987, Long range socioeconomic and marital consequences of adolescent marriage in three cohorts of adult males, *Journal of Marriage and the Family*, Aug 49(3), 499-506.

Tjaden P.G., 1988, Pornography and sex education, *Journal of Sex Research*, 24, 208-212.

Tokareva E.K., [Marriage ties and bonds of freedom], *Sotsiologicheskie Issledovaniya*, Apr 14(2), 83-91.

Trent K., 1994, Family context and adolescents' expectations about marriage, fertility, and nonmarital childbearing, *Social Science Quarterly*, Jun 75(2), 319-339.

Tucker R.K., Marvin M.G., Vivian B., 1991, What constitutes a romantic act? An empirical study, *Psychological Reports*, Oct 69(2), 651-654.

Turner B.F., Adams C.G., 1988, Reported change in preferred sexual activity over the adult years, *Journal of Sex Research*, May 25(2), 289-303.

U.S. Department of Commerce, 1985, *1980 Census of the Population*, Volume 2 Subject Reports, Marital Characteristics, U.S. Government Printing Office, Washington, DC.

U.S. Bureau of the Census, 1992, *Money Income of Households, Families, and Persons in the United States: 1991*, U.S. Government Printing Office, Washington, DC.

Uhl S., 1989, Making the bed: Creating the home in Escalona, Andalusia, *Ethnology*, 1989, Apr 28(2), 151-166.

United Nations, 1984, *Demographic Yearbook 1982, Special Topic: Marriage and Divorce Statistics*, United Nations, New York.

United Nations, 1987, *Demographic Yearbook 1985, Special Topic: Mortality Statistics*, United Nations, New York.

Veenhoven R., 1983, The growing impact of marriage, *Social Indicators Research*, 12(1), 49-63.

Veevers J.E., 1984, Age-discrepant marriages: cross-national comparisons of Canadian-American trends, *Social Biology*, Spr-Sum 31(1-2), 18-27.

Vera H., Berardo F.M., Vandiver J.S., 1990, Age irrelevancy in society: The test of mate selection, *Journal of Aging Studies*, Spr 4(1), 81-95.

Wagner M.E., Schubert H.J., Schubert DS, 1985, Family size effects: A review, *Journal of Genetic Psychology*, Mar 146(1), 65-78.

Watt J.R., 1988, Marriage contract disputes in early modern Neuchatel, 1547- 1806, *Journal of Social History*, Fal 22(1), 129-148.

Weber E., 1976, *Peasants into Frenchmen, The Modernization of Rural France, 1870-1914*, Stanford University Press, Stanford, California.

Weis D.L., 1985, The experience of pain during women's first sexual intercourse: Cultural mythology about female sexual initiation, *Archives of Sexual Behavior*, Oct 14(5), 421-438.

Weisheit R.A., Hopkins R.H., Kearney K.A., Mauss A.L., 1982, Substance abuse, nonconformity, and the inability to assign problem responsibility, *The Journal of Drug Issues*, Spr 12(2), 199-209.

Wenz F.V., 1984, Household crowding, loneliness and suicide ideation, *Psychology, A Quarterly Journal of Human Behavior*, 21(2), 25-29.

West K.K., Morgan L.A., 1987, Public perceptions of the ideal number of children for contemporary families, *Population and Environment Behavioral and Social Ideas*, Fal 9(3), 160-172.7

Willits F.K., 1988, Adolescent behavior and adult success and well-being: A 37- year panel study, *Youth and Society*, Sep 20(1), 68-87.

Wrigley E.A., 1987, *People, Cities and Wealth*, Basil Blackwell, Oxford.

Yi Z., Coale A., Choe M.K., Zhiwu L., Li L., 1994, Leaving the parental home: Census-based estimates for China, Japan, South Korea, United States, France, and Sweden, *Population Studies*, 48(1), 65-80.

NOTES

[1] In a survey of six European nations (The European, 21 -23 Jan, 1991), of 14 high-importance activity areas, the *family* came out on top in every country, with on average 88% saying they have a 'very strong' attachment. *Freedom* came second at 86% on average, followed by *rights of man, equality, democracy, work, culture, solidarity, marriage, the nation, free enterprise, Europe, money* and, lastly, *religion*. Although the actual percentages varied from country to country, the ranks of values were not very different. Notice that freedom is immediately followed by three related concepts, thus emphasising the role of independence in the modern world. However, there is an incongruous distancing between *family* and *marriage*, demonstrating that society is confused about the true nature of both concepts.

In a survey of students, when both emotions and activities, such as love and freedom, were used as value areas, the relationships varied, depending to a certain extent on social status and age (Sugarman 1980). *Happiness* was the most important characteristic for both polytechnic students and high school students. However, *freedom* followed by *mature love* were important for the former, but an *exciting life, mature love, pleasure* and *true friendship* were all equal in importance after *happiness* for the latter, with *freedom* only then appearing as a concern. Perhaps younger people see freedom as not an important question since their actions are limited by parents and by law. College students would have more of a reason to value freedom since their potential for autonomy lies to a large extent in their hands. In any case, younger people value happiness most (when asked) and then love and freedom; older people value family (instead of love) then freedom, and associated concepts of equality and rights.

² Eastern Europe during its Communist period still had significantly more people marrying young, and had lower divorce rates, than Western Europe. This might very well change in the near future, as nations install some form of democratic government.

³ In speaking of sets of traits, people, whether they know it or not, often make a keen distinction between gender and sex, with the nature of this distinction varying from one social segment to another. The gender of a person is a set of attributes that one can take on. The sex of an individual is often considered to contain innate aspects. Thus, society can definitely look at the physiology of a person and deduce whether they are male or female, based on examination of physique, skin, hair, internal organs, external organs, blood and genetic material. However, gender is more difficult to define as this term is comprised of aspects that are relevant to a particular society. The universality of sex is beyond dispute, but there is no way to legitimately claim that a trait is considered truly 'masculine' everywhere and at all times. In this work, when 'sex' is mentioned, it can be determined from the context whether it concerns sociology or biology, behaviour or physique. This differentiation is simply a more formal assignment compared to the one we often in ordinary life. For example, a person who is distinctly physically 'female', might be 'male' in gender because most of her attributes and activities are likelier to occur in people that are distinctly physically 'male'.

⁴ The rule of similarity is of course not without exceptions, as observation reveals a nature's constant encounters with diversity. Such variety in the wild can only be based on one factor: Survival, both for the individual and the species. This multiplicity of engagements might be related to an instinctual need for reducing the chances of being victimised by predators by leveling out the probability of errors. In reproduction, the male of the species might take several females, possibly for

reasons of avoiding inbreeding through genetic variation. Human beings also have an innate need for diversity, which has two manifestations, biological and intellectual.

[5] On *Tugend und Untugend*, Naxos CD-8.553352, 1995.

[6] Tambs & Moum, 1992.

[7] Uhl, 1989.

[8] Although the literature on family life is voluminous, there is astonishingly little on modern courtship practises. Research is particularly sparse on European cultures other than that of England, America, France or Spain. One does not know why there is this paucity of research. Perhaps courtship is too commonly thought of as a 'ritualised process' and since dating practises leading up to marriage are hardly this, 'courtship' is seen as no longer existing. Even if courtship is not highly structured, there is little doubt that it does form a pattern. The very absence of restrictions or guidelines on dating is part of courtship pattern and must be investigated.

[9] See Appendix A, Friendship and Late Marriage.

[10] See Appendix A, Extroversion and Opposite Sex Friendships.

[11] Ibsen quoted in *Love's Comedy* (1862) the proverb: 'A friend married is a friend lost'. Percy Bysshe Shelley lamented: 'When a man marries, dies or turns Hindoo, his best friends hear no more of him.'

[12] De Sanctis, 1982.

[13] In most crimes the perpetrator and victim know one another. For example, for the year 1990, in only 14 % of murder cases known to police was the perpetrator a stranger, and in 33% he or

she was an acquaintance or friend; in 35% of these cases the relationship between victim and offender was not known (p 399, Table 3.140, T.J. Flanagan, K. Maguire, 1992, Sourcebook of Criminal Justice Statistics- 1991).

[14] Mersmann, 1986, p 185, p 191.

[15] Feld, 1991.

[16] See for example K. Doheny, Desperately seeking...anyone; single people are going to unusual lengths to meet peoples. Can people blame them? These days it takes creativity to find the perfect partner, *Los Angeles Times*, Nov 14, 1994.

[17] Sprecher & McKinney, 1987.

[18] Quote from *The Maid of the Mill* (1765) by Isaac Bickerstaff (c. 1735-1787).

[19] Rifkin & Timms, 1985, p 18.

[20] As presented for example in Ozment (1986), Mersmann (1986), and Kermode & Kermode (1995; especially letters 3, 19, 23, 25, 34, 61, 192).

[21] Germans of the 16th century were not reluctant about showing great devotion to their wives, to marriage, and to domestic life (Ozment, 1983, p 65). And perhaps the most 'wintry' people of all, the Puritans, were hardly averse to praising emotional attachment and deepest love and affection in marriage. 'Such marriages were commonplace among the Puritans. They were grounded in a union not of this world but of the world to come'. (p. 269; J. Adair, 1982, *Founding Fathers, The Puritans in England and America*, J.M. Dent & Sons, Ltd, London).

[22] Ozment (1983) makes this clear when he says that 'Several recent studies...argue that little genuine affection existed in the early modern family...for wives and children the traditional family was a kind of bondage that stifled self- realization' (p 2). Gillis (1997) maintains that many, if not most concepts of marriage, sex, family, and children are of fairly recent invention, since they evidently incorporate 'civilised', and therefore untraditional, views empathetic of personal rights.

[23] Burguière, 1987.

[24] The top five reasons as to why people would divorce are: Infidelity, loss of affection, emotional problems, financial problems, physical abuse. Relatively few will escape experiencing these predicaments as less than 60% of contemporary couples will still be together after 20 years of marriage (Chadwick & Heaton, 1992, C1-3., p 86; C3-5., p 97). It would appear that although modern people claim that marriage is only based on love, finances are also of great concern, no doubt as they were in the past. It is ironic that people of the present day think that their ancestors laboured in loveless, stifling marriages, racked by financial woes when they *themselves* suffer from precisely this fate. Perhaps a classic case of psychological projection?

[25] Admittedly, it is difficult to determine the parameters of the everyday life. People undoubtedly made their most intimate thoughts known in their letters, but few of these are published. Instead scholars have sought to bring forward into public view supposedly more interesting matters relating to politics, government, economics, law and so forth. But what could be more important than human relations of the most spiritual kind? No doubt there are thousands of letters and diaries, from people of all classes, revealing all sorts of deep emotional sentiments, gathering dust in archives. Until scholars have the resources and see the necessity for exhuming them, we must do with what we

have. What is clear, however, is that when people speak of affection, and give it central place in their personal writings, they do not see it as curious or unusual, or something that needs to hidden because decent people would find it inappropriate. If we are to consider the writers to be normal with respect to reflecting the tastes and standards of the time, we then have some idea as to the current customs.

26 For examples, see Blum, 1974.

27 We can see similar problems that anthropologists face in their observations of primitive peoples. For example, Margaret Mead's work on the Samoan people (as described and critiqued in E.F. Torrey, 1992, *Freudian Fraud*, HarperCollins, New York, pp 72-74) has been rendered dubious following subsequent investigations by others, who found a culture quite different from the one she describes. It would appear that Mead's bullying tactics and difficulty with the language, as well as the natives' purposely inaccurate statements (made often as 'jokes'), all yielded a highly artificial view of their a society, which was then further processed through a disposition of mind which favoured those ideas that fit in with a personal and political agenda. The resulting 'culture' was as mythical as anything the Samoans themselves could have invented.

28 There is little doubt that contemporary observers could be confused or mistaken, and from this we find apparent contradictions. For example, whereas early to mid-19th century observers found the peasantry of southern France dressed in rags, vulgar, hardly civilised, brutal, hardly better than animals (Weber, 1976, p. 4), early 17th century Languedoc and Provence contained villages and towns where women had who dress in many different materials colours, so much colour in fact that some observers found them excessive (S. Kettering, 1978, *Judicial Politics and Urban Revolt in Seventeenth-Century France*, Princeton University Press, Princeton, p 14-15). Further, depiction of

peasants in various Books of Hours of the 15th century depict the French people as basically well-fed, well- dressed, in colourful, perhaps nearly 'bourgeois' clothing. Are these differences a reflection of changes over time, are they the result of faulty observation, or are they simply a result of our own prejudices not allowing us to accept the concept of the 'prosperous peasant'? There is no doubt that many farm families were very poor, but a well-to-do rustic? Is that beyond belief? It would appear that in Europe there has almost always existed a standard-of-living scale with many gradations, not only amongst town-dwellers, but also amongst the country people. Authors writing about the cultures of their own time not infrequently gave widely different assessments of living conditions of the same land, as for example in the cases of early 19th century England, France, Poland, Hungary and Romania.

[29] Using the criteria discussed, statistics derived from Flinn (1981) of parish data from different regions from different nations (England, France, Germany, Scandinavia, Switzerland), show in general great similarity when it comes to marriage age, illegitimate births, and premarital conceptions, but not so with age- specific fertility, birth intervals and age of birth of last child. When it comes to testing for the existence of free deviation and choice from the norm, we do find positive evidence in virtually all recorded life areas, except for illegitimacy. Economic expediency certainly might explain some or all of the variation. We are constrained, however, from being more certain about this, since we do not know the economic conditions that applied in these diverse areas. Furthermore, when it comes to something like premarital conceptions (and by connection ideas about courtship, fondness, and affection), economics does not seem particularly relevant, and thus individual choice might be quite germane as an explanatory mechanism.

30 Chapter IX, Twenty-Fourth Session; Schroeder 1978, p 189.

31 Catholic Church, 1908, p 401.

32 Wrigley, 1987, Figure 9.5, pp 232-233.

33 Weber 1976, p 18. This correlation disappeared by 1876, however, perhaps due to less concern about the impact of economics on satisfaction in married life.

34 Flinn, 1981, pp 118-123. France and Germany, but not England, were below 20% for premarital conceptions.

35 Hajnal, 1965.

36 Alter, 1991. The main challenges revolve around the inability to explain why late marriage persisted so long in the cities when economic opportunities facilitating early marriage were present. Indeed, because of the strong economic growth and urbanisation throughout Europe, there should have been an overall *lowering* of marriage age in the 19th century.

37 Kuklo, 1991.

38 Kuklo, 1991. The figures were calculated after those of 'unknown' marital status were removed.

39 Wrigley, 1987, pp 281-283. In France, many men would marry women older than themselves as a way of limiting fertility, including middle-age widows (Weber, 1976, p 185). Aphorisms about this were contradictory, showing to a certain extent the ambiguity that surrounded the issue; popular sayings put in relief pragmatic concerns against the background of emotional needs.

[40] Wrigley, 1987, p 257.

[41] Spagnoli, 1983.

[42] Segalen, 1991.

[43] See Weber, 1976, pp 167-191.

[44] Weber, 1976, pp 134-135.

[45] Miller, 1985, pp 54-60, pp 402-409.

[46] Mitchell, 1975.

[47] Guinnane, 1991.

[48] Landale & Tolnay, 1991.

[49] Industrialisation, regardless of its net effect on the economy, might have encouraged impartible inheritance. As men could find work by themselves in the town and cities, parents did not have to provide a living to children and land therefore did not have to be shared. This would have intensified the practise of restricting the inheritance of land to one only son, forcing younger or non-inheriting sons to leave.

[50] Watt, 1988.

[51] Flinn, 1981, Table 6, pp 121-123.

[52] Shorter, 1980, pp 113-120.

[53] Tokareva, 1987; Bernard, 1982.

[54] Veenhoven, 1983; suicide rates for the Netherlands.

[55] Blossfeld & Jaenichen, 1990.

[56] Elder & Rockwell, 1976.

[57] It would appear, though, that Catholics are hardly conservative in all matters. In a Gallup poll published on 16 May, 1985, when asked if premarital sex was wrong, 46% of Protestants thought is was compared to only 33% of the Catholics. One could argue that Catholics are willing to tolerate premarital sex precisely because they consider marriage such an important aspect of life. Cohabitation for the sake of 'trying out' various partners for a good 'fit' theoretically is consistent with the ideal of lifelong marital gratification, more so than marrying without experiencing prior intimacy. However, this does not work in practise, as those who cohabitate and then marry have a *higher*, not lower, chance of divorcing. It would appear that one can quite adequately obtain all the information necessary about a person without living with them, and that those who do cohabitate do so largely for reasons unrelated to love.

[58] Stycos, 1983.

[59] One should be careful not to conclude that the unmarried are generally more irreligious, as we are saying here only that there are more unmarried persons among those with weak *religious* beliefs. It is likely that people first become disenchanted with religion then become disenchanted with marriage; although the direction of cause and effect could work the other way, it does not seem to be the case.

[60] Hertel, 1988.

[61] Kilmann et al., 1993.

[62] Prokopec, 1977.

[63] Bolger et al., 1989. The frequency of domestic conflict is naturally dependent on individual reports, which are probably not entirely accurate

[64] Malony, 1988.

[65] Bachrach, 1980.

[66] Ramu & Tavuchis, 1986.

[67] Chadwick & Heaton, 1992, Table C3-5, p 97.

[68] Herlihy & Klapisch-Zuber, 1987, p 323.

[69] See Appendix A, Domestic Variables and Early Marriage.

[70] Buck & Scott, 1993.

[71] Wrigley, 1987, p 236-237, Figure 9.6.

[72] See Appendix A, Employment, Income per Capita, and Income Distribution in the Decision to Marry.

[73] U.S. Bureau of the Census, 1992, p xvi.

[74] It would appear that compared to other industries, the service industry in the United States is more unequal in terms of income distribution than in the rest of the Western world (see Appendix A, Effect of Service Industry Work on Income Distribution and Marriage Propensity). Greater employment in service industries *reduces*, not increases, income inequality throughout the Western world, by decreasing the income held by the top 10% of households. Moreover, working in a service industry makes it

less likely that women will remain permanently single. Working in such industries appears to attract women to marriage, which is consistent with the idea that equal distribution gives *more* hope for the future, and thus acts to facilitate marriage.

[75] Temple & Polk, 1986.

[76] Jencks et al., 1983.

[77] Teti et al., 1987.

[78] Blossfeld & Jaenichen, 1990.

[79] Buck & Scott, 1993.

[80] Goldscheider & LeBourdais, 1986.

[81] This might very well contribute to the high dissolution rate for marriages where one partner is below 21. There is justifiable uncertainty as to whether the decision was made by 'adults' or mere 'children', although the married life and the consequences of divorce most assuredly require a mature disposition.

[82] Goldscheider & LeBourdais, 1986.

[83] Goldscheider & Goldscheider, 1989.

[84] Buck & Scott, 1993.

[85] See Chadwick & Heaton, 1992 (Table D3-1., p 119) for evidence that the percent of never-married women with one or more children has grown greatly since 1960, regardless of education. Furthermore, even in married households, parental absence is not at all unlikely; less than 6 in 10 marriages can be expected to last 20 years, that is, for the whole childhood of even

the oldest child (ibid, Chart C1-3., p 86). Similar statistics can be adduced for many other Western nations.

[86] Buck & Scott, 1993. National figures for unemployment are evidently more daunting than local figures. At least if local unemployment were high, the possibility remains of finding a job outside the area, but if national joblessness is a problem, then the chance of finding work anywhere is low.

[87] Data taken from Leppel, 1987. The table, labels (Conservative and Liberal), and the discussion that follows, are my own.

[88] Leppel, 1987.

[89] Grigsby & McGowan, 1986.

[90] See Appendix A, Living Arrangements and the Propensity to Marry (a).

[91] See Appendix A, Living Arrangements and the Propensity to Marry (b).

[92] See Appendix A, Living Arrangements and the Propensity to Marry (c).

[93] See Appendix A, Living Arrangements and the Propensity to Marry (d).

[94] Koller & Gosden, 1984.

[95] Palisi, 1984.

[96] SA:690.

[97] SA:1233.

[98] SA:1235.

[99] Carter & Glick, 1970, p 138.

[100] It is important to note that although high housing prices might *not* alter the desire for a separate residence. In the Spain of the late 1970s, people adjusted their timing of marriage rather than the context of marriage itself. Marriage in such situations is deferred until adequate money is saved (Stycos, 1983). In contrast to Spain, people living in Eastern Europe might put a premium on marrying early and/or having children, and thus will do what they can with regards to housing, even if it means living with family. Clearly, the decision to live alone is a function of individual temperament, and is not that amenable to cultural pressure, unless cultural principles are the product of the collective Will allowed to legitimately express itself. Thus, the desire for companionship, the desire for children, the desire for privacy, housing prices, and savings rates, are all relatively independent factors that must be connected in the correct causal sequence.

[101] Ideally, there should be little or no correlation between housing and marriage rates. This, however, is rarely, if ever, attained. Nonetheless, society should stand firm in keeping housing reasonable, instead of allowing prices to rise, as they did in the 1970s. Since residences are allowed to be bought and sold freely on the market in most places in the Western world, the blame for the inflation in house prices can be laid on both buyers and sellers. If young couples are strongly motivated to obtain a place of their own, they would be willing to sacrifice a greater share of their income rather than go without that first independent residence. Yet, once having gotten their own home, these same couples will then complain that they do not have enough money to make ends meet. The psychological dynamics behind consumer pricing strategies is worthy of study, because it appears that people do not act rationally in balancing their interests.

[102] See Appendix A, Housing Costs and Propensity to Marry.

[103] See Appendix A, Higher Education and its Effect on Information Acquisition.

[104] Those who watch *C-SPAN*, *Nightline*, and Sunday morning politically- orientated interview programmes such as *Meet the Press*, are normally from the higher income and educational echelons.

[105] SA:708.

[106] SA:378.

[107] SA:396

[108] SA:708.

[109] SA:396.

[110] SA:396

[111] See Appendix A, Effect of Space on the Propensity to Marry.

[112] A series of questions was given in 1978 in seven Western European nations, to young people ages 18 to 24, with an average age of about 21 (Gallup, 1978, pp 373-402). Although the details of our analysis are not reproduced here, we can conclude that *greater* communications and education (* denotes statistical significance): **increases* the desire to live one's life as one likes (independence ethos); **increases* willingness to attribute dissatisfaction with home life to inadequate *living space; increases* likelihood of saying that morals are lax; **decreases* overall

dissatisfaction with household life; *decreases* discontent with present household income; reduces willingness to say social rank, position or *wealth are important to attain personal success or are major goals; *decreases* willingness to say one can only carry out mechanically one's job at work; *increases* willingness to see a good future development for the nation.

For the thinking of a population with an average age higher than that above, we obtained survey data from 12 nations (Hastings & Hastings, 1987, pp 562-587). We find that *increased* communications and education are associated with: a *lesser* belief that there will be war in the future; *more* happiness; a *greater* desire to defend the current political system against change; *less* desire for a *radical change to the system or to associate with extreme left-wing politics; *more* satisfaction with democracy; *closer* affiliation with political parties; *less* willingness to fight in a war; *less* certainty about whether one is proud of one's nation or not.

113   Unlike the mainstream media's frequent coverage of the effect of films and television on society, academia's interest is much more spotty. The theme of autonomy in particular seems overlooked, although there is good evidence to show that it is one of the top philosophical concerns behind plots and characters. In surveys, Western culture puts great emphasis on freedom, family, rights of man, and democracy (see Chapter 1, note 1). It is therefore not surprising to find that of various themes, the French believe that freedom is the most meaningful thing in life, with work and love forming a second tier of interest, and then money, happy family and friendship (Hastings & Hastings, 1987, p 511). Consequently, the autonomy of children, portrayals of the ideal woman and disintegration of the family were common subjects on French public television programmes. Further, two main categories emerge in relation to these subjects: social problems relating to exclusion and

problems involving disintegration of relationships (Chalvon-Demersay & Libbrecht, 1995).

Hence, the themes of independence, youth, family, and rebellion are often interrelated. Genre films that focus on robust, determined actions, can address these basic subjects better than other, more general, types of film. For example, Americans enjoy Westerns because they unabashedly portray an ideal life consisting of freedom and closeness to nature, which is unique and a well-established part of the nation's history (Shively, 1991). This scenario is hardly a utopia, however, as various forces constantly intrude and threaten to destroy family and individual. Horror films take the fears in Westerns and bring them out into the open. Common themes such as alienation, confrontation, separation from family, as well as autonomy, are often successfully presented (Farquhar, 1992). How much the concept of autonomy is supported is difficult to determine, but it would appear that films find it weakening, since one of the dilemmas consistently returning to haunt characters is to have their masculinity under attack (Lipsitz, 1990). Certainly, breaking free of restraints (such as most developments in a modern person's life) is a bold enough step requiring a more characteristically male response. One could say that ruggedness, alienation and disruption of relationships are invariably related to the struggle for autonomy, and so it would make sense to link these topics in fictional works.

Many observers of the film industry would argue that the primary purpose of the movie, indeed of any fiction, is to present an escape from ordinary life, a temporary diversion, mere entertainment. The audience member wants to get lost in someone else's problems for a change, he wants to see the 'little guy' win, but he has no interest in seeing anything relevant to his own life on the screen. However, considering the theme we are discussing, it seems unlikely that people would be quite content to sample something so elemental as liberty or autonomy only in movies and not want it in their own lives. Of course, in the case of genre movies, many plots involve situations that are not part of the average person's life, and people do not expect to be confronting Apache Indians or killers wearing hockey masks anytime in the near future, but even there they *do* identify with the need to lash out at whatever is holding them back in life. People can and do abstract the major themes from a particular context, whether in a film or in life, thus building a bridge between reality and fiction. In fact, if films are designed to connect with a person's experiences rather than offers an escape from them, we would precisely expect them to focus on *freedom* and not fantasy as a major concept. There is compelling evidence that both concepts are popular, but more socially relevant and critically acclaimed films usually possess the former.

As powerful a medium as theatrical films are, it is no longer the most socially important form of art, competing with television (Liehm, 1975). The range of sources that propagate the above themes has been enlarged. The superior availability of television compared to major motion pictures makes the themes presented therein to be even more influential. Television, it has been found, is powerful enough in assisting young people in forming an identity and developing ideas about autonomy (Corset, 1995). Ideas about independence have been successfully inculcated, at least in part, through the frequent depiction of high- status, supposedly highly autonomous occupations; the audience encounters characters holding such occupations more often than they would in real life. Lower status occupations, when portrayed, are also unrealistic, in that they contain more latitude than is true in real life (Berk, 1977).

Obviously, a substantial work could be devoted to the theme of independence in films, television, magazines, novels, newspapers, and so on. What is clear is that the theme is so prevalent that one could be justified in saying that it is omnipresent. Whether it is cowboys on the range, defending themselves against encroachments by the big ranchers, or hustlers trying to stay alive in a grimy New York environment, or men encountering nearly invincible creatures in the depths of space, film and television consistently show the individual in challenging situations. As Hitchcock observed, his movies were basically about ordinary people in extraordinary situations. Modern stories all in one way or another feature a loss of rights, liberties or opportunities, which could be due to illness, an escaped convict, a major corporation, officials working as part of a government conspiracy, or simply fate dealing a poor hand. Whatever the details, the story must present the individual struggling to retain his dignity, social position, and sometimes his very life. Any significant loss of freedom is a loss of identity not only for one person but for all people; 'giving in' to the 'dark' forces in any way endangers us all. The whole edifice of the media attempts to link individual struggles with the universal struggle for autonomy, by showing that your life problems are really not that different from the ones you see on the screen. Television and theatrical films have recently tried to take the impact a step further by often saying their production has been 'based on real events', or a 'fact-based story' or is 'inspired by a true story', making even the most incredible situations that much closer to the life of the viewer. Whether the source is film, television, book, or magazine, the contemporary fictional story strikes a responsive chord in the viewer or reader using a variety of devices, and the anxiety the individual feels is almost always more to do with a subconscious fear about the loss of independence than worry about characters, or identifying with a storyline.

[114] Buck & Scott, 1993.

[115] It would appear that when people are heavily exposed to the media, as well as being more desirous of independence, they become more aware of the social environment. For example, women who watch television more heavily tend to be more socially orientated; they would also like to be more aggressive and to show more leadership (Gutman, 1973). The medium

provides nourishment to the extroverted and gregarious seeking ideas about trends, issues and fashion. Clearly, leaving home to marry or live with someone is a social statement, decisive, and perhaps more than a little bold, thus neatly tying together the various desires kindled by television. A small living space would be sufficient impetus for this process.

[116] Gilmartin, 1985.

[117] Gilmartin, 1985.

[118] Wagner et al., 1985.

[119] Elder & Rockwell, 1976; Trent, 1994.

[120] Wagner et al., 1985.

[121] See Appendix A, Effect of Fertility on the Propensity to Marry (a).

[122] See Appendix A, Effect of Fertility on the Propensity to Marry (b).

[123] In Chapter 2 we mentioned that Ireland was ahead of other countries in its 'modern' fertility rates. Although it had achieved relatively low birthrates by the turn of the 20th century, these rates decreased little compared to the declines occurring in the rest of Western Europe. Ironically, by the 1970s, Ireland had the *highest* fertility rate of any Western European nation. Occasionally, one finds oneself somewhat embarrassingly the subject of attention, not because one has moved into the open, but because the other members of one's group have taken two steps back. The grave situation of the 19th century, which forced the birthrate down, gave way to a more stable times which stopped the birthrate from falling. If the twin evils of

overpopulation and famine had never occurred, then it is quite possible that Ireland would have been similar to other nations in its birthrates in the period between the mid-19th century and early 20th century.

124 On the other hand, if we were to believe that fertility induces early marriage age for women (something that the analysis above does not support), leaving Ireland in the set *reverses* the dynamic. Having a small to moderate family of origin makes women marry later, but having a distinctly larger than average family of origin would induce women to actually marry young. Thus, when families are not too large, then the Profamilial Model applies, but if they go beyond a certain size, the Antifamilial Model is applicable. Although this is a reasonable assertion, after judging the evidence in the contemporary context, it appears that this dynamic if it exists is not especially strong.

125 One of the problems we encounter is in the definition of 'large family.' Obviously, there is no clear dividing line between 'moderate size' and 'large size.' Our statistical analyses demonstrate a smooth linear correlation, meaning that we are not dealing with conscious 'grades' of family size, but rather that the dynamics of the family itself increase proportionately with its size. Further, there is no convenient way to determine 'early' or 'late marriage.' These can only be considered approximate gauges of marriage propensity.

126 Wenz, 1984.

127 The problem of divorce is hardly recent On top of an already disturbing trend, the number of divorces rose sharply during and just after the Second World War, then dropped back down to the pre-war trend (CHADWICK & HEATON, 1992, C1-1., P 85). In other words, the divorce rate in the 1950s and 1960s would probably have been at the levels recorded even if the war in

Europe had never occurred; the dislocation of war (and carelessly arranged, rushed marriages) simply accelerated the pace of divorce for a time, but the trend had started all the way back in the 1880s. The temporal depth, and hence the complexity, of the divorce dynamic is quite extraordinary, and a call is made for the careful scrutiny of a most remarkable phenomenon. Moreover, it would appear that many men, women and children were already being heavily affected by marital dissolution in the middle part of the 20th century.

[128] Another factor that determines how people look at marriage is the structure of the household itself. If a mother is at a distinctly lower level than her husband, female children might opt to delay or forego marriage. From their personal experiences, they have formed a negative view of marriage and they would prefer their freedom over having a husband dominate them. This scenario is made more likely if a mother wanted to work but was forbidden to do so, or if she wished to have other activities outside the home but was thwarted. Whether such actions are typical is less important than what the individual perceives (rightly or wrongly) about her future.

[129] HS:H972; HS:H1006.

[130] Coleman et al., 1985.

[131] In this analysis, death rates and marriage rates will centre around the mid- 1980s. The effects of a death would be nearly instantaneously manifest on those remaining. There might come years between that death and the decision to marry, so a person marrying in 1987 might be reacting to a death that occurred in 1977. We should point out that this lag should not be a major problem, since a country's rate in one particular year is probably indicative of a fairly stable tendency, which is precisely what we seek to understand. Although indicators often change in absolute terms, they do not often change in rank. A nation, when

compared to other nations, might have had a relatively high death rate earlier in this century, and it would probably have a relatively high death rate again at the present time. However, that nation's rate has decreased considerably in absolute numerical terms. Thus, a nation's death rate for a particular year shows it mortality 'tendency' (or propensity) as much as its marriage rate show a marital 'tendency' (or inclination). Rates might decrease in numeric terms, but the tendency for an action remains the same as long as ranking remains the same. Correlations between rates are only to be taken as approximate indicators, not precise guides.

Further, we should keep in mind that age of marriage in modern European cultures does not necessarily mean age of first marriage. Our ability to determine whether delaying marriage helps people form better marriages, with lower probability of divorce, is confounded by the fact that divorced people who remarry tend to be over the age of 30. As most marriages break up from age 30 and up, and since most of these people remarry, a substantial proportion of these late marriages might be second marriages. The correlation between marriage at the age of 30 or older and divorce is positive and significant (MARR30F x DIV.MAP, R^2=.3598, p=.0031, $F(1,18)$=11.68). This dynamic hampers to an extent differentiating between the reasons for marrying. For example, is one marrying late because marrying for a second time usually comes later in life, or is one marrying late because one is delaying a first marriage? In most countries, however, divorce, as of the mid-1980s, was not so high as to render our results invalid. It would also appear that even when people remarry, they might do so as a reaction to loss of a parent or other figure, since many after divorce will rely upon, or even live with, such people. In essence, they go back several steps in life, to the time before their marriage.

[132] See Kuklo, 1991, for evidence in the decrease in celibacy rates in Warsaw after the rise in mortality caused by the war, floods, famine and plague of the mid-1790s.

[133] See Appendix A, The Effect of Parental Loss on the Propensity to Marry (a).

[134] See Appendix A, The Effect of Parental Loss on the Propensity to Marry (b).

[135] See Appendix A, The Effect of Parental Loss on the Propensity to Marry. Females show less correlation with age-specific deaths than males, at least for late marriage, as shown in part (b).

[136] See Appendix A, The Effect of Parental Loss on the Propensity to Marry (d).

[137] See Appendix A, The Effect of Parental Loss on the Propensity to Marry (e).

[138] General death rate is not a good indicator of how people react to loss. Let us look at an example. There are two nations, A and B, where we assume that the death of a middle-aged parent leaves one child troubled. If Country A has a *higher* death rate for middle aged (45-49) parents than Country B, Country A will have relatively more people affected by this loss. However, if we looked at the two nations' overall death rates, they might actually be similar because of the difference in the *size* of this age group. Although Country A might have a higher age-specific death rate, the effect on the overall death is negated by the smaller percentage size of this age group in the population, compared to Country B. Thus, some effects will be obscured if we do not control for the size of age groups.

[139] One could look at the connection between mortality and marriage from the perspective of a life-prolonging influence engendered by living in close proximity with a sympathetic and supportive person. In this case, the opposite direction of causality might be appropriate, that later marriage might result

in a higher death rate. There is evidence for this dynamic and no doubt marriage has helped many people lead a more comfortable and longer life. However, the existence of one dynamic does not necessarily negate the existence of a dynamic whose causality lies in the opposite direction. Our analyses show that age-specific death rates are *positively* correlated with early marriage. If marriage has a clear beneficial impact on health, then there would be an even greater extension of life than is the case with marriage later in life; instead, there is a shortening of life for people who marry young. Both the death rate and percent who are over 30 at marriage variables are taken from the mid-1980s, very close to each other in time. It seems doubtful that the effects of marriage would manifest themselves in a lower death rate almost immediately; one would rather expect a lag of perhaps twenty years or more. Hence, the direction of effect should be the other way around, where deaths influence marriage behaviour. More likely, recent deaths of family members would have more of an impact on marriage practices, since the latter are far more flexible and amenable to change than matters of health, a notoriously intractable and slow- moving dynamic.

Consequently, it appears quite unlikely that one could derive some kind of mid-life prophylaxis from a marriage begun only a decade earlier as there is little evidence that health effects would manifest themselves so soon after marriage. Marriage would then be a lifesaver, indeed!

[140] See Appendix A, Combined Effect of Family Size and Loss of Parent on Propensity to Marry (a).

[141] See Appendix A, Combined Effect of Family Size and Loss of Parent on Propensity to Marry (b).

[142] See Appendix A, Combined Effect of Family Size and Loss of Parent on Propensity to Marry (c).

143 Although a very large country rooted in pre-modern traditions has many variants in regard to mate selection, it would appear that at least in some cultures in India stress that individuals select potential mates, but with parental approval. Choosing a mate involves careful analysis of personality and socio-cultural attributes, including personal income, religion and caste, whereas occupation is not important. However, these considerations do not seem to be as meaningful among Indian immigrants to America (Sharma & Rajlakshmi, 1979; Siddiqi & Reeves, 1986). Assortative mating in the more economically modern, but still socially traditional Orkney Islands included considerations of kinship, demographic, social and geographic factors (Brennan & Dyke, 1980). Around the world, the selection and final approval of a mate are becoming matters increasingly in the hands of the individual; because of this, probably more people will marry late, and more will not marry at all (Murstein, 1980). The most 'advanced' form of mate selection uses computers. For example, 1000 pieces of information (in 108 categories) are taken from each person, compared to ideals set forth by the individual, and then compared to an ideal put forward by a marriage counsellor. The computer can predict which areas are most likely to be most rewarding and which areas are most troublesome (Smith & Debenham 1979). Automatic matching efforts, whether ancient or modern, where people are paired off by simple rules, do not by themselves seem to yield lower divorce rates nor happier marriages, in spite of the millions using such procedures and services. It appears that only when the individual considering marriage and the matchmaker are from a relatively homogeneous cultural background does an 'expert system' work.

144 It is not surprising that many girls take on masculine characteristics and interests in order to ease the transition from same-sex friendship to opposite-sex friendship, and on to opposite-sex romance. Such disguises often bring difficulty with boyfriends later on when the need for complementarity arises.

[145] Scanzoni, 1968.

[146] Heer, 1974.

[147] Christensen & Barber, 1967; Bumpass & Sweet, 1972.

[148] Howard, et al., 1989.

[149] Bentler & Newcomb, 1978; Chadwick & Heaton, 1992, p 84.

[150] Bainbridge & Stark, 1981.

[151] Hansen & Hicks, 1980.

[152] The desire for and approval of homology between married couples is not new. Writers, divines and moralists endorsed similarity in religious belief, age, economic position and social background as early as the 16th century (Ozment, 1983, p. 59).

[153] Tambs & Moum, 1992.

[154] Argyle et al., 1985.

[155] The survey was broken down by education and sex in CHADWICK & HEATON (1992, pp 22-47). We cite only those answers where there is a clear change in the diversity of opinion due to educational attainment.

[156] U.S. Department of Commerce, 1985, Table 8, p 154.

[157] One could reasonably argue that a difference of only one position on the scale might not be significant. For example, on the issue of saving money before marriage, a husband holds a position of 7 (very important) and his wife holds a position of 6 (quite important). Is there that much difference between the two

positions that would lead to a major contretemps? It is not so much the absolute difference between two positions as it is the *degrees of certainty relative to the ends of the scale*. The fact that the largest percentages tend to fall on positions 1, 4 or 7 (especially for the poorly educated) indicates the ideological importance of these positions. Falling on one of these pivotal steps in the scale might be seen as a 'declaration', with even the smallest deviance a disavowal. Clearly, someone could find it irritating if he is very adamant about an issue (say holding a position 1 or 7) and someone else is only one step away. They might feel similarly if they are firmly in the centre (at 4), and someone else is only at 3 or 5.

[158] In this way, people will quickly know within a particular social context where someone stands even before meeting them, facilitating the socialising and marriage process. If the majority have easy access to people who share their views, and are not willing to date people who differ from their views, then the minority must set up an 'underground' to effectively meet others who share their views and who are as unconventional in beliefs as they are. The college environment both creates a convergence of opinion as well as provides a venue for those who diverge from this consensus.

[159] Rankin & Maneker, 1987; comparisons are for couples who have divorced.

[160] Jung, 1968, p 20.

[161] One could argue that since they have low income, women in this position could not leave the marriage, since they could not support themselves. This might be specious reasoning, as present income does not guarantee future earnings potential, the ease of finding employment or competence at work. A married woman who works only part-time could after a divorce go into

full-time employment and earn an income that secures an autonomous lifestyle.

[162] 'To my feeling, this deadness to the history which has prepared half our world for us, this inability to find interest in any form of life that is not clad in the same coat-tails and flounces as our own lies very close to the worst kind of irreligion. The best that can be said of it is, that it is a sign of the intellectual narrowness-in plain English, the stupidity, which is still the average mark of our culture.' George Eliot (Marian Evans), (quoted from Kermode & Kermode, 1995, p 346).

[163] Vera et al., 1990.

[164] People today are widely viewed as prisoners of their genes, reacting, especially in the deviant sense, to supposedly irrepressible urges, such as drinking, stealing, using drugs, sexual promiscuity and violence. The ongoing effort to prove the physical basis for much of human behaviour is quite conspicuously a major goal in the behavioural sciences.

[165] Hajnal, 1983.

[166] Veevers, 1984.

[167] Vera et al., 1990.

[168] Basavarajappa et al., 1988, Canadian data.

[169] If the idea of 'eternal youth' becomes fixed in society, then in the near future men and women will not be very different from each other even when both are older, because an adult will not be expected to give up many of his or her childhood interests or attitudes. Women will still be able to behave in a fairly 'tomboyish' way. Young and old should not be very different

and the tendency for older men to marry younger women might then not be as prevalent. Despite this increased similitude between youth and adult personalities, we should bear in mind that there will still be a distinction between the *obligations* of the married lifestyle and those of the single lifestyle.

[170] Archer, 1984.

[171] Peres & Meivar, 1986; study used sample of classifieds in Israeli newspapers.

[172] Hahn, 1983.

[173] As we mentioned in relation to films and the independence ethos, one defines and elucidates the masculine more easily and usefully, with the feminine left in some ambiguity. A critical part of the feminine is to express doubt, to raise objections to bold (ordinarily masculine) plans. The feminine can be characterised by caution, that is, a belief that a venture may not succeed in reaching its goal. Perhaps because of the female tendency to focus on maintenance and local control, women can be indecisive and passive when it comes to social matters. On the other hand, masculinity typically involves clear processes and methods, new ventures and original concepts. The coming together of a 'sex-typed' man and woman can produce interesting results. Men in such a situation see the *absence* of mental and physical energy as 'feminine' and a counterpart to their own decisiveness. This might make the male-female relationship far more attractive to a man than a same- sex friendship, because there is the opportunity his unique abilities to be appreciated. Further, a woman can be the place where he projects all that he finds uncertain, equivocal or enigmatic, thus removing these features from his own character. Women end up being the 'injured innocent', giving men the role of a 'knight', a guardian and leader ready to endure the failings of his companion (Jung, 1959/68, paras. 169, 183). After a loss or

disappointment, husbands can routinely blame their wives for being too timid and not taking chances, when in fact it might primarily be the husband's fault. The husband then has responsibility taken off of his shoulders.

[174] Atienza Hernández, 1989.

[175] Armstrong, 1986. Contemporaries noted the common attitude of focussing attention on pleasure and materialism. The youth became much more independent- minded and were considered to be undisciplined and anti-authoritarian. Patterns of courtship and sexual activity changed also. These observations correspond well to the evidence provided by social statistics where available (Shorter & Schmalfuss, 1972).

[176] For an interesting foretaste of feminism and the breakdown in relations between the sexes, see the exchange of letters between Abigail and John Adams, (Kermode & Kermode, 1995, letters 85 and 86), wherein Abigail entreats here husband to pass laws that curtail the power of Man, who is 'Naturally Tyrannical', and to use the power given to men for the women's 'happiness'. John laughs off such suggestions but says that the 'Masculine systems' that give men power are never used in full force, because in reality 'We [men] are the subjects' of women.' This is a common theme of our Enlightenment era, where men deflect discussions about the loss of chivalry and the precarious, uncertain position of women by resorting to flattery, specifically, professing a constitutional weakness for the Fairer Sex. It evades the issue of whether there is any kind of real superiority, in general or in precise areas, of the male over the female. Men must convey convincing reasons why a dominant role should be assigned to them, and why women should not fear this authority is going to be exceeded. It is understandable that women are reluctant to say that their fears have been allayed, when the only thing standing between civil and uncivil use of power is a pretty face or a charming manner.

[177] Anderson, 1986.

[178] Shorter, 1987.

[179] Quote from *A Woman of No Importance* (1893).

[180] For a description of these changes see Hawes, 1985.

[181] Hawes, 1985, p 57.

[182] Quotes taken from Hawes, 1985.

[183] Wrigley, 1987, Fig. 10.5, p 258.

[184] See for example American data in HS:B42-B48, which shows, by modern standards, an amazing diversity in household types.

[185] HS:B42-B48; SA:101.

[186] Chadwick & Heaton, 1992, p 111, Table D1-7., p 113, Table D1-9.

[187] See HS:D60.

[188] Just as decisions about family size varied from family to family, they probably varied from community to community, and region to region. If one could look across the cultural map of any nation, one would see a hodge-podge of practises and tendencies which reflected the traditions, exigencies and innate temperament of the people. Since we rarely have anything resembling a complete set of cultural ideas for a community, let alone a region, scholars often resort to using language as a marker for culture; and where culture changes, so does language. Even though France is renowned for its centralised government, a vast assortment of dialects and languages existed

in the nation well into this century. There were many who spoke no French or spoke it badly, but nonetheless they believed French should be used for solemn occasions, for higher culture, and for sermons. The government encouraged the use of French as the exclusive language for all social strata, using the school system as its main agent. Older terms were either abandoned or remained as names for certain common objects. Some peasants had difficulty making the adjustment because there were sometimes no words in French that were comparable to ones in their own dialect or language (Weber 1976, 67-94). The extensibility of the local language reflects other aspects of culture; one could use French when necessary, and another language when it suited the individual and the situation. The homogenisation of France was a necessity if the country was to prosper (communications is critical in the development of any modern economy) but at the same time the people lost the ability to speak effectively, since the words that arose from a culture close to their hearts and minds were no more. The new language was instrumental, just as was the common national culture, but the old language and old ways which could preserve many nuances of attitudes, behaviours, and utilisation, were useful in a human sense. One wonders if the current lack of precision in vernacular speech in countries such as America might not be due to this imposition of a common dialect, leaving people who vary from the average temperament and experience without convenient words. In the same way that words and expressions give us an easy way to convey our desires, so too do cultural ideas, through maxims, legends, and events taken from previous generations. Hence, the loss of diversity in speech parallels the homogenisation of culture. The same that was said about language can be said about culture: people search for precise cultural answers to their personal difficulties, but are only offered rough and clumsy generic solutions. It is a paradox to say that modern people usually find satisfactory ways of doing most things, but are still frustrated by the inability of the common culture to give them the information and reassurance needed to reach their personal goals.

[189] West & Morgan, 1987; they also mention better birth control, although this is largely a function of the other two.

[190] Eisenberg et al. (1991), p 854.

[191] Eisenberg et al. (1991), p 856-857.

[192] Speicher, 1992.

[193] Boyes & Allen, 1993.

[194] Bar-Yam et al., 1980.

[195] Muram et al., 1992. Soap operas and erotic films often feature self-centred activities where moral thinking has no role, only immediate sensual gratification. A person without regard for morals would not only find the themes acceptable in these genres, but would also have his own views reinforced.

[196] Weisheit et al., 1982.

[197] Schab, 1991.

[198] Christopher, 1988.

[199] Chadwick & Heaton, 1992, Table E1-4, p 139.

[200] One suspects that even parents somehow know that they have not delivered the guidance and affection that their children need when they tolerate and even encourage early dating. Outwardly, they fear their boy or girl is somehow socially 'flawed' if they are not socialising with the opposite sex by an early age. However, the truth might be that parents do not so much fear what society thinks, but fear what they will think of themselves as parents. That unloved children often turn out to be rebellious and deviant is understood by everyone, but no one

appreciates this more poignantly than parents who are guilty of withholding affection. Hence, they privately wish that someone else will give their children what they have been unwilling or unable to do, before it is too late. Perhaps a boyfriend or girlfriend can bring a meaning to their child's life that has eluded them so far.

[201] Cameron et al., 1989.

[202] Calculated from Hastings & Hastings, 1987, p 500.

[203] Netting, 1992.

[204] Gordon & Miller, 1984.

[205] Chadwick & Heaton, 1992, C3-6, p 98.

[206] Knox, 1985.

[207] Downey, 1990-91; Kandel et al., 1991. Intoxicants of the stronger variety, such as cocaine and drugs other than alcohol or cannabis, are particularly likely to increase despondency.

[208] As with so many other things in the world, the route to marriage has become reduced to a well-ordered, scientific 'procedure' that nevertheless requires professional 'guidance'.
Such unnecessary complexification makes marriage that much more threatening, and makes love that much more difficult to uncover. In this regard, see J.P. Decker, 'Wedding checklist: Couples add premarital counseling', *The Christian Science Monitor*, May 2, 1996, and M. Jordan, 'A short course on courting', *The Washington Post*, Feb 14, 1994.

[209] U.S. Department of Commerce, 1985, Table 7, p 141.

[210] Diehl, 1986. There is surprisingly little research into the symbolism of mazes or labyrinths. Carl Jung referred to the subject only once in his extensive works. Yet, the maze must have considerable psychological power, considering that it was prominently used in Gothic cathedrals, with the largest example at Chartres. The perfect enclosure of the traditional maze, the unified system within well-established unchanging boundaries, gives one confidence but only *if* one believes that it represents life. Perhaps the transformation inherent in the symbolism of the maze is an all too disturbing concept now that the goal of life is not located at a detectable, unshifting centre, but somewhere outside. If there is anything that modern man desperately seeks, it is stability, and the maze, now a hated word in the post-Reformation interpretation, offers an articulation only of the pathological doubts that plague our times.

Printed in the United States
2132